Charles Leonard
South Africa's Forgotten Revolutionary Leader

Simon Winter

Footprint Press

Published in 2021 by Footprint Press

Website: www.footprintpress.co.za

Copyright © Simon Winter

Cover design and page layout by Anthony Cuerden

e-mail: ant@flyingant.co.za

ISBN 978-1-920704-49-0

Printed by Pinetown Printers (Pty) Ltd; Pinetown, KwaZulu-Natal

All rights reserved. No part of this publication may be reproduced, stored, manipulated in any retrieval system, or be transmitted in any mechanical, electronic form or by any other means, without the prior written authority of the publishers, except for short extracts in media reviews. Any person who engages in any unauthorised activity in relation to this publication shall be liable to criminal prosecution and claims for civil and criminal damages.

*For Catherine, Daisy and Violet, whose love sustained Charles,
and
for Lee, Katherine and Janice, whose love sustains me.*

CONTENTS

1	Preface	1
2	Chapter 1 : Roots (1575-1856)	7
3	Chapter 2 : Formative Years (1856-1876)	25
4	Chapter 3 : Scaling the Legal Ladder (1876-1888)	41
5	Chapter 4 : A Beachfront Home (1880-1888)	57
6	Chapter 5 : A Highveld Home (1888-1891)	69
7	Chapter 6 : The Reformist (1890-1892)	81
8	Chapter 7 : Between a Rock and a Hard Place (1892-1894)	99
9	Chapter 8 : Kruger Must Fall (1894-1895)	113
10	Chapter 9 : Consternation (December 1895)	129
11	Chapter 10 : Cool Heads and Hotheads (Dec 1895-Jan 1896)	145
12	Chapter 11 : Up, Down and Away (January 1896)	159
13	Chapter 12 : At Sea and at the Grand (January-February 1896)	171
14	Chapter 13 : Home and Abroad (January-February 1896)	187
15	Chapter 14 : In the Dock and Before the House (1896-1897)	201
16	Chapter 15 : Gaining a Son and Losing a Brother (1897-1909)	219
17	Chapter 16 : Losing His Wife and Losing His Life (1910-1921)	239
18	Chapter 17 : Kith, Kin and Co-conspirators (1922-1987)	253
19	Chapter 18 : A Great Son of South Africa (1856-1921)	261
20	Acknowledgments	271
21	Select Bibliography and List of Illustrations	273
22	Index	285

18 and 19 Kensington Palace Gardens. Charles Leonard and his family lived at No. 18 (on the left) at various times between 1904 and 1911.

PREFACE

*I must simply be content to let the truth come out later on,
and in the meantime a clear conscience is my strength.*

— Charles Leonard in a letter to his wife, 1896

What do Grand Prix supremo Bernie Ecklestone, Iranian property developer David Khalili, founder of the Reuters news agency Paul Reuter, Indian steel tycoon Lakshmi Mittal and the Rothschild family all have in common – besides being outrageously wealthy, of course? They've all owned the mansion situated at 18 Kensington Palace Gardens, West London, on what is known as Billionaires' Row, where the average house fetches in excess of £20 million. Number 18 is the most valuable of the lot, and is currently regarded as the fifth most expensive private home in the world.

Now add Charles Leonard to the list of owners. Charles who? Haven't heard of him? I'm not surprised. Even in his homeland he's virtually unknown. Ask any South African to rattle off the names of those who conspired to overthrow the government, and they'll give you names like Nelson Mandela, Walter Sisulu and Oliver Tambo, but I'm prepared to wager that not one of them would mention Charles Leonard. They've never heard of him. I hadn't either until I came across the following snippet of information while researching the history of Green Point, the suburb of Cape Town that I call home. It piqued my interest, as I trust it will pique yours.

In the early hours of 19 January 1896, as the moon slipped behind a cloud, a shadowy figure crept out of Bordeaux, a mansion on the Sea Point beachfront, mounted a horse and made his way past the dark expanse of

Green Point Common to the Alfred Docks, where he boarded a steam ship and sailed away to England and to safety. That man, clad in a disguise, was the remarkable Charles Henry Brandt Leonard, the leader of South Africa's first band of revolutionaries.[1]

It needs to be stated at the outset that he would have objected to being remembered as such, but history has a knack of overriding our wishes. In Charles Leonard's case, this is particularly true because historians have generally maligned him. As Shakespeare puts it: *The evil that men do lives after them; the good is oft interred with their bones.* At the risk of disturbing those bones, I began unearthing what I could about Charles Leonard, and soon found myself digging deeper and deeper into a life that has, quite frankly, been crying out to be written so that the record might be set straight.

Initially, I doubted whether I should be the one to take on this task: after all, though interested in both fields, I am neither an historian nor a politician. However, I am a writer who finds human drama compelling, and it is the human drama of Charles Leonard's life that gripped me and continues to do so. Furthermore, there is nobody alive today who knows the man as well as I do and, to be perfectly honest, I feel as though I've been placed in the position of Horatio, whom his dying friend Hamlet tasked with salvaging his tarnished reputation:

> O God, Horatio, what a wounded name,
> Things standing thus unknown, shall live behind me!
> If thou didst ever hold me in thy heart
> Absent thee from felicity a while,
> And in this harsh world draw thy breath in pain
> To tell my story.

For the British biographer Michael Holroyd, biographers are the messengers of the dead calling to us out of the past, asking to be heard, remembered and understood.[2] Of course, I cannot hope to reveal Charles Leonard as he was, in all his complexity, but no biographer would dare to make such a claim. What I have done is to place him in his historical and political context and have sought to explain how the world in which he lived shaped his life, and how he, in turn, reciprocated through his involvement in some of the tumultuous events of his day.

---

[1] Murray, Marischal. *Under Lion's Head,* 139-40.
[2] Holroyd, M. *Works on Paper: The Craft of Biography and Autobiography,* 19.

Preface

In 1895, Charles Leonard, a prominent and popular Johannesburg attorney, was elected Chairman of the Transvaal National Union, a cosmopolitan group of activists who initially petitioned President Paul Kruger and his Boer[3] government for reforms, but then plotted to overthrow the regime in an armed insurrection. In this, they had the secret but full support of Cecil John Rhodes, then Prime Minister of the Cape, and leading members of his British South Africa Company, as well as the tacit support of the British Secretary of State for the Colonies, Joseph Chamberlain. Then, at the eleventh hour, disaster struck. In the ensuing pandemonium and international diplomatic crisis, Charles Leonard managed to escape, leading most historians to label him a coward. This book critically examines the facts and challenges their verdict.

George Cory, the eminent South African historian, once wrote:

> It is no more than the grateful duty of a succeeding generation to revere the memory of those who bore the heat and burden of the days long gone. But better than merely holding in one's individual mind the memories of departed heroes is the placing on permanent record the account of their lives and works.

In recording the facts, however, I could not help but comment on them and interpret them. This is, after all, a biography, not an entry in an encyclopaedia, and the reader requires (and deserves) more than what merely lies on the surface. It is both the public and the private personae that interest us. Understandably, there were times when I was tempted to indulge in speculation, but I have tried as far as is humanly possible to confine myself to interpretations and suppositions based on evidence.

In his inaugural lecture as Professor of History at the University of South Africa, Alex Mouton highlighted the value of biography for historiography:

> The crucial contribution of biography is that it humanises history as it reflects life – its heroism, nobility, endurance, folly, ignorance, weaknesses and brutality... As G.M. Trevelyan hauntingly summarised it, '...the poetry of history lies in the quasi-miraculous fact that once, on this earth, once on this familiar ground walked other men and women, as actual as we are today, thinking their own thoughts, swayed by their own

---

[3] Boer is the Dutch for farmer, and was originally applied only to that class, though in later years all Republican inhabitants of the Transvaal were proud to be known as Boers.

passions, but now all gone, one generation vanishing into another, gone as utterly as we ourselves shall shortly be gone, like ghosts at cock-crow'[4].[5]

I'd go further, however, and claim that precisely because our forebears walked this earth before us, they may have something of value to teach those of us still on the road of life, particularly if they left written records. They may well have lived in a bygone era very different from our own, but the human condition is such that we face many of the same challenges and experience all of the same emotions as they did. As a result, their insights often have universal applicability. Certainly – as I'm sure you'll come to agree – Charles Leonard has much to teach us, even though almost a century has passed since he departed this life. Fortunately, he left behind a collection of his private papers and public documents, which shed light on his thoughts, decisions, actions, and feelings.

Those readers who are not particularly interested in his ancestors or his childhood are advised to skip the first two chapters. However, as the quotation at the start of Chapter 1 so aptly puts it, a man cannot be properly understood without some reference to his roots, and so I would encourage readers to bear with me.

For those interested in such things, I've included copious references to my sources, a comprehensive index, and a select bibliography, but this isn't intended primarily as a work of scholarly erudition. It is aimed at lay readers – those who until now had never heard of this truly remarkable man.

If, having read this book, others feel that they have come to know Charles Leonard (as I have done) and, more particularly, are persuaded that he deserves – belatedly – to be accorded his rightful place amongst South Africa's leading historical figures, I shall feel that I have done right by his bones.

SIMON WINTER
Green Point
January 2021

---

[4] Cannadine, D. *G.M. Trevelyan, A Life in History*, 190.
[5] Mouton, F.A. "'The good, the bad and the ugly': Professional historians and political biography of South African parliamentary politics, 1910-1990" Inaugural address at Unisa, 27 October 2009.

Preface

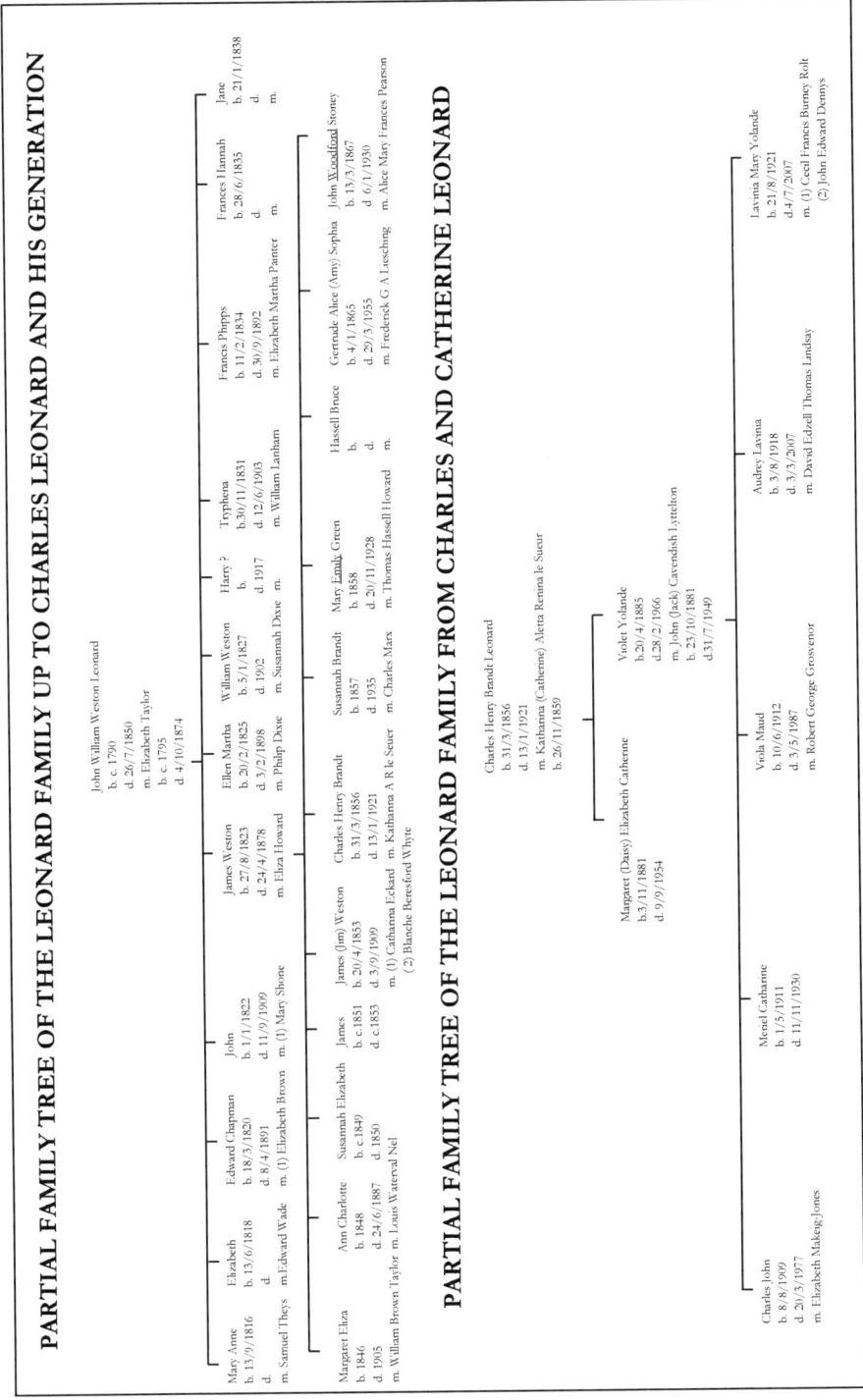

Gin Lane, an etching by William Hogarth

CHAPTER 1 : ROOTS
(1575-1856)

We all grow up with the weight of history on us. Our ancestors dwell in the attics of our brains as they do in the spiralling chains of knowledge hidden in every cell of our bodies.

– Shirley Abbott

Charles Leonard may have lived in one of London's most expensive mansions, but ninety years earlier, in 1818, his grandparents were renting accommodation in one of the city's most notorious slums. Market Street in St George's parish bordered Bloomsbury Square, a noisy and filthy market, which, besides being rat-infested, was crowded with thieves, pickpockets, prostitutes, vagrants and drunkards. Sixty years earlier, William Hogarth had captured the spirit of the place in his etching *Gin Lane*, in which St George's steeple is visible in the background. Small groups of vagrants lounge about drinking, while the skeletal young man, the hanging suicide, the hasty burials, the infant about to fall to its death, and the drunken woman with syphilitic sores all reflect in exaggerated detail the depravity of this part of London.

> The lanes here were narrow and dirty, windows of decaying tenements were stuffed with rags and paper, while the interiors were damp and unwholesome. The walls were sagging, the floors covered in dirt, the low ceilings discoloured by mould; their smell was indescribable.[6]

---

[6] Ackroyd, Peter. *London: The Biography*, 137-8.

This is a description of the Rookeries in St Giles's parish, a few streets to the south of where the Leonards lived in Market Street, but St George's was no different. This part of London was also known as Little Dublin or The Holy Land because most of the tenements housed poor Irish immigrants. They were not all debauched, of course; many were trying to earn an honest living as manual labourers, street-sweepers or vendors.

Charles's grandparents were not Irish immigrants, as it happens. To the contrary, his lineage has been traced back to a member of the English landed gentry, one William Phipps, who bought Yarnton estate in Oxford in about 1575. Comprising a farmhouse and two yardlands, the estate had formed part of Yarnton Manor, which Henry VIII had sold to George Owen, his physician, in 1538. Our interest in the line begins in 1713, when Elizabeth Phipps married John Weston. We shall see how the Phipps and Weston surnames crop up repeatedly as Christian names in the subsequent Leonard family. As the only surviving child of the late Robert Phipps, Elizabeth inherited Yarnton farm, but, after falling on hard times, she, her husband and son sold the estate to Exeter College in 1739, although they continued to lease the farmhouse. It was their daughter Sarah, born at Yarnton, who married into the Leonard family when she exchanged vows with William Leonard of Market Lavington, Wiltshire.[7]

William and Sarah then settled in Abingdon, just to the south of Oxford, where they raised a family. Two of their sons graduated from the University of Oxford and became Anglican priests, but it is another son, Phipps Weston Leonard, in whom we are most interested since he grew up to father John William Weston Leonard, born in 1790 or 1791.[8] John was Charles Leonard's grandfather and deserves the credit for having changed his family's fortunes.

In 1815, at the age of 25, John married Elizabeth Taylor, 20, at the church of St James, Paddington.[9] Their first child, Mary Anne, was born the following year and a second daughter, named after her mother, entered the world two years later.[10] John was a tanner or, to be more precise, a currier by

---

[7] www.thequietzone.com/genealogy/documents/leonardtree.doc Retrieved 9 September 2015.
[8] www.southafricansettlers.com/?cat=22&paged=21 Retrieved 9 September 2015.
[9] Sue Mackay, citing the London Metropolitan Archives. www.eggsa.org/1820-settlers/index.php/additional-information/i-surnames/1588-leonard-john-extra-data Retrieved on 6 July 2015. Another genealogist claims that John William Weston Leonard married a different woman: Elizabeth Howard, 21, of Brackley in 1814. www.thequietzone.com/genealogy/documents/leonardtree.doc Retrieved 9 September 2015.
[10] *Ibid.*

Chapter 1

trade and presumably managed to eke out a living.[11] However, following the end of the Napoleonic Wars, the nation's economy was in a precarious state, with returning soldiers and sailors swelling the ranks of the unemployed, particularly in London. With a growing family to support, John must have worried that he might soon be unable to keep the wolf from the door. Besides his financial anxieties, he must also have been concerned about his family's health and safety. As if the squalor of Bloomsbury Market were not sufficient cause for concern, a few years earlier, in October 1814, a great vat of porter had exploded at the nearby Horse Shoe Brewery off Tottenham Court Road, releasing thousands of pints of beer into the surrounding streets. Stalls, carts and walls were washed away in the flood, and the beer poured into cellars, drowning eight people, most of them Irish immigrants.[12] Who knew what calamity might descend on the Leonard family?

Then, in 1819, with another baby on the way, John read an article in *The Times* which announced that the Government intended introducing a settlement scheme in a colony far across the sea. It trumpeted: 'Our noble station at the Cape of Good Hope has the finest soil and climate in the world; it is the centre of both hemispheres – it commands the commerce of the globe – it produces in unparalleled abundance all the necessities of life.'[13] The name of the colony alone was enough to inspire confidence. To be honest, the Cape of Good Hope sounded like paradise. Shortly thereafter, John was given a handbill which announced that a meeting was to be held at 8 p.m. on 9 August at the Crown and Anchor Tavern on the Strand for those interested in 'Colonizing the Cape'.[14] After talking it over with Elizabeth, John decided to find out more.

As he neared the Thames, he fell in with an acquaintance, James Leader, who was also considering emigrating. When they reached the tavern, they found it packed to capacity and struggled to force their way inside. The atmosphere was thick with smoke and the crowd was making such a din that the two newcomers gave up trying to converse. The men were angry that the convener of the meeting had failed to arrive, and then rejected the proposals put forward by a hastily elected committee. Fortunately, a civil servant named John Bailie managed to restore some sort of order. As he rose to speak, he was greeted with the predictable smattering of jeers and gibes. He smiled and

---

[11] *Ibid.*
[12] Ackroyd, Peter. *op. cit.*, 133. However, the date was 1814, not 1818, as he has it.
[13] Bell, May. *They Came from a Far Land*, 9.
[14] Nash, M.D. *Bailie's Party of 1820 Settlers*, Plate 2.

raised his hands for silence. Some choice Cockney insults from the floor succeeded in silencing the loudmouths.

Bailie spoke stirringly about his plans to gather a party which might emigrate to the Cape under a new scheme under-written by the Government. At this, a group of Radicals disrupted the meeting, loudly opposing the scheme, arguing that Britain needed to provide for her unemployed masses, not ship them overseas. Bailie was not to be deterred, however. If he were successful, he shouted, his party would be given free passage and each member would receive a one-acre plot of land in a planned village and a hundred acres of land capable of being farmed. This announcement was received with whoops and prolonged cheers and applause. Six hundred people applied to join Bailie's party that very evening.[15]

John, too, was tempted to put his name down there and then but decided to discuss it with Elizabeth first. However, as he left the tavern, he was called aside by Leader, who was accompanied by two other men, whom he introduced as James Hoole and William Nobbs. He told John that Hoole intended forming a party of his own and that he and Nobbs had agreed to throw in their lot with him. John listened as Hoole outlined the advantages of joining his party, but, if truth be told, John needed little persuading and Hoole soon had another volunteer. One can only hope that Elizabeth was also swept along in the wave of enthusiasm. What is certain is that the prospective settlers had no idea of the dangers they would face on the eastern frontier of the Cape.

From the early 18th Century, Dutch *trekboers*[16] had begun migrating eastwards along the southern coast of the Cape Colony in search of better pastures and to escape the unwelcome attentions of first the Dutch and then the British colonial authorities, who sought to tax them and impose other restrictions. At the same time, the amaFengu and amaXhosa tribes, who were also nomadic herdsmen, were migrating south-westwards as part of the *Difaqane*, the diaspora of tribes fleeing the slave raiders from Delagoa Bay and the incursions of King Shaka and his amaZulu warriors further to the south. The *trekboers* and tribesmen confronted each other near the Great Fish River in the Eastern Cape, and neither was prepared to capitulate. So began what used to be called the Xhosa or Frontier Wars but have more recently come to be known as the Wars of Dispossession. The refusal of the amaXhosa to give up their land without a fight caused headaches for a series of British

---

[15] *Ibid.*, 20.
[16] Migrating farmers.

Governors at the Cape, who regarded it as their duty to expand the boundaries of the British dominion, but not at unreasonable cost, either in terms of lives or money.

> The politicians hoped that their scheme to flood the frontier territory with colonists might, by sheer force of numbers, secure the border region both from the predations of native tribes and also from the expansionist designs of the Dutch and other European states. From the government's point of view, the frontier needed to be settled and defended at a cost which was manageable, and settlers were cheaper than military garrisons. There had already been some settlement by a few hundred men in 1817, but those settlers had caused more trouble than they were worth, dispersing into the fledgling towns of the colony and refusing to move to the frontier zone where life was uncomfortable and dangerous.
>
> This time, in 1819, things were more organised. Twenty-six vessels were chartered by the Government. All that the settlers were told was that there was a wonderful climate, with limitless opportunities for occupying land of their own (without cost), and a landscape of lush green meadows and parkland.[17]

John and Elizabeth thought that they had nothing to lose and much to gain. There were no ties holding them back, and they were still young and energetic. As things turned out, several families dropped out of Hoole's party and others were refused permission to travel, so it looked for a while as though the Leonards' hopes might be dashed, but similar problems had beset Bailie's party, so he invited the remnants of Hoole's group to join his.

> The Articles of Agreement of the party bound its members to mutual assistance… A village was planned with provision for public amenities, and ground was to be cleared at first and houses built by communal labour. Tools and implements and a library were to be held as common stock, and the purchase or employment of slaves and the sale of spirituous liquor were strictly forbidden.[18]

---

[17] brian-angelmountain.blogspot.com/2012_12_01_archive.html. Retrieved 9 April 2015.
[18] Nash, M.D. *The Settler Handbook*, 39.

A few months later, probably in late November, in a state of nervous anticipation, the Leonard family said their farewells and boarded the transport at Deptford. Their party of 256 had been allocated to the sailing ship *Chapman*, which, after a delay caused by the Thames icing up, set sail from Gravesend early in December.[19] After dropping the pilot and some seasick passengers off at the Downs, the *Chapman*, accompanied by the *Nautilus*, steered a southerly course into the Atlantic and the old country was soon far astern. Many of the emigrants, like Harry Hastings, a semi-fictitious character conceived by John Ayliff, must have had mixed feelings:

> I sat alone on the poop and watched old England recede from my view till it became a speck and when it seemed to sink into the sea, I felt the tears start from my eyes, and I do not know how it is, that tho' remembrances of charity sermons, taxes, workhouses etc. caused me to feel glad that I am getting away from a region so poor and cold, yet after all, that little speck I have just seen sink into the ocean seems to me as 'the loveliest land on the face of the earth'.[20]

Whatever exuberance or regrets the Leonards might have felt as they set off on their adventure would soon have been forgotten as the harsh conditions aboard ship took their toll.

Heading down the Channel, they ran into a terrific storm, which John Mandy on the *Nautilus* described thus: 'It came on to blow tremendously hard, the sea running mountains high.' Then 'our troubles began, the sea breaking over us in all directions, tables, chairs, boxes, plates and dishes, men, women, and children all mixed together, tumbling over one another, and all dreadfully seasick... At half-past eight our pilot informed us we were out of danger.'[21] But the pilot was wrong. The *Nautilus* ran aground on the dreaded Goodwin Sands and the *Chapman* had to sail on, leaving the *Nautilus* to her fate. Fortunately, the tide soon lifted the stranded ship free and a few days later, she caught up with the *Chapman*, much to the respective passengers' delight. The ships completed the rest of their 6,000-mile voyage within sight or hailing distance of each other.[22]

Life below deck continued to be taxing, however. Louisa Biddulph

---

[19] Bell, May. *op. cit.*, 11.
[20] Ayliff, John. *The Journal of Harry Hastings – Albany Settler*, 38.
[21] Bell, May. *op. cit.*, 13-14.
[22] *Ibid.*, 14.

described the accommodation aboard the *Chapman* thus:

> The after-cabin was allotted to the use of the principal passengers, about fifty in number, twenty-five of whom were children. This cabin was divided at night by a canvas screen – sixteen ladies slept on one side and fourteen gentlemen on the other. Unless you have been on board a transport you can have no idea of the miserable situation we were in.[23]

If she considered the accommodation of the principal passengers miserable, one can imagine what conditions were like for the remaining two hundred. During the four months that they were at sea, an epidemic of whooping-cough carried off six young children. Six women gave birth as well.[24]

> There was also considerable friction amongst the passengers, not only because of the cramped conditions and illness on board, but also because Bailie's authoritarian manner created resentment. In addition, there was a greater social mix on this ship than on any of the others, and the gentry were not used to living cheek by jowl with skilled artisans, tradesmen, farmers and labourers.[25]

Unlike the directors of the other large settler parties, Bailie had not sought permission for a clergyman to accompany the party, which turned out to be an unfortunate oversight. If there had been a man of the cloth on board, he could have relieved the captain of the unpleasant duty of conducting the funerals of the deceased (whose mortal remains were consigned to the ocean) and he might have been in a more advantageous position to mediate in the conflicts.

On 23 December, the ships passed the island of Madeira, and on New Year's Eve, the Cape Verde islands of Sal and Boa Vista. Two days later, they ran into a severe thunderstorm and the *Chapman* lost her topsail sheet, much to the passengers' alarm. On 12 January, the ships anchored off St Jago and the following day the passengers were allowed ashore, where they enjoyed stretching their legs on *terra firma* and bartered with the islanders for oranges

---

[23] Pringle, John and Hudson-Reed, Sydney. *1820 Settler Sails & Tales*, 54.
[24] Nash, M.D. *The Settler Handbook*, 40.
[25] brian-angelmountain.blogspot.com/2012_12_01_archive.html. Retrieved 9 April 2015.

and lemons. Fresh supplies of water and livestock were also taken aboard. After a few days, the ships resumed their voyage. They made steady progress until the first week of March, when they were becalmed in the tropics for a few days. Water had to be rationed, even though the passengers were experiencing excessive heat and thirst.[26] The captain took pity on his charges and ordered boats to be lowered so that those who wished to could be rowed round the ship. It must have been a welcome distraction.[27]

At last, on 15 March, they had reason to rejoice as the magnificent spectacle of Table Mountain came into view. The *Chapman* dropped anchor at the Cape of Good Hope, but the passengers' hopes of disembarking were quickly dashed as the ship and all aboard were placed under quarantine. A few exceptions were made: Sarah Reed, accompanied by her father, went ashore to marry the ship's captain, John Milbank; Dr O'Flinn needed to stock up with medical supplies; and a man whose printing press had been confiscated by the colonial authorities, went ashore to petition (in vain) for its return.[28]

It was while the *Chapman* lay at anchor off Cape Town (on 18 March) that Elizabeth Leonard gave birth to her first son, who was later christened Edward Chapman.[29] The ship set sail shortly afterwards, but only as far as Simon's Bay, on the other side of the Cape Peninsula, where she remained until 26 March, presumably to take on some last provisions before proceeding to her destination in Algoa Bay.

On the slow voyage along the foot of Africa, the passengers had the opportunity to view their new homeland from the port rail. Thomas Pringle, the poet, journalist and philanthropist, a man who later fought for the freedom of the press and who was instrumental in bringing about the abolition of slavery, was aboard the *Brilliant*. He described the voyage thus:

> As we passed headland after headland, the sylvan recesses of the bays and mountains opened successively to our gaze, like a magnificent panorama, continually unfolding new features… The aspect of the whole was impressive but sombre; beautiful but somewhat savage… Seated on the poop of the vessel, I gazed alternatively on that solitary shore, and on the bands of emigrants who now crowded the deck or leaned along the

---

[26] From a letter written by Louisa Biddulph, published in the *Port Elizabeth Advertiser* of 23 April 1884, and quoted in Nash, M.D. *Bailie's Party of 1820 Settlers*, 125-6.
[27] Bell, May. *op. cit.*, 14.
[28] Nash, M.D. *Bailie's Party of 1820 Settlers*, 29.
[29] http://www.1820settlers.com/genealogy/getperson.php?personID=I104428&tree=master. Retrieved 2 July 2015.

gangway; some silently musing, like myself, on the scene before us; others conversing in scattered groups and pointing with eager gestures to the country they had come so far to inherit.[30]

When the *Chapman* rounded the last headland in fading daylight on 10 April 1820, thereby becoming the first settler ship to enter Algoa Bay, the emigrants on board stood looking at the land that was to be their home with very different feelings from Pringle's. John Centlivres Chase wrote:

> Our first impressions of the country at which we had at length arrived were anything but cheery. From the deck of our vessel we descried a coast lashed by a broad belt of angry breakers, threatening, we feared, death to a large proportion of our numbers. The shore was girt with an array of barren sandhills, behind and close to which appeared a series of rugged and stony acclivities and, in the distance behind these, the dark and gloomy range of the Winterhoek mountains frowned upon us.[31]

One wonders whether John and Elizabeth Leonard stood arm in arm on deck as daylight faded and whether their meditations were in any way comparable with those of Thomas Pringle:

> It being too late to go ashore that evening, we continued gazing on this scene till long after sunset – till twilight had darkened into night, and the constellations of the southern hemisphere, revolving in cloudless brilliancy above, reminded us that nearly half the globe's expanse intervened between us and our native land – the homes of our youth and the friends we had parted with for ever; and that here, in this farthest nook of Southern Africa, we were now about to receive the portion of our inheritance, and to draw an irrevocable lot for ourselves and for our children's children.[32]

Early the following morning – 11 April 1820 – the passengers and cargo were ferried ashore by surf boat, an extremely hazardous enterprise in the notorious breakers along that coast, but miraculously not one capsized. John, Elizabeth and their children stood on the shore of Algoa Bay as members of

---

[30] Quoted in Bell, May. *op. cit.*, 25.
[31] *Ibid.*, 26.
[32] *Ibid.*, 31.

the first party of settlers who would face the rigours – and the endless possibilities – of their new homeland.

Bailie's Party did not have to camp in tents on the beachfront for long, as subsequent settlers had to do, because on 17 April, they and their worldly goods were loaded on to 96 ox wagons and escorted to their designated location between the Wellington and Palmiet Rivers, where they constructed the village that came to be known as Cuylerville.[33] A few members of the party did not accompany the rest, however: John Leonard and Daniel Hockly, following the example of William Cowper, applied for and were granted the Landdrost's permission to settle in the nearby town of Uitenhage, because they had been offered employment there.[34] However, there is no record of the Leonards in Uitenhage, so it seems more probable that John was offered a job at Papenkuils Fontein, later known as Cradock Place.

> Five miles from the sea, in the midst of scrubby, dreary veld, stood this unexpected and beautiful estate. It belonged to the now wealthy Frederick Korsten, who had left the Dutch navy and settled here, and had all the trade of the district in his hands. He had built a large white house in the gracious, old Cape Dutch style, with figured tiles from Holland and furniture from far and wide; in his garden were palms and roses, an artificial stream, and long rows of oak trees. Besides this he had a tannery, … a mill, and the only store in the neighbourhood.[35]

With his experience as a currier, John was surely offered employment at Korsten's tannery. If this was indeed the case, he did not stay there for long. By late 1821, he had taken his family inland and had settled in the village of Cradock, which had been established about a decade earlier by Sir John Cradock, the Governor of the Cape at the time. He had intended it to be the northernmost point in a line of fortifications aimed at containing the Xhosa to the east of the Great Fish River, which had been proclaimed the eastern border of the Cape Colony. Although intended as a fort, Cradock never saw conflict because the Xhosa confined their raids to the coastal plain.[36] Perhaps it was the threat of or even an experience of such an incursion at Korsten's estate that had convinced John to move his family inland to the relative safety

---

[33] *Ibid.*, 30.
[34] Nash, M.D. *Bailie's Party of 1820 Settlers*, 40.
[35] Bell, May. *op. cit.*, 39.
[36] www.thegreatkaroo.com/listings/tourism_info/eastern_cape/great_karoo/cradock/history Retrieved 11 June 2015

of Cradock. Alternatively, a member of the family may have been consumptive or asthmatic, in which case John could have been advised to settle in the dry interior for health reasons.

After labouring up the escarpment in their wagon and finally having reached the top at Daggaboersnek,[37] John and his family, like most Europeans confronted by the Great Karoo for the first time, would have stared in awe at the dwarfing scale of the landscape. The valley below them stretched away to a series of ridges and mountain silhouettes, which receded one behind the other into the hazy distance. They would have been struck by the silence, too, the sense of peace being enhanced by the clarity of the dry air. Once they had descended into the valley, John would have noticed how the sparse vegetation struggled to conceal the elemental ironstone rock. The searing heat and lack of rainfall in this arid region are enough to deter all but the most determined of farmers. The writer, poet and academic Guy Butler, who grew up in Cradock, astutely wrote that it takes a man with a bit of ironstone in his heart to farm here. Fortunately, John was such a man. He acquired some land and set about building a rudimentary farmstead. His family would have had to sleep in the wagon until the roof was up.

John and Elizabeth 'must often have lain awake listening to the savage sounds of the night, wondering to what sort of country they were bringing their children. The shrill yell of the jackal and the hyena's howl ... "were the regular nightly serenade"; and even by day, the leopard's "deep bass sounded for hours together among the *krantzes*, and the ominous responsive call of the wild dogs as the pack ranged ravenously".'[38]

Winters on the Karoo plateau are severe and dry, and the nights bitterly cold. As darkness fell, the Leonards would no doubt have huddled closer to their fire, singing, chatting, or telling stories. They must have marvelled at the panoply of stars overhead, so different from those in the northern hemisphere and so much more numerous. Due to the lack of humidity and the absence of competing earthly lights, the stars in that region stand out against the darkness in startling clarity. On crystal cold mornings the family sometimes woke to find the mountaintops white with snow.

As the days lengthened during October and into November, they would have waited through days of intensifying heat for the rains to come. 'Only those who have lived in a semi-desert region know of the annual hope and anxiety with which the inhabitants scan the skies for the first cumulus cloud,

---

[37] Literally, 'Marijuana farmer's neck'.
[38] Bell, May. *op. cit.*, quoting the 1820 Settler Isaac Dugmore, 36.

no bigger than a man's hand, which will grow and be joined by others until a great mass, impenetrably purple below, rises high into the firmament.'³⁹ John would have warned his children not to venture out of doors once the wind began to whip up the dust and rattle the windows.

> The atmosphere darkens as for an eclipse. The sheep and cattle make for shelter – some seek it in the dongas, which will soon be drowning-deep. [The farmer] orders the men (mainly his sons) to bring the stock near the homestead to shelter, and to drive the beasts out of the watercourses… The first thunder comes like a sinister drumroll mustering a barbarous host in the remote hills; then much closer, a growling lion's roar… [Then] the storm, a great dark blundering beast, breaks loose… Drops of water smack into the dust… The lightning flashes and stabs, thunder cracks and rumbles… Water comes down on the roof so loud that you have to shout to be heard. Darkness closes in. Lamps are lit… Gutters, runnels, sluits, dongas, rivers, receive the flood that has cut and carved them, which is cutting and carving them now… One by one the men come back…soaked to the skin… The water has released a fragrance from the earth… Later, the thunder passes into the distance, the sky splits into fragments reeling across a calm, remote moon… A few hours later…the river has come down – a strange paradoxical phrase, quite inadequate to describe what has happened. The little trickle that connects the silver pools has disappeared under a cataract of dark brown, rough-backed water stampeding…with a force which carries millions upon millions of tons of topsoil to the sea.⁴⁰

Into this harsh environment, the Leonards' fourth child, John, was born on New Year's Day, 1822, and was baptised in the nearby town of Graaff-Reinet three months later, presumably because there was as yet no suitable church any closer to home. John was followed by another son, James Weston, who was born in Cradock on 27 August 1823.⁴¹ Since he grew up to become Charles Leonard's father, we shall return to him later.

Soon after the birth of their sixth child, Ellen Martha, early in 1825,⁴² the Leonards packed up their belongings once more and moved to the newly

---

³⁹ Butler, Guy. *Karoo Morning*, 17, 77, 111-2 (edited).
⁴⁰ *Ibid.*, 78, 111-12 (edited).
⁴¹ http://archiver.rootsweb.ancestry.com/th/read/SOUTH-AFRICA-IMMIGRANTS-BRITISH/2010-12/1292266200. Retrieved 11 June 2015.
⁴² *Ibid.*

established town of Somerset (its name changed to Somerset East from 1857 to distinguish it from Somerset West near Cape Town). A few years earlier, the Governor of the Cape, Lord Charles Somerset, had established an experimental farm at Agter Bruintjes Hoogte,[43] as the place was then called, but he had recently decided to close it down. The farm had subsequently been parcelled up into 91 erven, which were sold in April 1825, with more than half being bought by British Settlers.[44] Tucked into the forested Boschberg Mountains, this little town is surrounded by fertile farmlands.[45] It was a fertile place for Elizabeth Leonard, too, for she produced three more children while living there: William Weston in 1827, Harry (date of birth unknown) and Tryphena in 1831, bringing the number of her children to nine.[46]

Soon after Tryphena's birth, the Leonard family moved once again, this time to Grahamstown, where they joined many other 1820 Settlers and their families who had left farming to establish themselves in more secure trades. By 1833, the population of Grahamstown was estimated to be about 6,000.[47] In a few decades it became the Cape Colony's largest town after Cape Town and was traditionally the capital and English-speaking cultural centre of the Albany district. John started a tannery business and fathered three more children: Francis Phipps in 1834, Frances Hannah in 1835, and – finally – Jane in 1838. All three, with Tryphena, were baptised in St George's Anglican church (now Cathedral), Grahamstown, on 10 January 1839.[48] One has to pity John Heavyside, the poor chaplain! For Elizabeth to have successfully given birth to twelve children over a period of twenty-two years, and for all of them to have survived childhood, was a quite extraordinary achievement. It is thanks to their fecundity that the Leonards' countless progeny continue to populate the Eastern Cape and further afield to this day.

Unfortunately, in 1841, the patriarch of the line, John William Weston Leonard, was declared insolvent and seven lots of ground belonging to him in

---

[43] Literally, 'Behind Little Brown Height'.
[44] www.thegreatkaroo.com/all/eastern_cape/great_karoo/somerset_east. Retrieved 11 June 2015.
[45] www.southafrica.net/za/en/articles/entry/article-southafrica.net-somerset-east-eastern-cape. Retrieved 11 June 2015.
[46] www.geni.com>people>John-Leonard Retrieved 11 June 2015.
[47] *Roberts, Edmund. Embassy to the Eastern Courts of Cochin-China, Siam, and Muscat, 388.*
[48] http://archiver.rootsweb.ancestry.com/th/read/SOUTH-AFRICA-EASTERN-CAPE-L Re: [ZA-EC] JohnLEONARD . British Resident 1795-1819CapebyPeterPhillips based on the Cory Library Repository, MS 14 878-2, transcribed by Lynn Couperthwaite as part of the eGGSA project from photographs by William Jervois. Retrieved 9 September 2015.

Grahamstown were put up for sale. It is not clear what happened to Elizabeth and the children at this time, but it seems that they moved back to Somerset East, where friends must have taken them in. We do know that John became a transport rider or carrier, but that he died in a wagon accident near Burgersdorp (or Burgher's Dorp, as it was then known) on 26 July 1850 at the age of 60.[49]

Many years before, as young parents, he and Elizabeth had made the courageous decision to start a new life in a distant land and, no matter what one's opinion of colonialism may be, there can be no denying that they had tried to make the best of a challenging set of circumstances. They had both inherited the Protestant work ethic and no doubt instilled it in their children. In addition, they were almost certainly pragmatic, applying themselves to solving problems, rather than entertaining romantic aspirations or indulging in philosophical musings. They were also blessed with stoicism, not only enduring hard times, but doing what they could to rise above whatever sufferings, disappointments and setbacks life threw at them. Many of these character traits would have been passed on to their children and must have stood them in good stead during their adult lives. We know from later events that their grandson Charles had such qualities in abundance.

In the mid-1840s, their son, James Weston Leonard, who was by now in his early twenties, married a young woman named Elizabeth (or Eliza) Howard. She had been born on 16 February 1826 while her parents were living in the barracks at Fort Willshire, right in the heart of the dangerous frontier territory.[50] Eliza's elder sister, Susannah Brandt, had died in 1835 at the age of 14 and her younger sister, Sarah Ann, died eleven years later at the age of 5.[51] The Howards were also 1820 Settlers, having arrived as members of Thornhill's party aboard the *Zoroaster*. Eliza's father was John Hassell Howard, a chemist, druggist and apothecary, and her mother was Susannah Howard, née Brandt.[52] This accounts for Charles Leonard's rather unusual third name, Brandt, given to him in honour of his maternal grandmother.

A photograph survives of James and Eliza taken early in their married

---

[49] Nash, M.D. *op. cit.*, 150.
[50] Baptismal register, 1826. Commemoration Methodist Church, Grahamstown.
[51] EC Genealogical Society Newsletter, May 2005, N. 73, cited by Becky Horne in 'British Settler Cemetery, Somerset East – Part II', dated 29 May 2005, http://archiver.rootsweb.ancestry.com/th/read/SOUTH-AFRICA-EASTERN-CAPE>2005-05>1117391707 Retrieved 6 July 2015.
[52] www.1820settlers.co.uk/genealogy/getperson.php?ID:I87877&tree=master. Retrieved 11 June 2015.

life.[53] Comparing this photograph with those later taken of Charles, one is struck by the strong resemblance between father and son. They both have dark hair, a straight brow, smooth skin, slightly hooded eyes, a neat nose, prominent lips, fleshy earlobes, a strong jaw and an upright carriage.

James was clearly determined to make up for his father's shortcomings and took to business in earnest. He bought a number of erven in Somerset East, including a large property at 10, Charles Street, which is where he and his family lived.[54]

> At one time he [James Leonard] was almost omnipotent; of high talent, amazing information, and unrivalled powers of persuasion, he was the leader of every movement, and scarcely any scheme was organised for the benefit of the town in which he was not a prime mover.[55]

1846 was a good year for the Leonard family: on 15 April, the 29-year-old Elizabeth, second daughter of John and Elizabeth and elder sister to James, married Edward Wade of the prosperous Glen Avon Farm in Somerset East;[56] and James and Eliza welcomed their first child, Margaret Eliza, into the world. A second daughter, Ann Charlotte, was born two years later.[57] But then the couple suffered two tragic losses: their third daughter, Susannah Elizabeth, died in 1850, aged 14 months; and their first son, James, died at 20 months.[58] The first son to survive childhood was James Weston, born on 20 April 1853.[59] To avoid confusion with his father, who had the same names, he was called Jim or Jimmy. He was to play a significant role in his younger brother's life and a leading role in the public affairs of his country, so more of him later.

---

[53] Hagley Hall Archives. No catalogue number.
[54] KAB, MOIB 2/1414, 166. Leonard, James, Insolvent Liquidation and Distribution Account, 1858-78.
[55] *Somerset and Bedford Courant*, 1 May 1878, 2-3.
[56] http://archiver.rootsweb.ancestry.com/th/read/SOUTH-AFRICA-EASTERN-CAPE>2005-02>1107815511 Post by Sue Mackay. Retrieved 6 July 2015.
[57] http://archiver.rootsweb.ancestry.com/th/read/SOUTH-AFRICA-IMMIGRANTS-BRITISH/2010-12/1292266200. Post by Johann H. Claassen. Retrieved 11 June 2015.
[58] EC Genealogical Society Newsletter, May 2005, N. 73, cited by Becky Horne in 'British Settler Cemetery, Somerset East – Part II', dated 29 May 2005, http://archiver.rootsweb.ancestry.com/th/read/SOUTH-AFRICA-EASTERN-CAPE>2005-05>1117391707 Retrieved 6 July 2015.
[59] Anon. 'The Hon JW Leonard KC' (1905) 22 *South African Law Journal* (hereafter *SALJ*) 132142.

James and Eliza's next son, who would grow up to lead an even more eventful life than his elder brother, was born in Somerset (later Somerset East) on 31 March 1856. He was christened Charles Henry Brandt Leonard.[60]

---

[60] Cape Archives Repository (hereafter KAB), MOOC, 6/9/1894, 186. Leonard, Charles Henry Brandt Leonard, Estate Papers, 1921.

Chapter 1

James and Eliza Leonard, Charles' parents, c. 1850. Charles inherited many of his father's features.

Annie, Eliza and Charles Leonard, c. 1867, before Annie's wedding. Charles was about 12 years old.

The Reverend Templeton's school in Bedford as it looked in its foundation year, 1867. Both Charles and his elder brother Jim – as well as a host of boys who went on to become legal luminaries – attended this remarkable school, which is still in existence today.

Fertile farmlands of Somerset East with the Boschberg in the distance

CHAPTER 2 : FORMATIVE YEARS
(1856-1876)

I was given a good life in a lovable world among remarkable people.

– Guy Butler, writing of his childhood in *Karoo Morning*

As a boy, Charles Leonard must have been immensely proud of his father. Not only was he a successful and wealthy businessman, but he was also one of the most respected and public-spirited members of the community. For many years, he was Chairman of the Municipality and one of the Directors of the Somerset East Bank, which had been built on one of his properties in the town. He was the moving force behind the erection of the Fish River Bridge, while his scheme for bringing piped water into the town was postponed only until the increase of the population rendered it possible. He was also a keen politician, regularly speaking his mind on public platforms.

> On all these occasions Mr Leonard displayed oratorical prowess of the highest order, and on one of these his rare command of homely Dutch, and that real English love of fair play, that made him translate an opponent's speech as truthfully as if it had been a friend's.
> …
> But it was for his efforts on behalf of the natives that Mr Leonard was most distinguished. For many years he managed the Native School. By his influence a succession of first-rate teachers, such as Messrs Frost and Gordon conducted it, and, the expense thereby incurred, came in

great measure out of his own pocket.[61]

He was pastor to about two hundred local 'natives', leading them in worship and teaching them in a chapel, which he himself had built. He was even appointed their marriage officer by the Governor of the Cape himself.[62]

Eliza Leonard was devoted to her husband and children, working hard to provide them with a comfortable home and striving to bring up her family in the tradition of their English forebears. She 'set great store by observing the proprieties, for she had seen some families degenerate into poor-whiteness from having to live in houses with mud floors and unglazed windows… [She] made a point of using the family silver and best linen every day and she allowed no untoward conversation at table… One of her regular admonitions was, "You will preserve your respectabilities if you keep your furniture and nice things about you."'[63]

It is apparent from letters that Charles wrote in later life that he grew up in a closely knit and loving family. He was no idealist to believe in the sanctity of marriage and in the mutual love and support of husband and wife, as well as in the strength of sibling love and loyalty. He had had personal experience of all of these during his formative years. Besides his three elder siblings already mentioned, Charles soon had five younger brothers and sisters: Susannah Brandt (called Susie), Mary Emily Green (known by her second name), Hassell Bruce (who seems to have died between 1878 and 1903), Gertrude Alice Sophia (known as Gertie Amy), and John Woodford Stoney (known by his second name and as Woodie by his family).[64]

When Charles was seven years old, there was great excitement in the Leonard household because the eldest daughter Margaret was to marry her beau, William Brown Taylor of Vine Park, Uitenhage, and late of East Lothian, Scotland. The wedding took place in the parish church on 8 September 1863,[65] with the groom no doubt appropriately attired in his clan kilt and sporran. There may well have been the skirl of bagpipes in the church or at the reception, but it is unlikely that haggis was served. Early in their married life, William took his wife back home to Scotland, where they settled

---

[61] *Somerset and Bedford Courant*, 1 May 1878, 2-3.
[62] KAB, CO 4115, 278. Memorial. James Leonard. Application to be appointed marriage officer amongst kaffirs [sic] at Somerset East, 1860.
[63] McMagh, Kathleen. *A Dinner of Herbs: Being the Memoirs of Kathleen McMagh*, 65-6.
[64] KAB, MOOC 6/9/163, 5293. James Leonard Death Notice, 1878.
[65] www.eggsa.org/newspapers/index.php/grahamstown-journal/1171-grahamstown-journal-1863-3-july-to-september Retrieved 11 June 2015.

at Seafield, Banffshire. In 1872, Margaret gave birth to a son, christened Harry James Charles.[66] Another son, Bertram Alexander Leonard, was born there nine years later.[67] Margaret also produced three daughters, who are identified in the records merely by their married names: Mrs Lindsay (4, Murrayfield Gardens, Edinburgh), Mrs Campbell (Shian, Woodcote Road, Wallington, Surrey) and Mrs Frederick Walford (living with Mrs Lindsay).[68]

A photograph survives of Charles, his elder sister Annie (as she was known) and their mother Eliza, taken when Charles was about twelve years old.[69] He was tall for his age, with full lips, a slightly upturned nose and a widow's peak. He also appears to have been of serious demeanour, but it may just have been the custom not to smile in photographs. They are dressed in their Sunday best, which may also account for their sombre mood. Sunday was observed as the Christian Sabbath, a day devoted to worship and rest, and Mr Leonard or the local Presbyterian minister would have chastised any laddie or lassie who dared do anything which might be construed as work or fun on the Lord's Day. On Sunday mornings, Charles would have attended church with his family and every other member of the community, after which he would have moped about the house with nothing to do but irritate his siblings or read the Holy Bible, which would not have been shut away in a bookcase but would have been left open on a table. As an adult, he was wont to quote from the Good Book.

For a young boy finding his way in the world, Somerset East held many attractions. Early travellers considered the Boschberg to be the most beautiful mountain in southern Africa. Cascading waterfalls and clear streams nourish forests of Yellowwood, Wild Olive and Cape Chestnut, as well as more than eighty indigenous tree species which grow on the slopes. Besides the wealth of flora, the mountain is home to many types of buck, and close to a hundred bird species, including the Piet-my-vrou, Knysna Loerie, Booted Eagle and

---

[66] "Scotland, Births and Baptisms, 1564-1950", Index, FamilySearch (https://familysearch.org/arki/61903/1:1:XYBQ-2XZ), Margaret Eliza Leonard in entry for Harry James Charles Taylor, 27 Jun. 1872; citing Seafield, Banff, reference n167 p6; FHL microfilm 6,035,516. Retrieved 9 April 2015.
[67] "Scotland, Births and Baptisms, 1564-1950", Index, FamilySearch (https://familysearch.org/arki/61903/1:1:XT6B-6XY), Margaret Eliza Leonard in entry for Bertram Alexander Leonard Taylor, 25 Apr. 1881; citing Seafield, Banffshire, Scotland, reference n167 p6; FHL microfilm 232,630. Retrieved 9 April 2015.
[68] KAB, MOOC 13/1/4643, 224. Leonard, Charles Henry Brandt, Liquidation and Distribution Account, 1922.
[69] Hagley Hall Archives. No catalogue number.

Crowned Eagle.[70] Charles must have revelled in exploring such a wonderland, though he would have had to beware of wild predators, snakes, spiders and scorpions.

From an early age, he would have learnt to ride a horse and to shoot, both regarded as indispensable accomplishments for boys and girls on the frontier. He would no doubt have had his own dog (in later life he owned a number of dogs and horses). With his siblings, he would have had to help about the house, for children knew what hard work meant and were taught to fend for themselves, if needs be. Most of them married before they were out of their teens.

Charles's second sister Annie is a case in point. On 16 September 1867, she married Louis (or Lewies or Luis) 'Waterval' Nel, who lived in the Somerset East district on the farm Rietfontein.[71] He and Annie were only nineteen years old when they wed. Over the next two decades, she was to bear him eleven children, two of whom would die in infancy (Lorna at fourteen months and Leonard Weston at three weeks).[72] As a matter of interest, her husband's younger sister Ydie married Gysbert Reitz Hofmeyr, who later became Administrator of South West Africa.[73]

Annie's marriage to Louis raises the question of the relationship between settlers of British and Dutch ancestry on the eastern frontier of the Cape Colony, and of the attitude of one group towards the other. The British had, after all, recaptured the Cape from the Dutch in 1806 and Lord Charles Somerset had polarised Dutch and English colonists by imposing a policy of Anglicisation, banning the use of the Dutch language throughout the Colony, even in the Dutch Reformed Church. That is why Scottish Presbyterian ministers such as Dr Andrew Murray had been invited to come to South Africa: while 'Dutchmen' had no choice but to listen to English (or a dialect that purports to be English) in their churches, at least they would be spared from listening to 'Papist' doctrine!

Then, on 1 December 1834, slavery was abolished in all British colonies and slaves were emancipated. This was one of the major causes of the Great

---

[70] www.places.co.za/html/somerset_east.html. Retrieved 11 June 2015.
[71] Ancestry.com, Rootsweb: Archiver>SOUTH-AFRICA-IMMIGRANT-BRITISH>2010-12>1292266200 Retrieved 12 April 2015.
[72] Gravestone of Annie Nel, Kerkstraat Cemetery, Oudtshoorn. www.eggsa.org>library. Western Cape, OUDTSHOORN, Kerkstraat cemetery – eGGSA home. Photograph of tombstone contributed by Alta Griffiths, 29 June 2009. Retrieved 11 June 2015.
[73] af.wikipedia.org/wiki/Gysbert_Reitz_Hofmeyr. Retrieved 11 June 2015.

Trek, in which a number of Dutch farmers (Boers), who regarded it as their right to own slaves, loaded up their ox wagons and, with their families, slaves and livestock, headed off into the dangerous and uncharted interior of the country.

As a result of all these measures, it would come as no surprise if the Dutch settlers in the Eastern Cape resented their English neighbours and refrained from associating with them, but this was not the case. They knew that most of the English settlers also objected to interference from colonial officials, but it was not only this shared antipathy towards authority that broke down any barriers that might have existed between them; it was their common struggle against the natural elements and their having to defend themselves against marauding tribes that united them. These shared challenges and experiences forged bonds of mutual respect, trust, reliance and friendship, even to the point of intermarriage.

Charles Leonard may have been descended from English settlers, but his roots were buried deep in the African soil, so much so that he called himself an Afrikander.[74] He certainly shared none of the common English-speakers' prejudice towards the Boers; to the contrary, he later counted a number of them amongst his closest friends. He would in all likelihood have echoed the sentiments of Olive Schreiner, one of South Africa's foremost novelists, who in the late nineteenth century worked as a teacher on Boer farms in the Cradock district:

> For… years I lived among them…, sometimes among the more cultured, and sometimes among the more primitive but not one whit less lovable and intelligent, class. I… was brought into the closest contact with them which is possible… Watching them in all the vicissitudes of life, from birth to marriage and death, I learnt to love the Boer, but more, I learnt to admire him. I learnt that in the African Boer we have one of the most intellectually virile and dominant races the world has seen; a people who beneath a calm and almost stolid surface hide the intensest [*sic*] passions

---

[74] The term *Afrikander* (also spelled *Africander*), a word of Cape Dutch origin, was originally used to imply an African native, then a half caste, then a South African white of Dutch speech and sympathies, but it eventually became enlarged to mean any South African-born white. Only later did it become *Afrikaner* and refer only to those who speak Afrikaans, the indigenous South African language derived from Dutch and other influences.

and the most indomitable resolutions.⁷⁵

Charles himself had this to say about his Dutch-speaking compatriots in 1892:

> I have many firm friends amongst the Dutchmen in this country. I am a South African born, and my parents were born here, and I claim to be as good a South African as any of them. I yield to no man in my admiration of the good qualities which the Dutch population undoubtedly possess. The Boer is prejudiced, and has not had the opportunity for the wider culture which many of us have enjoyed, and we should assist him and not blackguard him too heartily.'⁷⁶

In 1897, he added, 'I had no dislike for the Boers; I am South African born, and I had lived amongst them all my life; and had more than a friendly feeling towards them.'⁷⁷ Charles may have grown up to accept and like the Boers, but what was his attitude towards black South Africans? It would not have differed markedly from that of white people who had had a similar upbringing, and which is described with such unflinching candour by Guy Butler in *Karoo Morning*:

> Whites gave the orders; the rest obeyed as servants and labourers…we were seldom aware of the…injustice. How should we be? We grew up into it, almost unquestioning. It was all we knew – we had no standards of comparison. It had always been so. It would change for the better, of course, gradually, particularly for the blacks and Coloureds, who would slowly, and at a pace which would not make a single white ever feel threatened or uncomfortable, become civilised like us… A favourite argument was: It took us (whites) 2000 years to get where we were. And we were a clever lot. The blacks must be patient, particularly with themselves. After all, they had only just met civilisation – a mere 200 or 300 years ago.⁷⁸

---

⁷⁵ Quoted by T.S. Emslie, the editor, in his Introduction to *Karoo Moon*, a compilation of Olive Schreiner's novels, xii-xiii.
⁷⁶ Leonard, Charles. *Papers on the Political Situation in South Africa 1885-1895*, 166. http://www.ebooksread.com/authors-eng/charles-leonard/papers Retrieved 4 May 2015.
⁷⁷ *Ibid.*, 383.
⁷⁸ Butler, Guy. *op. cit.*, 205.

Chapter 2

This shockingly paternalistic, but – for the time – prevalent, belief in racial supremacy would have been inculcated in Charles, his friends and siblings, not only by their parents, but by their teachers as well, in what might euphemistically be labelled a Eurocentric approach to education but was in fact undeniably racist.

According to the *South African Law Journal*, Jim (and presumably Charles and his siblings) attended the local school, where their first schoolmaster was the Reverend Peter Wither, who is described as a Scottish *dominie*[79] of the old school, not sparing in his use of the birch. It is claimed that from him the Leonard boys derived their love of the classics, which they were wont to quote in later public life. We do not know how the younger brothers and sisters took to their studies, but it seems that Jim 'in his early boyhood…showed himself anything but a studious pupil'.[80]

The boys completed their schooling at the public high school in the nearby town of Bedford, founded in 1867 by the Reverend Templeton. They may have boarded at the school or stayed with a relative in the area, at least on weekdays, since it would have been too arduous to travel the 60-mile (100 km) return journey between Somerset East and Bedford daily. Their uncle, Francis Phipps Leonard, owned a farm in the Bedford district, so he and his family possibly took the boys in.

The first impression one has of Bedford, founded in 1854, is of the green-striped mountain looming over it. Indeed, the San (Bushmen) who had inhabited these parts many years earlier, called these mountains *kaga* ('stripes', the same name they gave to the zebra, and from which the name quagga is derived). The name stuck. The Kaga Mountain, encircling the town as it does, ensures that Bedford has a more moderate climate and better groundwater than its neighbours. The decidedly English character of the town is largely due to the influence of the 1820 Settlers' Pringle party, who settled and farmed in the nearby Baviaans River Valley.[81]

During the course of one decade (from the early 1860s to the early 1870s), Reverend Templeton's small upcountry school produced a string of exceptional achievers, almost all of whom became lawyers, and went on to make their mark in their homeland and beyond. Besides the remarkable achievements of the Leonard brothers (which will be revealed later), two of

---

[79] In Scottish English, the word *dominie* is used to refer to a schoolmaster. In Afrikaans it means a minister in one of the Reformed Churches.
[80] Anon. 'The Hon JW Leonard KC' (1905) 22 *SALJ* 132142.
[81] www.southafrica.net/za/en/articles/entry/article-southafrica.net-bedford. Retrieved 11 June 2015.

the past pupils became Chief Justices of South Africa and were knighted for their services to the Crown. They were Sir James Rose-Innes and Sir William Solomon. The latter's brothers were also knighted: Sir Edward Solomon, who became a leading lawyer and politician in the Transvaal; and Sir Richard Solomon, who besides being a leader at the bar, became Attorney-General at the Cape and Union High Commissioner in London. Another past pupil, William Otto Danckwerts, became a leader of the bar in London and fathered a future Lord Justice of Appeal. Then there was William Schreiner, the brother of the acclaimed author Olive, who became Attorney-General and Prime Minister at the Cape and later South African High Commissioner in London.[82]

Having obtained an M.A. with honours from Glasgow University, Robert Templeton emigrated to the Cape Colony and taught at Lovedale College until 1864. While he was there, he married Elizabeth Calderwood. He then became a Presbyterian minister and taught in Uitenhage before establishing his own school at Bedford, which exists to this day and is named after him, helping in some degree to commemorate the great service which he rendered to the cause of education.[83] His former pupil, Sir James Rose-Innes, later paid this tribute to Templeton:

> He was a born teacher who threw his whole soul into his work. Endowed with a clear and logical mind, he had the gift of imparting knowledge, as well as the power of stimulating thought. Frail in body, he possessed an indomitable spirit and a personality which energized the whole school. By nature quick-tempered, he was by grace self-controlled, but there was a glint in his eye when roused which restrained the hardiest spirit. Two faults there were which never failed to rouse him, untruthfulness and impertinence. In dealing with these, his methods were short, sharp and decisive. Yet his patience with even the dullest pupil was unbounded. He was a strict disciplinarian, but always just, and, though we regarded him not only with respect but with a certain awe, we all loved the *Ou*.[84]

---

[82] McSporran, Jane. *Great achievers educated at a small East Cape village school* (cited in www.genesreunited.co.uk/boards/board/general_chat/thread/1140724) Retrieved 7 July 2015.
[83] *Ibid*.
[84] Tindall, B.A. *James Rose-Innes, chief justice of South Africa, 1914-27, Autobiography*, quoted in Butler, Guy. *When Boys Were Men*, 270.

Another to prioritise the education of local children was Dr William Gill. He had arrived in Somerset East in 1829, having been appointed District Surgeon there.

> Dr Gill was a kindly man who never pressed his patients for payment so he did not make a fortune from his profession. He was, however, a keen farmer and it was from his merino-sheep farm near Cookhouse that he made his money; and he was determined that his fortune should be devoted to the education of poor boys who might not otherwise have an opportunity in life. So he instructed his friend James Leonard to draw up his will and to see to it that bequests were made available for this purpose. Dr Gill decreed incidentally that his legacy was not to be used for the erection of school buildings, and he named seven men to form a 'Gill College Corporation'. One was James Leonard and another was Dr Langham Dale, then Superintendent of Education of Cape Colony.
>
> The building of the school was a considerable undertaking, as the people of the village and district who had pledged to pay the costs were to suffer from droughts and subsequent depression, but eventually on Christmas Eve in 1868 Gill College opened its doors for the first time.[85]

Gill College was initially an institution of higher learning, becoming only a high school in 1903. Jim Leonard, who was one of the first students to be enrolled there, obtained the second-class certificate of the Board of Examiners, which was equivalent to the B.A. degree of the Cape University.[86]

In its foundation year, the former headmaster of Shaw College in Grahamstown, Peter MacOwan, was appointed head of natural sciences at Gill. His special area of interest was botany and he worked with local farmers to understand which plant species were favoured by which animals. He received most help from James Leonard, who had recently taken up farming, having acquired the farm Hartebeest Leegte. Already as a child, he had come to know 'the names of the varieties of plants, the seasonal flowers, the birds and their nesting-places, their characteristic cries and flight – small buck, ground squirrels, meercats and other small mammals – reptiles, snakes, lizards and tortoises – the veld, a perennial source of delight, mainly sunlit, dry and still, sometimes overcast and damp, or windy, the shrubs shaking, and cirrus

---

[85] McMagh, Kathleen. *op. cit.*, 66-7.
[86] Anon. 'The Hon JW Leonard KC' (1905) 22 *SALJ* 132142.

clouds streaking the blue overhead'.[87] Now, as an adult, his close observation of the habits of his animals and of the shrubs and grasses which fed them brought him success as a livestock farmer.

> Mr Leonard was of considerable assistance to Professor MacOwan in developing the Botanical resources of this division. His quick intelligence and powers of observation enabled him to form an idea of what Mr MacOwan wished to find, and its probable *habitat*, and then he grudged no labour and expense to discover it.[88]

MacOwan began to publish on Cape plants, economic botany, veld management, and the history of botanical exploration. He was rewarded in 1880 with the appointment as Professor of Botany at the South African College (which later became the University of Cape Town) and as Curator of the Cape Town Botanical Gardens.[89]

Sadly, when Charles was fifteen, he discovered that his father had been carrying a heavy secret for a number of years: James Leonard was in dire financial straits. He had spent a fortune on building dams and enclosing his fields but had not been able to make his expenditure pay. Charles would have been aware that fires in 1867 and again in 1869 had hit his father heavily, and that stock thieves were a constant thorn in his flesh, but it must still have come as a shock when his father surrendered his estate on 11 October 1871 and was, like his own father before him, declared insolvent. The Provisional Trustee, Thomas Holland, wrote the following in his report:

> The difficulties of the Insolvent appear to have been of long standing and to have had their origin in losses on wool, and by bad debts dating back as far as 1863. In 1864 he discontinued his trade transactions and from that time to the date of his surrender he appears to have divided his attention between his sheep farming establishment at Biesjes Fontein and an extensive agency business at Somerset.[90] ... His credit up to a comparatively recent period appears to have been good, and he was enabled to obtain large assistance from his friends in the shape of accommodation Bills, and with their help to stave off for a considerable

---

[87] Butler, Guy. *op. cit.*, 58.
[88] *Somerset and Bedford Courant*, 1 May 1878, 2-3.
[89] Beinart, William. *The Rise of Conservation in South Africa: Settlers, Livestock, and the Environment 1770-1950*, 118.
[90] Letting property.

time the inevitable crisis in his affairs.

...

A sum of £75 was granted to the Insolvent for the support of himself and his family by the former Provisional Trustee, Mr Leppan, with the consent of the Chief Creditors. The present Trustee has supplemented this grant with a further sum of £15. The Insolvent has applied for a further sum of £32.10.0.[91]

James had even pledged all 53 shares he held in the Somerset East Bank to different creditors as security for their claims against him. The Trustee reported that the Insolvent's gross debts amounted to £23,555.9.5.

It must have been both an humiliating and sobering experience for Charles and his siblings to see their father's assets being auctioned or sold for cash to settle his debts. A wagon, plough and other farming implements, together with a horse and a few cows, were sold by auction on 5 April 1872 and realised £116.11.6 gross. Some articles of furniture, worth perhaps £25 or £30, were also disposed of. The family was fortunate that the furniture in their farmhouse was considered of such little value that the Trustee recommended that James be allowed to retain possession thereof.

The farm Hartebeest Leegte was sold for £3,337.2.3; the previous owner of Biesjes Fontein, J.J. Nel, proved on the Estate for the purchase money and outstanding interest owed on the farm; the buildings and grounds at 10, Charles Street, Somerset East, were sold to three different buyers for £2,878.8.8 gross; five other erven in the town were sold for £1,276.13.2 gross; and four erven in Bedford were sold for £40 gross. This still left a shortfall of almost £16,000.[92] The Leonards were, to use a colloquial expression, in Queer Street. Fortunately, their friends William and Alice Turner of the nearby farm, Brakfontein, took them in.

Conversely, the fortunes of South Africa took a dramatic upward turn in 1871 when news reached the outside world of the discovery of diamonds at Kimberley. Sir Richard Southey, the Colonial Secretary at the Cape, declared: 'Gentlemen, this is the rock on which the future success of South Africa will be built.'[93] The diamond rush had begun. Thousands flocked to the diggings, including Jim Leonard, who was only eighteen. As men dug deeper into what

---

[91] KAB, MOIB 2/1414, 166. Leonard, James, Insolvent Liquidation and Distribution Account, 1858-78.
[92] *Ibid.*
[93] http://en.wikipedia.org/wiki/Richard_Southey_(colonial_administrator). Retrieved 11 June 2015.

became the Big Hole, chaos reigned, with fights and riots becoming commonplace. Jim quickly decided that the life of a digger was not to his liking, so the following year he returned to the Karoo, to the northern village of Richmond, where he joined the staff of the local newspaper, the *Richmond Era*.[94] Richmond was not then as sleepy and run down as it is today. It was a popular health resort for wealthy Europeans suffering from breathing difficulties.[95]

We have no way of knowing what his motives were, but on 15 July 1873, he married a 32-year-old widow. Sixteen years earlier, when Jim was only four, Catharina Elizabeth Coetzee (or Kotze), aged sixteen, had married a local farmer's son, Johannes Henricus Eckard. Their only child, Agnes Sophia, had been born shortly thereafter, but then Johannes had died.[96] We can only speculate on Jim's reasons for marrying the widow and on what his parents and siblings might have made of the match, but from our vantage point it does seem a strange decision: besides the gap in their ages, there was also the cultural gap between those of English and Dutch extraction.

The wedding took place at Richmond, so it is likely that Jim's parents and siblings attended the ceremony. He continued living in the town with his wife and stepdaughter (who took his surname) and soon became editor of the *Richmond Era*, a position that he held for the next three years. He also became proprietor of the newspaper, which is said to have become something of a political power during this period.[97]

Jim soon tired of journalism, however, and set about gaining the Ll.B. degree, which would qualify him to practise as an advocate.[98] His wife was said to have sat on the doorstep at night to prevent his friends from disturbing him while he studied.[99] He graduated in 1876 and invited Charles to visit him at Richmond, where he informed his brother that he would be relinquishing ownership and editorship of the newspaper and moving to Cape Town in December, having been called to the Cape bar.

Charles had been trying his hand at farming, working on a farm in the Graaff-Reinet district, but after doing this for a couple of years, he too had

---

[94] Anon. 'The Hon JW Leonard KC' (1905) 22 *SALJ* 132142.
[95] Rogers, Owen. *Lawyers in Turmoil*, 19.
[96] http://archiver.rootsweb.ancestry.com/th/read/SOUTH-AFRICA-IMMIGRANTS-BRITISH/2010-12/1292266200. Retrieved 11 June 2015.
[97] Anon. 'The Hon JW Leonard KC' (1905) 22 *SALJ* 132142.
[98] In Britain, the equivalent would be a barrister, and in the Transvaal, where he later practised, a solicitor.
[99] Nathan, Manfred. 'The Republican Bench and Bar', 88.

Chapter 2

had enough. He confided in Jim that he would also like to make a fresh start in Cape Town but wondered what he could do as he had no qualifications. Jim persuaded him to apply for a position in the Civil Service and helped him draft the letter. Addressed to the Colonial Secretary in Cape Town, it is dated 7 November 1876 and reads as follows:

> Sir
>
> I have the honour respectfully to inform you that I am anxious to procure an appointment in the Civil Service of this Colony, and should feel very grateful to you if you could confer any such appointment upon me.
>
> I can, of course, not say much concerning my own qualifications; but beg to refer you to the Revd Mr Woodrooffe, of Somerset East, who will, I am sure, be glad to give his opinion as to my fitness for a post in the Service of the Government.[100] The Honourable Mr Brownlee is also, I believe, in some measure, acquainted with my qualifications, and I should be glad if you would refer to him on this subject.[101] I may also state that I am about twenty-two years of age. [This is incorrect: he was only 20.]
>
> Hoping you will be able to give me a favourable reply to my application,
>
> I have the honour to be your obedient servant,
>
> Chas. H. B. Leonard

This letter was referred to the Civil Commissioner at Richmond on 14 November and to the Civil Commissioner at Somerset East on 5 December for confidential reports.[102] These reports must have been favourable because Charles received a letter shortly thereafter informing him that his application had been successful and that he was to take up a clerical position in the Department of Native Affairs in Cape Town early in 1877.[103]

So it was that Charles left the rural district of the Great Karoo, which he had known all his life, and made his way to Cape Town with his brother and his family. In so doing, Charles revealed something of the courage and

---

[100] The Reverend Henry Reade Woodrooffe was rector of Somerset East until 1885. He was a co-translator of the *Book of Common Prayer* into isiXhosa.
[101] Charles Brownlee was the first Secretary for Native Affairs in the Cape Government, having previously served as Civil Commissioner in several districts on the eastern frontier of the colony.
[102] KAB, CO 4191, L31, Memorial, CHB Leonard, requesting appointment in the Civil Service, 1876.
[103] *The Cape Argus*, 13 January 1921, 5.

pioneering spirit of his Settler grandparents. He had not yet come of age, but he was mature enough to know that his prospects of advancement would be greatly improved in the Mother City. He and Jim could be grateful that their upbringing in the harsh Karoo had prepared them for the rocky road ahead.

THE KARROO [*sic*] – Anonymous, June 1890.[104]

> A strange land is the Karroo,
> Abounding in deserts, in mountain-sentinelled solitudes,
> Bare rocks, stones, scraggy bushes,
> Dry river-beds all bathed in sun-dried air, and dazzling sunshine.
> A strange, strange land, oft apparently dead,
> And not welcoming human children
> Rashly to make it their home.
> …
> This land so vast, so lone, so desolate,
> Has messages most deep for the soul of man:
> …
> 'Judge not alone from the bare baked surface.
> Dig deep, dig deep my children,
> …
> In that same stern school have I taught them
> That pain and suffering are sore,
> But are God's agents
> By which His fine human steel has ever been tempered;
> Because work now lies before them
> That these gifts will enable them to accomplish,
> Water must they bring from the stony rock,
> And make of the desert a living blooming garden.'

---

[104] Excerpts from 'Scraps from an Old Diary. I.' in *Chronicle of the Family*, August 1914. moltenofamily.com. Retrieved 6 May 2015.

Chapter 2

Charles Leonard, Cape Town, c. 1878

Caricature of Jim Leonard as a lawyer

Cape Town as seen from Signal Hill when Charles Leonard arrived in 1876. Table Bay had not been pushed back by the reclamation of the foreshore, so Waterkant Street was, as its name suggests, at the water's edge. The railway line can be seen at the curve of the bay, passing between the Castle of Good Hope and the sea. The Lutheran Church can be seen in the right foreground, while the notorious Prestwich Street burial ground for slaves can be seen in the left foreground.

Longmarket Street, Cape Town, in the late 19th Century. Note the unpaved streets and the Temperance Hotel appropriately adjoining the Metropolitan Methodist Church. Beyond the church can be seen the turret of the Town House and beyond that at No. 141 were the chambers of Fairbridge and Arderne, the law firm where Charles Leonard became an articled clerk.

CHAPTER 3 : SCALING THE LEGAL LADDER
(1876-1888)

As to the essentials of a good lawyer… He should have a keen sense of right and wrong and a firm belief in basic moral values.

– Joseph T. Karcher

Charles Leonard – accompanied by his elder brother Jim, Jim's wife Catharina, and her daughter Agnes – travelled to Cape Town by stagecoach because the railway linking the Eastern Cape with the Mother City had not yet been completed. In 1876, Cape Town was a bustling port city, the capital of Britain's Cape Colony and the seat of government, with a cosmopolitan population of more than 33,000.[105] None of the new arrivals had ever experienced anything even remotely similar. Let us pause for a moment and stand in their shoes as they took in the sights, sounds and smells of the Tavern of the Seas.

The dominant sight for anyone visiting Cape Town for the first time has always been the towering mass of Table Mountain, one of the geological wonders of the world. It enfolds the city bowl within its protective embrace, its right arm being Devil's Peak to the south and its left arm Lion's Head and Signal Hill to the north. By 1876, the centre of Cape Town was no longer primarily a place of residence. It had become the commercial centre of the city, with shops, warehouses, banks and insurance offices having replaced

---

[105] Bickford-Smith, Vivian. *Cape Town at the Advent of the Mineral Revolution (c. 1875): Economic Activity and Social Structure*, 1.

most of the former homes. As a result, the dominant noise was that of human industry. From the locomotives and derricks operating in the harbour to the pedestrian and horse-drawn traffic in the dusty streets, there was a constant hubbub, which was regularly accentuated by the tuneless bray of fish horns as vendors plied their wares on carts and barrows. The dominant smell at that time was of fish and the sea, for Cape Town lies on the sweeping curve of Table Bay, which yielded a daily harvest, landed from numerous small fishing boats at Roggebaai.[106] The stench from the fish market would waft into the centre of town, unless the Cape Doctor[107] took pity on the citizens.

As he looked out across the bay, Charles may well have imagined the *Chapman* lying at anchor after its four-month voyage from the Old Country. Perhaps he paid a silent tribute to his grandparents, who had courageously ventured into the unknown in search of a better life. Sadly, his grandmother had recently completed her life's journey, having died at Retreat farm near Bedford on 5 October 1874.[108]

The Leonards would not have arrived at the Tavern of the Seas without prior arrangements having been made for their accommodation. Charles may have stayed with Jim and his family at first, but he was not one to impose on others, so he soon found lodgings in a boarding house or hotel, which was situated at 31, Roeland Street, at the upper end of town.[109] There is a photograph of Charles taken at about this time. He is a handsome young man, neatly groomed, with soft features and a smooth complexion, but his steely gaze and strong jaw dispel any notion of weakness.[110]

Early in January 1877, Charles reported for work at the Department of Native Affairs, which administered African tribal lands, such as Kaffraria and Basutoland, on behalf of the Cape Government. The Prime Minister, John Molteno, had appointed Charles Brownlee the first Secretary for Native Affairs in 1872, based on the fact that he was openly sympathetic to the Xhosa, understood their main issues and spoke their language. Under his leadership, the department succeeded in holding back white expansion into Xhosa lands, while offering equal political rights to black Africans who were citizens of the Cape. This liberal policy succeeded in pacifying the notoriously

---

[106] *Ibid.*, 6.
[107] The south-easterly wind is called the Cape Doctor, because it reputedly blows all smells, litter and contagion out to sea.
[108] www.1820settlers.co.uk/genealogy/getperson.php?ID:131198tree= Retrieved 11 June 2015.
[109] KAB, 316.87 CAP, General Directory of the Cape of Good Hope, 1880, Index.
[110] Hagley Hall Archives. No catalogue number.

Chapter 3

volatile frontier region, but it was a peace that was to be short-lived. At about the time that Charles Leonard joined the department, the British Colonial Office decided to pursue a disastrous confederation scheme, part of which entailed a plan to annex the remaining tribal lands. The resulting escalation of conflict soon led to the 9th War of Dispossession. The Cape Government strongly opposed the British plan so, in retaliation, the Colonial Office suspended the Cape's elected parliament in 1878 and once again assumed direct imperial control over Cape Colony. Charles Brownlee lost his job, as did Charles Leonard.[111]

Brownlee became Chief Magistrate of Griqualand East and his underling became an articled clerk in the law firm Fairbridge and Arderne. From the testimony of one of his friends, we know that Charles was ambitious. William Henry Somerset Bell was another young man articled to the firm, having joined at about the same time as Charles. Bell was a few months younger than his friend and also hailed from the Eastern Cape, having been born at Fort Hare in Alice.[112] He later wrote a commentary on members of the firm and provides these insights into Charles's character and lifestyle at the time: 'One of my fellow clerks was Charles Leonard; he was a man of great promise … He and I were great friends; we were equally ambitious and both equally "hard up"; and on many a day we made our lunch off two pennyworth of grapes – grapes were cheap in Cape Town in those days.'[113]

A new partner named Thomas Scanlen joined the firm at about this time. His family was of Irish extraction (then called Scanlan with an 'a') and, like the Leonards, had arrived with the 1820 Settlers. They had first settled on Longford Farm in the Albany District before moving to Grahamstown, but they had then moved to Cradock, which remained their home for many years. In 1856, Thomas Scanlen's father, Charles, was elected as the parliamentary representative for Cradock and, in 1870, he was succeeded by his son, who had been admitted as an attorney in 1866 and conducted a successful legal practice in the town. When Charles Leonard arrived in Cape Town, Thomas Scanlen was still the M.P. for Cradock and remained so until 1896.[114] Bell had this to say about Scanlen: 'He was a clever lawyer, unostentatious and self-controlled in manner, yet very quick to grasp the point in any legal problem;

---

[111] https://en.wikipedia.org>wiki>Charles_Brownlee Retrieved 26 February 2016.
[112] www.1820settlers.com/genealogy/getperson.php?personID=121258&tree=master Retrieved 26 February 2016.
[113] Bell, W. H. Somerset. *Bygone Days*, cited in MacSymon, Robert Massey and Linnegar, John. *Fairbridge, Arderne and Lawton: A History of a Cape Law Firm*, 93.
[114] http://en.wikipedia.org/wiki/Thomas_Charles_Scanlen. Retrieved 11 June 2015.

he was a hard worker and got through a great deal of night work.'[115] Charles and his fellow clerks were privileged to have worked under this great man, even if for only a few years. In 1881, Scanlen became Prime Minister of the Cape, at which point he resigned from the firm.

After moving to Cape Town, Scanlen and his wife had for a while been tenants of the firm's senior partner, Charles Fairbridge, who was regarded as one of the Cape's most erudite attorneys and public-spirited citizens. Already in 1854, he had been elected to the first Cape Parliament, and in 1874, he was elected once again. 'But, legal luminary and politician though he was, C.A. Fairbridge's real loves lay elsewhere: he was a connoisseur of old furniture and a keen collector of pictures, a scholar and, above all, a bibliophile.'[116] He and his family lived at Mimosas in Sea Point. 'What gave Mimosas its chief claim to fame was Charles Fairbridge's magnificent library, housed in a special wing erected for the purpose… No wonder that Mimosas came to be regarded as "a home of European stateliness and culture, to which any distinguished visitor to the Cape immediately makes his way".'[117] His friend, John Currey, wrote: 'His presence was so refreshing to the rougher colonial society in which his lot was cast. One felt that to converse with him was to breathe the bracing atmosphere of the early days of Victorian wits and humourists. He was undoubtedly one of the most cultured and universal men that this Sunny Land has yet known.'[118] His articled clerk, William Bell, expressed his admiration for Charles Fairbridge far less floridly: 'He was a very popular man both in and out of the office.'[119] After Fairbridge's death in 1893, his collection of books was donated to the South African Library in Cape Town, where it is housed to this day in the Fairbridge Wing.

Henry Arderne, the junior partner, qualified as a solicitor at University College, London, and served his articles with Fairbridge from 1852 before being admitted as an attorney in Cape Town in 1857. For most of his life he lived on The Hill, the estate his father had established in Claremont, an upmarket suburb to the south of Cape Town. 'The ground had a gentle slope, and in one corner a spring welled up and spilled into a small stream and even in summer kept the soil around it moist. Beyond the ground, like a majestic

---

[115] Bell, W. H. Somerset. *op. cit.*, 96.
[116] Murray, Marischal. *op. cit.*, 134.
[117] *Ibid.*, 133-4.
[118] http://www.fairbridges.co.za/fairbridges-200th-anniversary. Retrieved 11 June 2015.
[119] Bell, W. H. Somerset. *op. cit.*, 96.

backdrop, rose Table Mountain.'[120] It was the perfect place to establish a magnificent garden, which is what Henry's father did, collecting trees, shrubs and perennials from around the world. Henry shared his father's botanical passion and extended and improved the estate, which became widely known for its fine collection of exotic and indigenous trees and plants. It became the Claremont Public Garden in 1927 and was renamed the Arderne Gardens in 1961.[121] It remains an area of great botanical, scientific and environmental importance to this day.

How fortunate for young men starting out in the legal profession and in adult life to have been mentored by men with such wide-ranging interests.

Jim, in the meanwhile, was excelling in his new profession: 'It soon became evident that he had found his *métier*. Sir Thomas Upington was then the leader of the Cape bar, and Mr Leonard, to begin with, often acted as his junior. But, having once secured a footing, it was natural that his rare combination of effective speaking and sound law should bring him to the front.'[122] In 1883, after a mere seven years at the bar, James took silk, becoming one of the first three South African advocates to receive QC status. His practice was extremely busy: over the approximately five-year period that he practised as a silk at the Cape bar (1883-1888) he appeared as leading counsel in almost 200 reported judgments.[123]

Back in Somerset East, things were not going as well. James Leonard Snr had been laid low by a fever towards the end of 1877, and, still in a weakened state, had nonetheless moved to his newly acquired farm, Niekerk's Hill, in January of the following year. He continued to suffer ill health, however, afflicted by both rheumatism and diarrhoea.[124] On 1 April, fearing the worst, he signed a codicil to his will, leaving all his worldly goods (such as they were) to his wife.[125] His health continued to decline until he lost consciousness and passed away on 24 April 1878 at the relatively early age of 54.[126] A few days before his death, he had received official notification of his financial rehabilitation and, despite his ailing health, his mind had been busy with schemes for making a new start in life.[127] Notwithstanding his financial

---

[120] http://www.historicalmedia.co.za/?p=761. Retrieved 11 June 2015.
[121] www.ardernegardens.org.za Retrieved 11 June 2015.
[122] Anon. 'The Hon JW Leonard KC' (1905) 22 *SALJ* 132142.
[123] Rogers, *op. cit.*, 24.
[124] *Somerset and Bedford Courant*, 1 May 1878, 2-3.
[125] KAB, MOOC 7/1/381, 38 James Leonard Will, 1861.
[126] KAB, MOOC 6/9/163. James Leonard Death Notice, 1878.
[127] *Somerset and Bedford Courant*, 1 May 1878, 2-3.

difficulties, James had worked extremely hard to establish himself as a respected member of his community, and had done his best to provide for his family, so the inscription on his (and later Eliza's) tombstone in the Somerset East cemetery is most appropriate: 'And I heard a voice from Heaven saying unto me, write: Blessed are the dead which die in the Lord from henceforth: yea, saith the Spirit, that they may rest from their labours: and their works do follow them.'[128]

Jim and Charles had travelled to Somerset East to be at their father's bedside[129] and attended the funeral, which was conducted by Mr Hofmeyr on Friday 26 April.[130] Their father's death must have placed them in an awkward predicament. What was to be done about his grieving widow and three minor children, all of whom needed to be supported? They must have been relieved when their recently married sister Emily offered to take their mother and minor siblings into her home in Paulet Street, Somerset East. It is likely that her brothers offered to contribute something towards their keep, although Charles was hardly in a position to do so at this stage. He certainly did so later in life.

Following his father's death, Charles applied himself to his studies and qualified as a lawyer. In 1879, he was awarded the Certificate of Proficiency in Law and Jurisprudence by the University of the Cape of Good Hope[131] and was called to the Cape bar as an attorney the following year.[132]

During the course of 1881, Charles acquired a client who was to become a particularly close friend and confidant. David Pieter de Villiers Graaff had recently taken over the lucrative butchery of his great-uncle, Jacobus Arnoldus Combrinck. Having grown up in poverty as the son of a *bywoner* (farmhand) in Villiersdorp, Dawie (as he was known) had accompanied his great-uncle to Cape Town in 1870 when he was a mere eleven years old. During the day, he learned as much as he could about the meat trade and then spent his evenings with his books, learning *inter alia* to speak, read and write English. His brother

---

[128] Gravestone of James and Eliza Leonard, main cemetery, Somerset East. eGGSA library > Gravestones in South Africa > Eastern Cape, SOMERSET EAST/SOMERSET-OOS, Urban area > Eastern Cape, SOMERST-EAST, Main cemetery > L-VANNE::Surnames -L > LEONARD James 1823-1873 & Eliza HOWARD 1826-1903.
[129] Jim signed the official death notice.
[130] *Somerset and Bedford Courant*, 1 May 1878, 2-3.
[131] Report of the University of the Cape of Good Hope, 1879, 3.
[132] MacSymon, Robert Massey and Linnegar, John. *Fairbridge, Arderne and Lawton: A History of a Cape Law Firm*, 96.

Jacobus (Kobie) joined him when he turned twelve.[133] Now aged 22, David needed legal advice and was referred to Charles Leonard, who was only a few years his senior, but already a successful attorney. The fact that Charles could understand and converse in Dutch, an accomplishment stemming from his youth in the Eastern Cape, must have reassured the young butcher. Later, when times became tough for Charles, he could count himself fortunate that David – who had by then become a wealthy businessman and leading politician – was prepared to come to his assistance, at great risk to his reputation it must be said.

An indication of how influential Charles himself became may be surmised from the fact that the members of the side bar in Cape Town nominated him to represent them before the Select Committee appointed by the Cape House of Assembly to consider and report on the proposed Law Society Bill. On 15 January 1883, his friend William Bell had founded the Law Society of the Cape of Good Hope in the Eastern Province, with Charles Fairbridge elected its first President, a position that he held until his death ten years later. The Law Society Bill now aimed to establish an Incorporated Law Society for the entire Cape Colony. Charles was examined in the Committee Rooms of the House of Assembly on Wednesday 29 August 1883. He answered thirty questions put to him by the Attorney-General, Sir Thomas Upington, and submitted for the consideration of the Committee a memorandum, which he himself had written, in support of the promulgation of the Bill. In response to a question from the Chairman, Charles confirmed that he considered it 'eminently desirable that all matters relating to discipline, professional training, admission to the profession, and the general conduct of the professions of attorneys and notaries should be committed to one general body … in order to secure uniformity of practice throughout the Colony'.[134] The House was persuaded by his argument and the Bill was subsequently promulgated on 27 September.

In 1884, the Incorporated Law Society published Volume 1 of *The Cape Law Journal*, which included a contribution by Charles Leonard entitled 'Law Reform – Divorce'. Because it reveals so much about Charles's legal acumen, his intellect, his command of English and his character, as well as providing insights into an important social issue of the day, it is worth quoting most of the paper.

In the first paragraph, he explains his reasons for writing the paper and

---

[133] Dommisse, Ebbe. *Sir David Pieter de Villiers Graaff: First baronet of De Grendel*, 23-29.
[134] Report of the Select Committee on the Law Society Bill, Question 18.

diplomatically prods the judges to implement the reforms that he is about to propose:

> The process of the superior courts for obtaining divorce on the ground of malicious desertion is so cumbrous and expensive that the bare hope of rendering it less so is sufficient justification for these lines being written. The Judges have displayed laudable zeal in altering the procedure of the Courts, and have, in many instances succeeded in reducing costs to a considerable extent by abolishing useless and antiquated notices, &c.; and if their Lordships find any weight in what follows here, they will, I have no doubt, lose no time in serving the great cause committed to their charge by effecting the necessary reform.

In the second paragraph, Charles outlines the 'cumbrous and expensive' process as it existed at the time, which called for two court appearances:

> According to existing practice, any person who seeks to obtain a divorce on the grounds of malicious desertion is compelled to bring two actions. Of these the first is for restitution of conjugal rights, and declaration has to be filed, and notice of trial served as in any ordinary case. On the day of trial the plaintiff comes into Court, proves the marriage and desertion, and the Court grants an order for restitution of conjugal rights. This order has to be served on the defendant, who is very frequently absent from the Colony, and if he fails to obey it the plaintiff becomes entitled to bring an action for Divorce on the ground that the defendant has not returned. Another summons has to be issued, fresh service thereof has to be effected, another declaration has to be filed, and notice of trial has to be served on the defendant, just as if he knew nothing whatever about the first action and the order for restitution. The fees of counsel and attorney have to be paid of course, as well as Court fees and sheriff's charges, the last-mentioned being frequently very heavy. On the day of the trial the plaintiff comes into Court, proves the service of the order and the disobedience of the defendant, and the divorce is granted.

In the third paragraph, he proposes a more streamlined process and refutes potential objections:

> One cannot but think that this process could be very much simplified. Why should not the plaintiff be entitled to sue for and obtain a divorce at

once, on the ground of malicious desertion? The proposed alteration seems, at first sight, a bold one, but is there any sound reason why it should not be made? It is difficult to see what hardship could be entailed on a defaulting spouse by a final decree of divorce being granted as the termination of one, instead of two, actions. Malicious desertion must be proved as a fact just as adultery must be proved; and the defendant could not be prejudiced or say that he had no opportunity of entering an appearance, because service of the summons and all subsequent process on him would have to be clearly proved to the Court before it granted the decree. Any defence could be as conveniently made at the first as at the second action; and it is reasonable to assume that if the defendant would not trouble himself to appear to defend the action when he knew that the result of his non-appearance would be divorce, he would have paid no heed to the order of restitution, which indeed could not be enforced by committal for contempt; and it follows that the whole of the proceedings to obtain an order for restitution is unnecessary and useless.

In the fourth paragraph, he presents a moral defence and then reveals his motive – not principally to cut down on court time by streamlining the process, but to reduce the plaintiffs' costs. This is not something that a layman would normally expect of a lawyer, with all due respect.

In the vast majority of cases of this nature, the defendants are in default, have fully made up their minds not to return, and resolutely refuse obedience to the order for restitution; and the severance of the tie which has become so hateful is a positive relief. One may well be sceptical about the happiness which would result from reunion compelled by an order of the Court, and may question whether it is wise to try to bring spouses together again when one of them has taken the extreme step of suing the other on such delicate grounds. But what is more to the point is the fact that persons who cannot claim the privilege of paupers may be deterred by the expense of the two actions, from seeking divorce, and, not being able to rid themselves of the tie which has become a mockery, may pass their lives in misery or immorality, or may even be driven to commit crime. The experience of very many lawyers is that spouses who are compelled to seek the Divorce Court curse the law which may have been intended to bless, but which certainly in our day does not fulfil its object.

In the fifth paragraph, he argues in favour of compassion for the mainly female plaintiffs in such cases:

> It is worthy of note that in a very large proportion of cases the plaintiffs are poor people, many being women who have been deserted and left all but destitute; and though the law is no respecter of persons, and its administration should, in all cases, be made as inexpensive and convenient as possible, yet the fact of such poverty furnishes an additional argument in favour of hastening reform.

In the sixth paragraph, Charles modestly admits that he may be unaware of some legal nicety that would militate against his proposed reform, and, should this be the case, advocates a watered-down alternative, which would still be an improvement on the existing process:

> If, however, there should be some safeguard (which I am too obtuse to see) in retaining the practice of granting an order for restitution of conjugal rights, and allowing some time to elapse before the divorce is granted, or if conservatism should prevent the reform above advocated, it seems to me that great improvement might still be effected by issuing a summons, at once, for restitution of conjugal rights, and failing such restitution, for divorce on the ground of malicious desertion, and making the declaration contain two prayers in accordance with the summons. The Court could then, on the hearing, order restitution by a certain day, and further direct the defendant, in the event of his disobeying, to appear on a day named in the order to shew cause why a decree of divorce should not be granted. On the return day, if the order had not been obeyed, the matter could be set down in the same manner as a rule nisi, and the divorce could be granted on proof of the defendant's disobedience.

In the final paragraph, Charles raises one more question regarding the judicial process, this time with regard to a man's legal difficulties, and once again advocates reform:

> Before laying down the pen, I may be allowed to ask whether there is sufficient reason for the Judges being so particular in exacting the strictest proof of marriage before granting a divorce? It is not likely that a man would go to the expense of getting the Court to decree the

Chapter 3

dissolution of a marriage which never existed. And if he did, there would be no harm done to anyone but himself, though the Court might think it had been trifled with. But, seriously, is there any human probability of their Lordships being practised on in this manner, and would it not be sufficient for the plaintiff to state on oath that he was married to the person from whom he seeks to be divorced, and to put in a certified copy of the marriage register. I apprehend that the reason why such strict proof of marriage is required in England is that a co-respondent might be cast in heavy damages as the result of a conspiracy between a man and woman who, for the purposes of an action, might pretend to be married. But where there is no co-respondent who might be damaged, it would appear that the rule might be relaxed without danger.[135]

When one considers that Charles was not yet thirty years old and had been an attorney for only a matter of five years, it is astonishing that he displays such critical faculty, such compassion for the helpless, and such precocious self-assurance in presuming to advise Supreme Court judges on legal matters. Nonetheless, the respectful tone and measured argument of his article, as well as his high ethical standards, meant that others in the legal fraternity sat up and took notice. He was offered a partnership in another Cape Town firm, and when he accepted, the firm changed its name to van Zyl, Buissinnè and Leonard.

Mr Casper Henry van Zyl, the senior partner, came to be regarded as the leader of his profession in Cape Colony, eventually succeeding Charles Fairbridge as President of the Incorporated Law Society. He was the son of a Swellendam farmer, G.P. van Zyl, who had returned from fighting on the Kei River frontier with seeds of the Kei apple. In 1870, Casper moved to Sea Point and brought some of the seeds with him. In due course, his Kei apple hedges fringed almost the entire length of his property, which became known as Kei Apple Grove. It was an extensive property, stretching from Kloof Road down to Regent Road. It had previously belonged, separately, to two of Cape Town's most public-spirited sons, Howson Rutherfoord and John Fairbairn. Rutherfoord was a great philanthropist who donated large sums to charity. When the slaves were emancipated in 1834, he gave a dinner for nearly 300 people to celebrate the event. Fairbairn was editor of Cape Town's first newspaper, *The Commercial Advertiser*, and opposed Lord Charles

---

[135] *Cape Law Journal,* Volume 1, 1887, 80-83. http://heinonline.org. Retrieved 10 June 2015.

Somerset's attempts to limit press freedom. He later successfully led the Anti-Convict Agitation. Casper van Zyl's son, Gideon Brand van Zyl, followed his father into the legal profession and eventually occupied the highest office in the land, becoming Governor-General from 1945 to 1950, the first South African-born holder of this office.[136]

Cornelis Johannes Buissinnè, the other partner, lived in Wynberg, on the other side of the mountain. His son, William Templer Buissinnè, also entered the legal profession, later becoming President of the Incorporated Law Society.

It was perhaps inevitable that Charles Leonard, surrounded by so many legal luminaries, should himself scale the legal ladder, so that by 1886, he was regarded as 'one of Cape Town's outstanding attorneys'.[137] His elder brother, Jim, had become even more successful, however.

> In 1878, Mr [James] Leonard decided to stand for Parliament, but was defeated by a small majority in the contest to represent Richmond. However, he was returned for Oudtshoorn in 1879 and held his seat until 1888, when he stood down. His eloquence soon made him prominent in Parliamentary life, and at the age of twenty-eight he became Attorney-General of Cape Colony.[138]

James Weston Leonard served in the first Sprigg Cabinet and in that of Thomas Scanlen, being Commissioner of Crown Lands and Public Works. It had been a spectacularly rapid rise to the top of his profession and to the heights of political power. In 1882, he was able to buy 22 hectares of the sub-divided Rustenburg estate in Rondebosch for £2,500.[139] Given what we know of his imperialistic views, it is appropriate that Jim should have come to own part of the estate where the Dutch had signed their first surrender of the Cape to the British in 1795. The estate had also been the residence of the notoriously jingoistic British Governor, Lord Charles Somerset, for a while.

In September 1881, Jim took his wife and stepdaughter to England, sailing on the *Dublin Castle*. It was their first trip abroad.[140] A caricature of Jim

---

[136] Murray, Marischal. *op. cit.*, 118, 144.
[137] *Ibid.*, 139.
[138] Anon. 'The Hon JW Leonard KC' (1905) 22 *SALJ* 132142.
[139] KAB, DOC 4/1/44, 91. Leonard, James Weston, Mortgage Bond, 1882.
[140] www.ancestry.com,rootsweb.Archiver>SOUTH-AFRICA-EASTERN-CAPE>2004-10>1096842737 Posted by Becky Horne. Retrieved 10 April 2017.

Chapter 3

Leonard survives.[141] He has the same hooded eyes as his younger brother, but is arguably not as handsome, having large mutton-chop whiskers, a sharply upturned nose and a quizzical turn to his eyebrows. These features may have been exaggerated, as is typical in caricatures. A photograph taken some years later is far more flattering: the side whiskers have gone, he has grown a neat moustache, and his strong features convey an air of self-confidence.[142] His contemporaries certainly found him an attractive person, both in terms of appearance and in terms of character and personality.

> His eloquence, and the popularity resulting from his amiability, made him a force in politics… It was a pleasure to collaborate with him in a case…he was a sympathetic and courteous adversary. In his advocacy also it is pleasing to refer to the amiable elements in his character; the bullying of witnesses, for which the English common law bar has acquired an unsavoury reputation, was utterly alien to his nature.'[143]

One wonders how Charles responded to his brother's spectacular success and obvious popularity. It would have been understandable had there been at least some degree of sibling rivalry and resentment, particularly since they were employed in the same profession, but the facts as we know them do not provide any evidence of this. As will be shown, these brothers enjoyed a close relationship throughout their adult lives.

Their younger brother, Woodford, also studied law and, like Jim, became an advocate, but he became something of a burden to his elder brothers, as we shall see. Let us leave them pursuing their professional careers for the moment, while we catch up with developments in Charles's private life.

---

[141] JW Schroder Scrapbook, 1880. J.W. Leonard_QC_-_Cape_Colony_Parliament_MLA_for_Oudtshoorn_jpg
[142] *Illustrated London News*, 25 February 1896. Three Prominent Members of the Johannesburg National Reform Union.
[143] Anon. 'The Hon JW Leonard KC' (1905) 22 *SALJ* 132142.

Charles Leonard's boarding house in Roeland Street (left). Katharina (Catherine) Leonard lived with her siblings and widowed mother in Bouquet Street, which is situated on the mountain side of St Mary's Roman Catholic Cathedral.

Catherine's mother, Margaret le Sueur, known to the Leonard family as 'Oumatjie'

Charles Leonard named the first house he bought Weston Cottage, in honour of his father and grandfather, who shared the name Weston. Remarkably, it is still standing in lower Kloof Street, Cape Town.

Chapter 3

Catherine, Charles and Margaret (Daisy) Leonard, c. 1884

An old postcard of Fresnaye and Sea Point, c. 1887. The Leonards' spacious home is just visible on the beachfront in the distance. It was within easy walking distance of both the railway and tram termini and overlooked a sandy beach.

CHAPTER 4 : A BEACHFRONT HOME
(1880-1888)

It is a truth universally acknowledged, that a single man in possession of a good fortune must be in want of a wife.

– Jane Austen, *Pride and Prejudice*

From the doorway of his lodgings in Roeland Street, Charles Leonard would have faced St Mary's Roman Catholic Cathedral, standing tall on the opposite side of the street. Directly behind the cathedral, in Bouquet Street, lived Mrs Margaret le Sueur, the widow of Jacobus Johannes le Sueur Jnr, and her children. In a photograph, she looks statuesque, with a sweet smile.[144]

> Among the old families [of Cape Town] there were few so well known as the Le Sueurs…They were of Huguenot stock, various Le Sueurs… having fled to Holland during the religious persecutions of the seventeenth century… In 1360 the French Le Sueurs had been ennobled by the King of France (for their part in the Crusades, it is believed), and became the Lords of Fresnes… In 1729 one of these 'Dutch' Le Sueurs, the Revd François le Sueur, was sent to the Cape by the [Dutch] East India Company to take up the post of Assistant Pastor at the settlement there. He was the founder of the South African branch of the family.[145]

Margaret le Sueur's eldest daughter, Katharina Aletta Renina le Sueur,

---

[144] Hagley Hall Archives. No catalogue number.
[145] Murray, Marischal. *op. cit.*, 108.

was born on 26 November 1859.[146] Catherine (as she preferred to be known) was the niece of one of Cape Town's most prominent lawyers and accountants, Ryk le Sueur. In 1853, he had bought a farm at the far end of Sea Point, called Winterslust.

> The Le Sueurs soon established themselves at Winterslust. In place of the small homestead there a new house was erected. It was subsequently enlarged and became known as Fresnaye Villa [Fresnaye, spelt thus in archaic French, means 'ash-grove']. The slopes around and above the house were covered with protea bushes, and through the great stone-pine trees that surrounded the place one glimpsed the placid little village of Green Point, with the sea beyond. For children it was a paradise.[147]

As she blossomed into a teenager, Catherine would have run errands for her mother. Living as she did within 100 yards of Charles's lodgings, it was inevitable that their paths should have crossed. Howsoever they met, it seems that Charles was smitten and that the feeling was mutual. It might be a romantic notion, but it is tempting to picture Charles and Catherine falling more deeply in love on trips to Fresnaye.

> As the children grew older pleasures became more sophisticated – if, indeed, that term could be applied to dances in the big dining-room; musical evenings, followed (in the proper season) by *kreefpartijen*.[148] On certain nights when the moon was out – and, likewise, the rock lobsters – the young people would troop down to the sea to have a midnight picnic. While the young men were busy catching *kreef* the young ladies would lay the 'table' on the rocks. The midnight feast would then begin – and the revellers would get back home only when the early morning milk arrived. For recreation later in the day there was a cricket pitch outside Fresnaye Villa… Behind the house were two tennis courts, probably the first laid down in Sea Point.[149]

When they met, Charles would have been in his early twenties and Catherine in her late teens. It was not long before they committed themselves

---

[146] www.eggsa.org/newspapers/index.php/cape-and-natal-news-1860-1-january-april Retrieved 11 June 2015.
[147] *Ibid.*, 109.
[148] Rock lobster parties.
[149] Murray, Marischal. *op. cit.*, 109-110.

Chapter 4

to each other, for on 21 January 1880, soon after her twentieth birthday, Charles wrote Catherine an impassioned love letter in which he pictures their future lives together as husband and wife. She was spending a few days with her friend, Miss de Wet, at Stellenberg, a Cape Dutch farmstead in Kenilworth, which lies roughly eight miles to the south of Cape Town. Because this letter reveals so much of Charles's sentimental nature and his great love for 'Kitty', 'Rosebud' or 'Tatie' (as he called Catherine at the time), it is worth quoting it in full:

Cape Town
Thursday 22/1/80

My own darling 'Rosebud'

According to promise I am writing, but had I never promised it, it'd have been all the same, as my thoughts are so full of you. Last night I took your two portraits in my hand when I retired, and only removed my eyes from them when sleep overpowered me. I then put them under my pillow, & resigned myself to Morpheus and dreams of my pet. They were doomed to be waking dreams, though, for I had not been asleep an hour before Dr ____ and Mr ____ came hammering at my door and wanted me to join a convivial party in the Doctor's room. I refused point blank to go, and each party retired gracefully – they to their frolic, I to my bed, but not to sleep – at least for about three hours; but I did not grudge this in the least, as my thoughts were all of my dear girlie away at Stellenberg. You'd laugh to see the capricious manner in which I treat your photographs. One minute I kiss them, fondle them, and tell them all sorts of pretty little things;- the next I quarrel with them, grumble at them, and tell them they are not half so *nice*, or so *sweet*, or so *pretty* as the darling original;- in fact that they are a regular libel on her. But still, Kitty pet, I don't know what I should do without them – even when you are in Town. When you are away the place seems deserted, and the sun does not shine as brightly as it does when my Queen is here. Isn't it awfully hard to be parted for even a short while, old treasure? I know we both feel unhappy when we cannot see each other often. How I look forward to the day when I can claim you as my own darling bride, the wife of my heart, whose happiness is the only thing to be considered; and how I feel as if the very thought of you is enough to give me energy to move a world. The feeling which makes me cry to myself: 'Where is little Tatie!', with a sickening consciousness of the distance between her & myself, is the feeling which spurs me on to make a home for her, and to be worthy of her in every sense of the word. You are such a pure, good, innocent girl, Catherine, that I feel myself by comparison to be a very gross, worldly, sort of animal. I do feel though that your influence has made a change in me and my life; it has given me something to live for, & made me less selfish, & more thoughtful – thoughtful for the present and the future, and I earnestly hope the result of our mutual love will be perfect happiness.

My priceless pearl! I value you above everything the world can offer! Darling! I sometimes wonder whether we, who love each other so well and truly now, could ever in the time to come say harsh, unkind things to each other, and quarrel, as, alas! so many married people do – I say I sometimes wonder, but my heart answers passionately NO! NO! a thousand times *NO! Never* darling, will we?

My glimpses into the future show me a *happy* wife, and a proud husband, proud of the sweet creature, whose loving heart and gentle nature have become so intertwined with his life and very being that existence without her seems an impossibility, proud to work for her, care for her, and devote his life to her, in return for the happiness she has brought him, proud of the sunshine streaming in on both their lives from the fountain of devoted mutual love, and thankful to God for having given him such an inestimable treasure. She, the glory of her husband's life, passing on through her earthly pilgrimage beloved by all (for who could help loving her!) and blessed by all, who have the privilege of knowing her. I am no prophet, but I think this picture will be seen yet. You won't think me a sentimental fool, Kitty, will you, for writing this? Others might, but they do not know what it is to love as we love, and this letter is not for their eyes, but yours alone.

Let me change the subject. We (Reyneveld & I) went round the kloof yesterday afternoon, stopping at Camp's Bay to have a bathe, but I have not carried out my threat of going to Robben Island as there was some danger of the medical authorities there claiming me as one of their own,[150] & I still *ke* for you.[151] If there is a reasonable opportunity for doing so, I would very much like you to write and say whether you *ke* for me, and whose darling you are. You must also tell me *Hoekom is jy zoo en*

---

[150] The implication is that he might be considered a lunatic (Robben Island housed a mental asylum at that time).
[151] Charles is teasing Catherine about her pronunciation of *care*, as she tended to flatten the vowel.

Chapter 4

kleine pretty 'little maid'[152] & sundry other little things. I picture to myself what you are doing, Kitty, and trust that you will enjoy your visit as much as I wish you to, & come back looking better for the change. Remember how delighted I will be to hear from you.

Give my love to Miss de Wet & tell her to enjoy herself.

Now, darling, I must close with a thousand kisses and as much love as the train can carry for my own sweet darling Rosebud.

From her *own*

Charlie

I think of you constantly.[153]

Which young woman would not be swept off her feet by such an ardent declaration of love? It is likely, too, that members of Catherine's immediate and extended family would have complimented her on her 'catch', Charles being regarded as an eminently eligible bachelor.

From his letter, it is evident that Charles was still living in lodgings, for he speaks of being invited to join a party in a fellow resident's room. A few months later, however, in August 1880, he bought his first home, a newly constructed north-facing house in Kloof Street, in the Gardens area of Cape Town, on a plot of ground officially identified as Erf 94749. It cost him £1,350 and he named it Weston Cottage.[154] The following year, he sued the builder, William Beckam, for damages in the amount of £150, alleging that he had knowingly given fraudulent assurances regarding the construction of the roof. The court found in Charles's favour, but awarded him only £77.10 in damages.[155] He also complained about shoddy workmanship but did not seek compensation in this regard. Remarkably, despite its alleged defects, this house is still standing.

Early in 1881, Catherine informed Charles (probably in a state of panic) that she was pregnant, so it comes as no surprise that they announced their engagement almost immediately, since premarital sex was severely frowned upon in Victorian society and a young man who had impregnated a young woman was expected to do the honourable thing and marry her so that she would not be shamed. Their wedding took place on Wednesday 9 March 1881

---

[152] "Why are you such a small pretty 'little maid'".
[153] Hagley Hall Archives. No catalogue number.
[154] KAB, 316.87 CAP, General Directory of the Cape of Good Hope, 1882, Index.
[155] KAB, CSC 2/1/1/199, 57, Illiquid Case, Charles Henry Brandt Leonard versus William Beckham, 1881.

at the Le Sueur home in Bouquet Street.[156] After their honeymoon, Charles carried his wife over the threshold of Weston Cottage. Catherine gave birth to their first child, a daughter, on 3 November 1881.[157] She was christened Margaret Elizabeth Catherine Leonard, but was afterwards known as Daisy. A photograph taken of Charles, Catherine and Daisy in the early months of Catherine's second pregnancy is typical of Victorian family portraits: Charles is seated with Daisy on his lap, while Catherine kneels beside them.[158] They look thoroughly miserable, but appearances can be deceptive; in fact, they had reason to be happy because a few months later, on 20 April 1885, Catherine gave birth to their second daughter, christened Violet Yolande.[159]

In his letter to Catherine, Charles mentions that he and Reyneveld [*sic*] went swimming at Camps Bay. His friend was almost certainly Anthony van Ryneveld, who had been born in Graaff-Reinet, the son of Mr Daniel Johannes van Ryneveld, the mayor of the town. Anthony was five years younger than Charles, so it is unlikely that their friendship dated from the time when Charles was farming in the district. It must have developed after Anthony had arrived in Cape Town to study law. Anthony later founded the firm Dempers and van Ryneveld, with offices in St George's Street. The other founding partner, Herman J. Dempers, had been raised in Caledon and represented the district in the Cape Parliament. Van Ryneveld later became a Justice of the Peace and bought a house in Oliver Road, Sea Point, which he named Rynheath.[160]

Charles's marriage to Catherine and his friendship with 'Dutchmen', as they were still called, exposed him to their culture and perspectives on life. Since the departure of Lord Charles Somerset, British officials at the Cape had attempted to conciliate the Dutch speakers in the colony by giving them the right to operate within the Dutch language. This led to the establishment of a small but influential organisation known as the Afrikander Bond,[161] which initially formed to safeguard their political interests and extend their political influence, but also succeeded in having Dutch recognised as the second official language of the Cape in 1882. This was also partially achieved thanks to the efforts of another organisation calling itself the Genootskap van Regte

---

[156] *Cape Times*, 10 March 1881.
[157] www.eggsa.org/newspapers/index.php/cape-times/1177-cape-times-1881-4-october-december. Retrieved 11 June 2015.
[158] Hagley Hall Archives. No catalogue number.
[159] *Cape Times*, 22 April 1885.
[160] Murray, Marischal. *op. cit.*, 147.
[161] *Bond* means Union.

Afrikaners,[162] which, since 1875, had been campaigning to obtain official recognition of a written form of the vernacular Dutch spoken at the Cape. This dialect was known disparagingly as Kitchen Dutch, since it was considered inferior to pure Dutch due to the considerable influence of other European languages (particularly the French of the Huguenots), as well as the languages of indigenous tribes such as the Khoekhoe, and especially the languages of the Cape Malays. This new language, first called *Afferkaans*, later became known as Afrikaans, but it was some time before it received official recognition.

Considering all these ameliorations, one might have expected the Dutch-speaking population to have been relatively content with their lot. However, the first British annexation of the Transvaal and the First South African War of 1880-81 (otherwise known as the First Anglo-Boer War) had given them reason to be suspicious of the motives of the British. Extremists within the Bond now spoke openly of the need to create a united South Africa free from British rule. More powerful in the Orange Free State and Transvaal, it still developed a considerable following amongst the Dutch-speaking population of Cape Colony. As a result, it provoked some British residents to set up their own organisation in opposition to the goals of the Bond. Jim Leonard was one of those who launched the Empire League in order to support the ideology of British imperialism and to promote loyalty to the Crown. He was one of those who spoke stirringly at the inaugural public meeting.[163] This initiative led eventually to the founding of the British Empire League in London in 1894.

Although he was also a member of the Empire League, Charles was less concerned about British imperialism than he was about the polarisation of the community and the increasingly vitriolic exchanges between the factions. He had, after all, married into a French-Dutch family and both his elder sister Annie and elder brother Jim had married Dutch speakers. In addition, by his own admission, he 'had a number of friends at Cape Town, very influential friends, amongst the leaders of the Dutch party'.[164] He therefore regarded himself as ideally placed to act as a mediator, so he wrote a pamphlet entitled *England in South Africa*, which was issued by the Central Committee of the Empire League in 1885.[165] The following are some excerpts:

---

[162] Literally, the Society of Proper Afrikaners.
[163] *Standard and Diggers' News*, 22 August 1892.
[164] Leonard, Charles. *op. cit.*, 389.
[165] *Ibid.*, 3-20.

Let us look openly and honestly at the conditions under which we live, and ask ourselves whether there is any substantial reason why any one section of Colonists should regard with suspicion any other section; and, in discussing with each other, let reason, not passion or sentiment, govern us. So shall we learn that Heaven has cast us together in this land not to examine each other's pedigrees, not to discuss whether we are descended from English, Dutch, French, or German ancestors, but to live in brotherhood, to learn from one another, and to be rivals only in promoting the welfare of the country.

…

Now, truth requires that it should be said that there has been a breach formed between the two leading races[166] of South Africa which did not exist ten years ago, and that certain forces are at work tending to widen that breach. The Transvaal war seems to have raised a feeling which did not previously exist (at all events as anything worthy of notice), a feeling of antagonism between English and Dutch. The brave conduct of the Transvaal burghers not unnaturally awakened a feeling of pride and enthusiasm in the breasts of persons of the same blood in this Colony; it aroused the attention of the world; it stirred in the minds of Dutchmen, both in Holland and in South Africa, a dream of a future Dutch Empire which should renew the glories which have passed away from the Netherlands. But all this enthusiasm has worked this country incalculable evil, because it has set on foot intriguing between men in the neighbouring republics and this Colony. It has given designing men an opportunity of gaining their own ends by means of class distinctions, and has produced, or at least nourished the growth of, an association which, though its ostensible object is to educate the people to appreciate their political power and privileges, has indirectly had the effect of widening the breach between Colonists who should live side by side in mutual respect and friendship, helping, encouraging, and supporting each other. A house divided against itself cannot stand. A state torn by dissentions cannot prosper.

…

Many people who have not thought clearly what the phrase means, talk about a 'United South Africa under her own flag'… The several states

---

[166] The term 'races' was applied to those of different ethnic or cultural groups as well as to those of different pigmentation.

in this country are not now, and may not for a long time be, anxious to unite, and to talk about forcing a union is the surest way of producing irritation and distrust instead of confidence between us. If an Englishman were to propose such a union under the British flag, the cry would immediately be raised that an attempt was being made to deprive the Free State and Transvaal of their independence, and a feeling of hostility on the part of those states, as well as many sympathisers in this Colony, would at once be raised, which could not but hinder our progress. Do we ever hear of such a thing from Englishmen? Never.

...

Now, if we respect the flags which wave over our neighbours, we expect that the flag which waves over us shall also be respected. We have indicated that to impose our flag on the neighbouring republics could only lead to bloodshed, and it must be plain that to want to hoist another flag over us in this Colony could only end in the same thing, for we are not going to change the glorious flag of liberty under which we live for any other in the world.

...

Now, if this kind of agitation is persisted in, it must lead, not to union, but to civil war and political dissolution, destruction of property, ruin, and discord, from which it will take generations to recover. And we ask our fellow-Colonists to think carefully whether we are not right. We do not think that all the objects of the Afrikander Bond are evil, or that every man who belongs to it is an opponent of England. On the contrary, we wish it to be distinctly understood that, in so far as the Bond has awakened the people of this country to take an active interest in the legitimate concerns of the Colony, it has done good. We condemn it only for having branches in the neighbouring republics, and in so far as it has given utterance to, or fostered, the growth of anti-English feelings... But we believe that the great bulk of Bondsmen are not disloyal to the British flag... Can anyone be mad enough to suppose that any attempt to substitute for the flag under which we live any other would not be resisted by the great proportion of us to the bitter death? Where, then, would be the union?

...

Our sons and daughters are learning together at the same schools, worshipping together, playing cricket, football, and tennis together, intermarrying, and mixing with each other in every phase of Colonial life... This is the true way to be united, and it will be owing to influences such as these that we shall be able, when the time comes, as come it will, to say, Now we are indeed brothers. We can hasten or delay that true union. Will not Colonists prefer to hasten it?

Let us, the inhabitants of the Cape Colony, be swift to recognise that we are one people cast together under a glorious flag of liberty, with heads clear enough to appreciate the freedom we enjoy and hearts resolute to maintain our true privileges; let us desist from reproaching and insulting one another, and, rejoicing that we have this goodly land as a common heritage, remember that by united action only can we realise its grand possibilities.

There are important lessons to be learned from these excerpts, particularly in the light of future developments. As far as can be ascertained, this was Charles Leonard's first foray into politics and he reveals himself as not only a master of rhetoric, but also a man of obvious integrity: there can be no doubting the conviction of his appeal to his fellow colonists. As he presents his carefully reasoned argument, it also becomes evident that he writes with the assurance of a natural leader. He had already shown glimpses of these qualities in his appearance before the Law Society Bill Select Committee and in his article on divorce reform the previous year, but those had been on less public platforms. Finally, one should also note his attitude towards the independence of the Boer republics and the respect he shows for their flags. This is a significant theme to which we shall have cause to return.

Charles ends his pamphlet by reminding his readers that both factions belong to 'a home-loving stock' and that 'the peace and prosperity of every home in the land is at stake'. In 1887, two years after the publication of this pamphlet, Charles moved his family into a new home, 'known to be the best in Sea Point'. It had belonged to the late Johann Sebastiaan ('Bassie') Leibbrandt, the 'Governor of Sea Point', who had built it on property which he had bought on the Sea Point bulge (impinging on where the Marine Research Aquarium stands today). Charles bought the house and adjacent plots of land for £1,700.[167] The house itself was spacious, a charming single-storeyed home built in the mid-Victorian 'English' style. The property extended across the present lower Beach Road, which was then non-existent, on to a private beach, with a tidal pool suitable for swimming.[168]

---

[167] KAB, DOC 4/1/209, 157. Mortgage Bond, Charles Henry Brando [sic] Leonard, 1887.
[168] Murray, Marischal. *op. cit.*, 138-9.

Chapter 4

The rocky littoral on either side of this beach was visited by Charles Darwin in 1836 and named the Green Point Contact (it has since become more correctly known as the Sea Point Contact). Here he observed a rare geological interface of igneous and metamorphic rock: the dark granite has schists of lighter Malmesbury greywackes embedded in it, providing a striking example of the evolutionary nature of geological formations. Today a plaque on the promenade commemorates Darwin's visit.

The Leonards' home led straight on to these rocks at their highest point, right on the tip of the 'bulge'. The house was demolished in 1957 and the Ostende block of flats was erected on the site. To the south, the Leonards' neighbour was Mr J.J. Smuts, Clerk of the Papers at Parliament House, who had converted the stable buildings of the old Leibbrandt property into a compact villa, to which the name Scheveningen was subsequently given. This home, too, was demolished in 1957 and the Lisdale block of flats was erected on the site. Across the road stood Cassel Villa, the home of Mr Hurlingh, a good friend of Mr Smuts.[169]

We have no way of knowing whether Charles and Catherine opened their home to their neighbours, family and friends, or to Charles's colleagues and clients, or whether they preferred to raise their children more privately. Whatever the case, it is fair to assume that these were happy days for the young family. There was one cause of sadness, however, when Charles learned that the second of his sisters, Annie Nel, had died on 24 June 1887 at the age of 40, leaving her husband with nine children. Charles had lost contact with the Nels during his years in Cape Town, but the news of her untimely passing must still have come as a dreadful shock because they had been close as youngsters. She lies buried in the Kerkstraat Cemetery in Oudtshoorn.[170]

One might have expected the Leonards to have lived in Sea Point for many years to come, but within a year, they had sold their home and left the Cape. Events in the *Zuid-Afrikaansche Republiek*,[171] far to the north of Cape Town, had put paid to any prospect of a comfortable, civilised and peaceful life, surrounded by their friends, neighbours and extended family.

---

[169] *Ibid.*, 140-1.
[170] Gravestone of Annie Nel, Kerkstraat Cemetery, Oudtshoorn. www.eggsa.org>library. Western Cape, OUDTSHOORN, Kerkstraat cemetery – eGGSA home. Photograph of tombstone contributed by Alta Griffiths, 29 June 2009. Retrieved 11 June 2015.
[171] The South African Republic, commonly called the Transvaal.

Houses facing the newly established park in Gus Street, Jeppes Township c.1890. If these are representative of other houses in the vicinity, they are more spacious and ornate than most other contemporary homes in Johannesburg. It was a more affluent suburb, by all accounts. Charles Leonard had a house built in this street.

CHAPTER 5 : A HIGHVELD HOME
(1888-1891)

Our wives, our children, our homes are here,
and most of us are likely to live, and a great many to die, here.

– Charles Leonard, August 1892

In 1888, Charles Leonard was persuaded by his partners to give up his successful career in Cape Town in order to establish a branch of the firm in the Transvaal Republic, a thousand miles to the north. Two years earlier, promising seams of gold had been discovered on the Witwatersrand,[172] luring thousands of prospectors from all over the world to the burgeoning camp that soon came to be known as Johannesburg. The surrounding land was owned by Dutch farmers (Boers), who were prepared to sell if the price was right, but they were naturally wary. There was a fortune to be made by lawyers who could gain the confidence of the Boers and persuade them to sell their farms, and who could then have the subdivision of these tracts of land approved by the authorities and draw up the deeds of transfer to the prospectors who wanted to purchase the stands. Having grown up on a Karoo farm, Charles had the immense advantage of being able to speak Dutch reasonably fluently, and to understand the ways of the Boers, thus enabling him to win the farmers' confidence. He also possessed the requisite qualifications and expertise to handle the legal side of the sales. There was consequently no shortage of business. Charles soon took over the firm of Ford and Jeppe, but

---

[172] Literally 'White water's edge', commonly shortened to 'the Rand'.

it was not long before he realised that it would be far more lucrative if he set up his own practice. As a result, the firm of Charles Leonard, Attorney and Notary, was soon established with an office in the heart of the new commercial district – in Fraser's Building, 24 Commissioner Street, Marshall's Township.[173]

The initial confidence that the gold deposits would be more than a flash in the pan gradually gave way to disillusionment as the prospectors reluctantly came to accept that the seams near the surface had yielded all that they would. By the end of 1888, only 266,000 oz. of gold had been mined by those using primitive equipment.[174] From now on, only those with sufficient capital to outlay on the heavy machinery required for deep-level mining would make substantial profits. Most of those who had bought small stands in the first rush of blood now wanted to sell them to the big mining houses for whatever they could get. Once again, it was a lucrative market for lawyers. Within a very short space of time, Charles Leonard became extremely wealthy. By his own admission, his practice was worth about £10,000 per annum by 1895.[175]

Charles soon arranged for his wife and children to join him on the Rand. One wonders whether Catherine had any idea of just what awaited them there. We do know from a letter that she wrote many years later that she was reluctant to go: 'I sometimes wish we had never seen the Transvaal. You remember how much I was against going up there.'[176] The journey from Cape Town to Johannesburg would have been daunting in itself, irrespective of what they might find at the destination. The first part of the journey, from Cape Town to Kimberley, was by train and was comparatively comfortable, although the carriages would have been hot and stuffy, particularly during the tedious crossing of the barren landscape of the Great Karoo. Catherine would no doubt have struggled to keep up the spirits of her young daughters. The onward journey from Kimberley was by stagecoach, however, with frequent stops because the horses had to be changed every ten miles or so. There was no road; only a rough track over bumpy ground, and the cramped carriage would have jolted and rocked from side to side, jarring every bone in the passengers' bodies. The route also included a number of river crossings.

---

[173] 1890 Edwards General Directory of Johannesburg – Trades. http://archiver.rootsweb.ancestry.com/th/read/SOUTH-AFRICA/2014-02/1392824828 Retrieved 17 February 2014.
[174] Gutsche, Thelma. *Old Gold: The History of the Wanderers Club*, Ch. 3, 1. www.thewanderersclub.co.za/History Retrieved 15 May 2015.
[175] Leonard, Charles. *op. cit.*, 401.
[176] Hagley Hall Archives 201/2/31.

Chapter 5

Florence Phillips, the wife of Lionel Phillips, who later became President of the Chamber of Mines and played a leading role in Charles Leonard's political movement, described the hazards of the coach trip to Johannesburg thus:

> Capsizes were numerous, sometimes in the middle of a swollen river, and lives were occasionally lost. A not uncommon and exciting experience was when the coach arrived at a river too swollen to be crossed, and the unhappy passengers had to be hoisted across in a box. I have often sailed above the Modder River in that inhuman fashion. A rope would be stretched across, and a small packing-case hung thereto, which was worked by pulleys. It is a very curious feeling to dangle a hundred and fifty feet up in the air, with a roaring torrent beneath, and the knowledge that if the rope broke one would not be left to tell the tale. On one occasion, when soaring thus, the pulley would not work, and for a long time I remained suspended in mid-air.[177]

One certainly hopes that Catherine and her young daughters were spared such an ordeal. Even still, they must have been physically exhausted and emotionally drained by the time they reached the terminus in Loveday Street.

Once the necessary arrangements had been made, they moved into a tin-roofed house on a track called Gus Street in the newly laid out township of Jeppe's Town.[178] Life on the Witwatersrand in 1888 was exceptionally tough, even for whites. At that stage, there was no sewerage system and no piped water. Special carts and wagons brought water in barrels from Natal Spruit, the Fordsburg dip and from out towards Sans Souci near what is now the Show Ground. Ordinary folk paid 6d a bucket, but water was often in short supply, particularly during the dry season.[179] From May to November 1889, Johannesburg experienced the worst drought in its history, and starvation faced the town. Dust storms were common, with the suffocating clouds sometimes being so thick that one could not see across the street, and people could not venture out of doors unless they wore a veil.[180]

Then there were the locusts. In May 1891, '... a cloud of locusts half a

---

[177] Phillips, Florence. *Some South African Recollections*, 7-8.
[178] Johannesburg Residents Longland Directory 1893 and 1894. http://archiver.rootsweb.ancestry.com/th/read/SOUTH-AFRICA/2014-02/1392824828 Retrieved 17 February 2014.
[179] Gutsche, Thelma. *op. cit.*, Ch. 2, 2.
[180] *Ibid.* Ch. 4, 3.

mile wide and many miles long darkened the Johannesburg sky... *The Star* reported, "One walks on locusts, the walls are barnacled with them, but still they come, despite nipping frost in the mornings". Visitors complained of the sickening stench of thousands of dead locusts in the streets, mangled and trodden by traffic.'[181]

One can understand why Catherine resented having had to leave their home on the Sea Point beachfront and move to this dusty, windswept plain in the middle of nowhere. As a devoted wife and mother, she may well have put on a brave face and tried to make the best of things, but to be honest, it is difficult to rule out the occasional heated argument or outburst of tearful recriminations. One wonders if ever, in private moments, Catherine took out Charles's love letter and gently wept as she reread the following words:

> My glimpses into the future show me a *happy* wife... and I earnestly hope the result of our mutual love will be perfect happiness... I value you above everything the world can offer! Darling! I sometimes wonder whether we, who love each other so well and truly now, could ever in the time to come say harsh, unkind things to each other, and quarrel, as, alas! so many married people do – I say I sometimes wonder, but my heart answers passionately NO! NO! a thousand times *NO! Never* darling, will we?

The location of the Leonards' new home had one advantage, however: in 1888, St Mary's School for Girls opened its doors just around the corner in Park Street. Although the original admissions register has not been preserved, it is almost certain that Daisy and Violet would have been educated there. As a devout Calvinist, Catherine may have had reservations about entrusting her daughters to members of 'the English church', but there was no realistic alternative. As an interesting aside, the first headmistress, Mary Ross, resigned shortly after assuming duties to marry the priest who had founded the school, the Revd John Darragh. The school moved from Jeppe's Town to Belgravia soon after the turn of the century in order to make way for the railway, and thence, in the mid-1930s, to its present site in Waverley. Today, it is regarded as one of the most prestigious girls' schools in South Africa and counts the Premier of the Western Cape, Helen Zille, amongst its alumni.[182]

Like almost every other white family, no matter what their social status,

---

[181] *Ibid.* Ch. 5, 1.
[182] www.stmaryschool.co.za/aboutHistory.php. Retrieved 15 May 2015.

the Leonards would have employed at least one black servant, possibly as a char, but more likely as a live-in domestic worker. She would have had a small outside room at the back of their home, possibly only a wood and iron lean-to, with little space for more than a bed, and no ablution facilities other than a bucket of water and another for night soil. It would have been stiflingly hot in summer and freezing cold in winter. She would have done the cleaning, laundry and ironing, but might also have cooked and done the washing up if she lived on the premises. She would have been forbidden from entertaining friends, especially males, in her room after hours. Only on Sundays, which she would have had off, would she have been free to mix with her own kind. It was a hard and lonely life, barely distinguishable from that of a slave.

Catherine's life would have been comparatively more comfortable, especially as she would not have had to do the back-breaking menial chores, but she too would have had to make do without decent sanitation. She would also have been lonely, at least during the day once her children started attending school. She no doubt conversed with her 'help' while supervising her work, but friendships across the colour and class lines were considered inappropriate, so she would have known where to draw the line. The language barrier would also have prevented more than basic chit-chat. Catherine would have been housebound during the day since it was considered unsafe for women to venture out of doors, even to visit a friend in a neighbouring street. Florence Phillips wrote:

> What would women residing in peaceful England say to the fact that one cannot take a walk out of sight of one's own home in the suburbs of Johannesburg with safety? The [blacks],[183] who in other parts of South Africa treat a white woman with almost servile respect, there make it a most unpleasant ordeal to pass them, and in a lonely part absolutely dangerous.'[184]

The writer would not have considered for one moment the possibility that these men, starved of female company, were bound to take an interest in anyone wearing a dress. They would not have dared do more than stare or perhaps whistle, following the example of the lower class of white men, but

---

[183] Mrs Phillips here used a common 19th Century term to refer to black people. It means 'infidel' and is considered extremely derogatory and offensive. It is now classified as hate speech in South Africa and its use is punishable by law.
[184] Creswicke, Louis. *South Africa and the Transvaal War*, Vol. 1, 143.

even that would have been considered threatening behaviour by white women, who expected black people to 'know their place'.

Initially, there were few white women of Catherine's class in Johannesburg, the majority being barmaids or sex workers. Gradually, however, a better class began to join their husbands and the occasional entertainment was laid on at clubs such as the Wanderers, to which members' wives were invited, though they were prohibited from becoming members themselves. A dashing gentleman horse-trainer, Captain Hayes, who spent some time on the Rand with his equestrienne wife, wrote:

> When South African society has assumed a more permanent and a more cultured form than it has up to the present attained, and when its ladies have increased in number and have become less afraid than they are of each other, the Club committee-men will see the advantage of catering for the amusement of the members' womenkind by, for instance, allowing them the entrance of certain club-rooms during certain hours of the afternoon and evening, having lawn tennis courts at which they might play and getting up periodical dances. Such a deliberate consummation, outrageously improbable as it may now appear, will no doubt come to pass in time.[185]

Many of these reforms were soon implemented and the rules were relaxed to allow wives to accompany their husbands to performances by the Wanderers' Club 'Full Orchestra' under the baton of Francis Crane. Sadly, during their first Grand Concert at the Globe Theatre on 3 April 1889, the hail hammered on the tin roof so loudly that little else was heard. There were also performances by the Brass or Military Band under the baton of Charles Bain, the first Sunday Promenade Concert being held on the Wanderers' Ground on 16 April 1889. 'We used to have anything between 5,000 and 10,000 people on a fine Sunday evening when the band played outside,' Bain later recalled.[186] It is almost certain that the Leonards would have attended these concerts as a family, perhaps packing a picnic hamper as people do today when attending concerts in the park.

One can imagine Catherine's flustered excitement as she and Charles dressed in their finery to attend one of the popular Smoking Concerts held in the small hall under the new Wanderers' Pavilion during the winter of 1889.

---

[185] Gutsche, Thelma. *op. cit.*, Ch. 5, 8.
[186] *Ibid.*, Ch. 4, 2.

These really were 'Smokers', with liberal contributions from the oil lamps as well as the male patrons. The Leonards would have driven there in Charles's Cape cart or trap, passing under the ornate *porte-cochere*, and then, having entrusted their carriage to a groom, would have mingled with the other guests before taking their seats. Starved of genteel company, Catherine would have relied on Charles to introduce her to his friends and their wives, and to direct the small talk. The entertainment on stage ranged from polished performances by Francis Crane's orchestra to comic songs such as *The Man who struck O'Hara*, the star turn of the dapper Charles Aubrey Smith. As was customary, the evening closed with the audience standing and singing *God Save the Queen*, even though the Transvaal was a Boer Republic.[187]

Charles Aubrey Smith had captained the first English cricket team to tour South Africa earlier that year. A team of eleven tourists had played against a team of twenty-two local cricketers at the Wanderers at the end of January in a match that had engendered great excitement. Charles Leonard was a keen follower of cricket and would willingly have parted with the three guineas required to attend each day of the match with the privilege of a seat in the Pavilion. Having been dismissed for only 22 runs in their first innings, the tourists recovered to win the match. After the last game in Cape Town, Aubrey Smith returned to Johannesburg to become a stockbroker. He played cricket and football for the Wanderers' Club and also promoted and captained the first Transvaal Currie Cup cricket team. However, after suffering a life-threatening illness in September and being financially ruined by the crash of the following year, he returned to England, where he took to the stage with conspicuous success. Many years later, he went to Hollywood and became one of the world's most famous stars in both silent and sound films. He was knighted in 1944 and died at his home in Beverly Hills in December 1948 at the age of 85, having maintained his interest in South African sport throughout his life.[188]

In April 1891, the Wanderers hosted the Currie Cup cricket match between the Transvaal and Griqualand West, otherwise known as the Inter-Town Match between Johannesburg and Kimberley:

> The town lost its head completely and shops were closed at noon to allow all and everybody to attend the match which lasted the whole of a week…. Huge scores were made…, but at a crucial point, the Kimberley

---

[187] *Ibid.*, Ch. 4, 5.
[188] *Ibid.*, Ch. 4, 3-6.

crack batsman A. B. Tancred scored a duck. 'The excitement which all along had been great,' wrote a member of the Kimberley team, 'now became almost too intense to be borne. Conversation in the Pavilion and in the crowd round the ropes entirely ceased and all gazed mutely at the game, rigid and absorbed.'

On the last day (Saturday), the Transvaal had only one wicket in hand and 76 to make. An even bigger throng had assembled and 'every minute, cabs containing excited men and women dashed up to the Pavilion entrance so that the crowd soon became enormous … Many were wringing their hands and walking up and down, too worked up to sit still or to speak. Some were even crying with excitement.' But the bowlers prevailed and Kimberley won 'the most magnificently contested game ever seen in South Africa by 58 runs. If ever sane men were mad, the old Kimberley supporters were then – such a drinking of champagne, such handshaking, dancing, cheering and foolish antics! Such crowing, swaggering and persistent drunkenness!'

The madness continued for days. On the Saturday night, a dinner for both teams was given at the Rand Club… On the Monday, another dinner was given at the Rand Club…and meritorious players were presented with bats, medals, cups, diamond pins, travelling liquor cases and other rewards. On Tuesday, Barney Barnato, not to be outdone, gave a dinner at the Central Hotel…and presented gold medals, jewels and purses to the players.[189]

Charles Leonard was no doubt one of those swept up in this excitement, but he is unlikely to have witnessed the final days of this match because he had to set off on the long journey to Mossel Bay on the south coast, where his younger brother, Woodford, was to marry Alice Frances Mary Pearson in the Roman Catholic church on Tuesday 14 April.[190] How the groom's family felt about his marrying a 'Papist' are unknown, but having been brought up as Protestants, they must have harboured some unease. While there, Charles persuaded both of his brothers to move to Johannesburg. Woodford joined Charles's firm, while Jim bought a house in End Street, Doornfontein, and set up a law firm in the Mercantile Buildings, Simmonds Street.[191]

---

[189] *Ibid.*, Ch. 5, 4.
[190] *South Africa* magazine, 23 May 1891.
[191] Longland Alphabetical Street Directory, 311. RootsWeb: SOUTH-AFRICA-L [SOUTH-AFRICA] 1897 JOHANNESBURG Alphabetical Street Directory - SIMMONDS ST. by shirley paladin <shirlbp27@gmail.com> Retrieved 11 June 2015.

Chapter 5

Besides his interest in cricket, Charles was also a keen supporter of rugby, as the following attests:

> In August 1891, the high excitement of the cricket match was again evoked by the first visit of an English Rugby Team… It was welcomed in typical Johannesburg fashion… The coaches bringing the team from Standerton (they had been playing in Natal) were due on the 13th August and a large number of notabilities went out to meet them…leading lawyer Charles Leonard, stockbroker H.C. Trull and many others journey[ing] down the dusty Klipriviersberg road to reach the rendezvous.
>
> Of the visitors, there was no sign and those weary sportsmen who had failed to provide themselves with refreshment during the delay, descended like locusts on J.P. Meyer['s] farm and were duly revived. Eventually the heralding clouds of dust were seen and the coaches escorted into Johannesburg where a great crowd had assembled outside the Central Hotel.'[192]

The tourists crushed all opposition. Charles and his brothers were soon involved in organising another cricket tour:

> As 1891 ended, the Wanderers prepared again for a major event and…their committee joined with Lionel Phillips, the Leonard brothers and other notables to prepare for the visit of a powerful English cricket team early in 1892.'[193]

Once again, the tourists proved far too strong for local opposition. It is of significance that in these reports Charles is referred to as a 'leading lawyer' and that he and his brothers are classed amongst the 'notables' who helped with arrangements for the tour. They were becoming recognised as leading members of Johannesburg society.

On 20 December 1891, Charles and Catherine attended a Grand Costume Ball in the ballroom of the newly opened Wanderers' Club House to mark the thirtieth birthday of the club's vice-president, James B. Taylor.

The hall was lit (at a cost of £2,876) by the most beautiful incandescent lamps, used in Johannesburg for the first time (they also illumined the

---

[192] Gutsche, Thelma. *op. cit.*, Ch. 5, 5.
[193] *Ibid.*, Ch. 5, 6.

front of the building). [The host] was garbed as a Master of the Hounds and the president, Hermann Eckstein, as a Cavalier…and George Farrar was appropriately dressed as a jockey, having been chairman of the Turf Club since 1887.'[194]

Farrar was soon to become involved with Charles Leonard in a far more daunting enterprise. We have no record of what costumes Charles and Catherine wore, but as all the foremost citizens had been invited, they would undoubtedly have been there.

Other entertainment was provided at the Theatre Royal, opened by Luscombe Searelle in 1889 and at Frank Fillis's enormous Amphitheatre for circus and other performances, which opened in September 1889. The following year, the new Rand Club opened its doors just a street or two away from Charles Leonard's firm. He and Jim became regular members, with Jim once claiming that more brains were to be found in that club than anywhere else in the southern hemisphere. Then there were the Races, which we know attracted the Leonards.[195]

As 1891 ended, Charles was not to know that he would shortly have neither the time nor the inclination to watch sport; nor was Catherine to know that she would henceforth be attending very few balls or concerts. In fact, she was to see less and less of Charles as his time, talents and energies became consumed by politics.

---

[194] *Ibid.*, Ch. 4, 9.
[195] Jim Leonard was a steward of the Johannesburg Turf Club and of the Jockey Club of South Africa.

Chapter 5

President Paul Kruger addresses the large crowd of disgruntled Uitlanders from beneath an umbrella at the Wanderers Club on 4 March 1890. Charles Leonard was one of those who petitioned Kruger straight after this rally.

Fillis's Amphitheatre, early Johannesburg, the venue for the mass meetings of the Transvaal National Union, where Charles Leonard rose to political prominence during the early 1890s thanks to his stirring speeches.

From a cartoon strip by D. Marquard and P.W. Wheeler. Lionel Phillips and Percy Fitzpatrick were not co-founders of the Transvaal National Union, however.

CHAPTER 6 : THE REFORMIST
(1890-1892)

*The time is come when we have to stand up as men for our rights.
I believe the Boers will see the justice of our cause, and respond to our demands.*

— Charles Leonard, August 1892

Johannesburg was about to experience the worst year in its brief history.

In 1890, the Crash came. The market collapsed and towards the end of the year, three banks – the Union, the Paarl and the Cape of Good Hope – closed their doors despite frenzied efforts by Rhodes and other financiers to maintain them. Few escaped the debris. Many of the young men left Johannesburg, ruined and broken in spirit. 'Numbers of the richest and smartest men on the Rand,' wrote the *Transvaal Mining Argus* in its annual review, 'have been temporarily ruined on account of the confidence they have shown in mining and other ventures.'[196]

Charles Leonard was one of the lucky few whose wealth was reckoned not only in shares, but also in banknotes, which he had safely deposited in a reputable bank. On 4 March, President Paul Kruger came to Johannesburg to meet the suffering citizens and hear their grievances. They assembled at the Wanderers' Ground where a platform had been erected for Kruger to address the crowd. Even he seemed taken aback by the large number of people who had turned out, estimated at ten thousand.

---

[196] Gutsche, Thelma. *op. cit.*, Ch. 4, 8.

It was said that a large number of those present were starving hopeless young men, broken by fluctuating share values and the failure of the Government to introduce the facilities that would enable profitable gold production and stabilise the market. Be that as it may, they behaved outrageously. They sang 'Rule Britannia!' and when the President shouted '*Blij stil*'[197] they laughed at him. He stamped off to Captain von Brandis' house without addressing them and ugly incidents ensued, including insult to the Transvaal flag.' [The Vierkleur[198] was torn down from its flagstaff in front of the captain's house and trampled in the dust.][199]

Before the mob arrived, however, Charles Leonard and George Farrar had succeeded in gaining entry to the house, where they listed their grievances and told the President what they required of him. Kruger listened, shifting a little uneasily in his chair, and then raised his hand.

'You want me to withdraw many of the duties and then you ask me for large sums of money. Taxes must be removed, you say, and more spent on public works… Where is it all to come from, if you do not pay taxes?'

'It is hardly fair, Your Honour,' said Charles, 'that the present inhabitants should bear the whole burden of costs for roads and bridges that will be used by future generations.'

'The following generations will have enough to pay for on their own account, Mijnheer Leonard,' Kruger replied.

It was at this point that the angry mob converged on the house and it was only a show of force by thirty armed policemen that prevented further insult to the President.[200]

On 12 March, a meeting attended by some 300 people was held and a new political association was formed. The following week a provisionally elected committee submitted a constitution, which was ratified, and it was decided that the organisation should be called the Political Reform Association of the South African Republic. Jim Leonard was elected President of the Association.[201]

---

[197] Dutch for 'Keep quiet!'
[198] Literally 'Four colours', the name given to the ZAR flag.
[199] *Ibid.*, Ch. 5, 12.
[200] Crisp, Robert. *The Outlanders: The Men Who Made Johannesburg*, 143-146.
[201] Webb, C. *The Uitlander Movement in the South African Republic before the Jameson Raid*, 11.

Almost from the start, however, there was dissention in the Uitlander camp. Certain men whose wishes had not been accorded with at the early meetings of the Political Reform Association decided to form their own organisation, and a rival union, known as 'The Transvaal International Political Association', was duly created on 19 March.[202]

Despite attempts to patch up their differences, the two organisations remained unreconciled, and by early May had become moribund. Men were seemingly more concerned with keeping the wolf from the door than with political agitation. This political quietude continued through the latter half of 1890 and the first half of 1891, but it was the calm before the storm.

During 1892, there was an economic turnaround prompted by an important development in the mining industry. Stimulated by the promise of the McArthur Forrest cyanide process of extracting gold ore from rock, there was renewed confidence and the Corner House (headquarters of the Chamber of Mines) poured money into deep-level mining. 'Whereas in earlier years there had been a feeling of instability, there was now a sense of security and permanence… But with this altered outlook, their "grievances" began to loom larger than ever before in the eyes of the Uitlanders. If their futures lay bound up in the South African Republic, then the newcomers wanted reform of those features in the affairs of the country which they regarded as undesirable.'[203] 'They stood on the threshold of great developments and huge fortunes, but the Government crippled them with monopolies, concessions and restrictions and denied them the right to make their voices heard at elections.'[204]

In 1892, Lionel Phillips was elected President of the Chamber of Mines in place of Hermann Eckstein, who was worn out and had refused re-election. Hoping to win President Kruger over, Phillips invited him to visit Johannesburg and the inhabitants gave him a gala dinner in the Wanderers' Hall on 25 March. It was his first visit since the infamous Flag Incident. Unfortunately, in his speech, 'Kruger made no effort to conceal his distaste of the diggers and the *congerie* of gamblers, speculators, traders and felons who obscured the work and honest intentions of a new breed of professional men and public-spirited individuals.'[205]

---

[202] *Ibid.*, 11.
[203] *Ibid.*, 16.
[204] Gutsche, Thelma. *op. cit.*, Ch. 5, 7.
[205] *Ibid.*, Ch. 5, 12.

This disdainful attitude was once again in evidence a few months later when the Volksraad refused to grant a request for increased municipal powers by the Johannesburg Sanitary Board. In response, the Sanitary Board announced its intention of convening a mass protest meeting on Saturday 13 August. This meeting was held at Fillis's Amphitheatre, and directly it was adjourned, the assembled crowd proceeded to hold a political meeting. Speaker after speaker expressed the need for political organisation, and the decision was taken to hold a further meeting the following Saturday night, a committee being appointed to draw up a programme in the interim.[206]

The audience at the follow-up meeting on Saturday 20 August was estimated at 3,000. They resolved to establish the Transvaal National Union in order to agitate for reforms. They elected John Tudhope, a former Cabinet Minister of Cape Colony, as Chairman and a group of like-minded public-spirited men, including both Charles and Jim Leonard, to the committee. The objectives of the proposed National Union were spelt out very simply:

a) The maintenance of the independence of the Republic;
b) To obtain, by all constitutional means, equal rights for all citizens of the Republic; and
c) The redress of all grievances.[207]

This is how that second public meeting was reported, in the hyperbolic style typical of the period:[208]

AUGUST 22ND, 1892.

JOHANNESBURG'S AGITATION.

AN AMPHITHEATRE ASSEMBLY.

A PROGRAMME SUBMITTED.

THOUSANDS APPROVE IT.

'GIVE US OUR RIGHTS'

STIRRING SPEECHES.

NIGHT OF THE BIRTH OF FREEDOM.

---

[206] Webb, C. *op. cit.*, 19.
[207] Leonard, Charles, *op. cit.*, 42
[208] *Standard and Diggers' News,* 22 August 1892.

Chapter 6

THE LEONARDS RUB IT IN.

'WHAT THE WRETCHED DARE.'

AN HISTORICAL [*sic*] MEETING.

It is from such a gathering as the Amphitheatre held within its capacious walls on Saturday night, that the size and numbers of the Johannesburg of today can be grasped. A truly soul-inspiring scene! Commodious as the Colosseum-like structure is, it was packed to its uttermost dimensions with an audience of all that is enlightened, influential, and respectable in the town. The words 'mass meeting' conjure up vague thoughts of indelicacies; yet there was nothing approaching aggressiveness in the manner in which this huge assembly last Saturday gave vent to its grievances and its cry for political redress. Mass meetings in other climes may take pattern of Johannesburg in propriety and dignity of demeanour, even of that 'sensation-yearning' public which is in part made up of what Pretoria politicians scurrilously characterise as the lowest stratum of a passionate and impulsive society. There was a soupçon of suspense and pent-up excitement accompanying this ready response to the recently sounded reveille. During the week speculation had been rife as to the nature of the promised 'programme', there was a tinge of mystery surrounding it; Mr Jan Meyer was to be dished up as an entree in the political bill of fare, and Mr [James] Leonard, Q.C., was to be served up with the 'sweets'! Therefore long before the appointed hour the vast auditorium was fully filled, and as each prominent Pleader for the People appeared, the greeting accorded him was such as the Leader of a Party might obtain at the hands of his followers. The scene, as viewed from the proscenium, was extremely impressive and imposing. It had something about it of the great theatres of Ancient Greece, and one's thoughts unconsciously turned to Modern Spain with its Alhambras and bullfights. There was Toreador Tudhope and his henchmen intent on morally vanquishing the Boer Bull. They would presently rush into the Political Arena and grapple with the stubborn animal, and all the weapons they would use would be the justifiable protest of Intelligence and Enlightenment! A picture that would have been metaphorically complete save for the bull, serenely slumbering the sleep of the satisfied, miles away at Pretoria, and for the absence of a bright-hued costumed bevy of beauty in the boxes, to smile approvingly upon the politically disabled matadors.

Surrounding the Chair were to be found as carefully chosen and representative a gathering of Johannesburg's Uitlander[209] population as could be desired. They offered as irrefutable a proof of the unanimity of their clamour as the most jaundiced giber could demand. Every interest had sent a delegate, and the Committee of the newly formed National Union embodies essentially fit and proper representatives of Johannesburg's intelligence. Amongst those accommodated with seats on the stage were Messrs John Tudhope (Chair), James Hay, W.H. Rogers, Carl Jeppe, E. Hancock, E.P. Solomon, H. Solomon, W.P. Fraser, H. Adler, H. Langermann, E.H. Duning, A.H. Reid, H.A. Reid, J. Jeppe, Jun. The Law was represented by Messrs J.W. Leonard, Q.C., J.G. Auret, C. Leonard, and F.C. Dumat; Commerce by Messrs C. Malcomess, and D. Holt; and the Cloth by the Rev. D.W. Drew. The 'workers and producers' of the land were in full force beyond; as indeed was all Johannesburg in that assembly of 3,000 men.

The proceedings were commenced at 8.15, when Mr Tudhope, with the cool, calm, collected complacency of an old Parliamentary hand, opened the meeting in a succinct speech. The majority of the speakers who followed were becomingly nervous, a sensation which was not surprising, as in all probability none of them, save Mr J.W. Leonard, Q.C., had ever addressed so large, so influential, and so eager a gathering in their lives before; and in these circumstances the seriousness of the situation had the effect on the speakers referred to. We have excluded Mr J.W. Leonard, in that that gentleman was a prominent speaker on the occasion of the huge meeting in Cape Town some years ago, when the Empire League was formed, to counteract the then rabid Afrikander Bond, which has, however, since toned down, and developed into a useful and respected body [perhaps thanks to Charles Leonard's pamphlet].

STATING THE CASE.

The Chairman (Mr John Tudhope) who on rising was greeted with loud applause, said: Citizens of Johannesburg, this meeting has been called, as you are all aware, in consequence of a meeting held last Saturday night here, when it was thought desirable that a further meeting should be held,

---

[209] Literally 'Outlander' or 'Foreigner'. This was the Dutch term used by conservative Transvaal politicians to refer to those drawn to their Republic by the discovery of gold. It soon came to refer to all non-Dutch-speaking residents of the Transvaal.

at which meeting the people of Johannesburg should have an opportunity of expressing their views upon some of the most important questions of the day. (Hear, hear.) At that meeting several speeches were made, indicating what might be expected at the next meeting, and we have endeavoured, as much as possible, to shadow forth what would be the duties of the Committee nominated to work in the interval. The Committee thought a distinct programme should be given out before the night of the meeting. A number of programmes have been distributed amongst the audience tonight, from which you will see we have not been idle in the meantime. (Applause.)

Before I proceed with any observations I would like to make one or two remarks regarding this meeting, and will first ask you to be as orderly as possible, and uphold the decisions of the chair. (Hear, hear.) But I do so not because I think there will be any disorder in this meeting. Judging from the proceedings of last Saturday night I never attended a more orderly meeting, there was no danger in this direction, and I trust the meeting will be equally orderly here tonight.

We intend to be moderate; we intend to be firm. In all we do we shall appeal only to law and order, and our demands are so reasonable, and our programme such a comprehensive one it excludes no parties, that I believe it will be accepted by the public of Johannesburg and the Government of Pretoria. (Applause.) I think the originators of this movement can claim they have correctly gauged the feelings of the public of Johannesburg, when I look around and see this magnificent meeting. Still, they have only put into shape what has been in the hearts of men for months past. The subject of our grievances, the grievances of the apparently new population of Johannesburg, has been in the mouths of men wherever men have congregated together, and we have asked you here to-night to give that private expression public voice.

I have been asked what occasion there is, what exigency there was for calling this meeting; whether there was any special event that led up to it. I have replied, not only by a special event, but a great many of them. First of all, as mentioned last Saturday night, we have the attitude of the Volksraad[210] towards the people of Johannesburg. I shall only enumerate a few of these things in order to justify the proceedings here tonight.

First, we have the attitude of the Volksraad towards the mining

---

[210] Parliament (literally 'People's council'), which sat in Pretoria, the capital of the South African Republic.

industry in the matter of the dynamite question. (Applause.) Another matter was the neglect of our reasonable representations for a licensing Act, to be able to regulate the drink traffic with natives. They objected to have the licensing powers removed from a controlling power at Pretoria to use in Johannesburg. Then there was the deputation when our representatives were treated with scorn. (Groans.) Then the most important question: We asked that a Court of Justice might be established here; this was also refused. On another subject a resolution was taken with regard to our local self-government, and I suppose that was the last straw that broke the proverbial camel's back. The reply to this was that we would have to be satisfied with the general Municipal Act, which applies to the whole country. Another resolution was passed recently, by which a large number of the inhabitants were deprived of their votes. By the present resolution of the Volksraad only burghers of ten years' standing will be allowed to vote for the highest office in the land, that of President. Such are the sins of commission. We come now to the

SINS OF OMISSION.

First of these stands the neglect of education, and this point will be appreciated by all working men, because you have to pay a heavy tax and get hardly any return for it. (Applause.) We are not sufficiently protected by the police. How otherwise could it be possible that a murder could be committed on a bright moonlight night in one of the busiest thoroughfares of Johannesburg, and the murderer escape detection? Then look at the mines! What protection have the miners against accident and disaster? But it is not necessary for me to go further into this question. I think we are amply justified in calling you together to give voice to your many grievances.

...

Well, I do not like to keep you any longer. The programme which will be laid before you will show what we propose to do. It is, in a few words, to educate the people, not only the English-speaking portion, but the Dutch also, and by every possible means to disseminate information throughout the whole land. We shall try to stir up a political feeling among the population at large. As it was said during the Reform agitation in England 'Register, Register, Register!' So would I say 'Organize, Organize, Organize!' We do not say what we will do or what we will not do, but we rest our cause on its justice only, and I think that its justice will triumph. We shall be victorious in the end, but our victory will be peaceful. (Loud applause.) I shall now ask Mr Charles Leonard to propose the first resolution.'

Let us pause at this juncture to imagine how Charles must have felt as he made his way to the lectern. Never before had he addressed a public meeting, certainly not on this scale. The audience was comprised mainly of tough miners, who would quickly turn against a speaker who failed to say what they had come to hear or who spoke down to them. Charles had clearly taken care over the preparation of his speech and used some of the rhetorical devices that Shakespeare employs in Mark Antony's famous speech from *Julius Caesar*, in which he too addresses the rabble. Charles even quotes from the play at one point! This is how his speech was reported:

Mr C. Leonard, who was enthusiastically received, said it was very gratifying to him to see such a body of citizens gathered together to show their love of freedom and justice. He proposed the following resolution, which he hoped would commend itself to the meeting: 'That regard being had to the great influx of population into this State, the magnitude of their interests, the fact that the greater portion of the public revenue is contributed by them, while they have no voice in the legislation of the country, that many grievances and abuses call for redress, and that there is reason to fear that exclusion from political rights may develop into a source of weakness and danger to the State: it is desirable to form a Union to obtain political rights and the redress of grievances.'

A programme, he continued, will be laid before the meeting a little later on. That programme was very simple. Its main features were to maintain the independence of the State and to obtain equal citizens' rights for all. (Applause.) I need hardly say (said Mr Leonard) the Committee whom last Saturday night's meeting did the honour to appoint intend practically to adhere to that programme. Nothing will move them from it. They are not here to oppose anybody, not to go against the laws of the country. (Hear, hear.) They are here to simply ask for that which reason approves and right demands.

With regard to a few words which fell from me on a previous occasion, I should like to say a few more. I think it is only due to me. I uttered a somewhat epigrammatical and possibly true expression when I described the ruling power in this country as an unintelligent minority. I wish to qualify that, as I do not think it was quite just, and I regretted that I did not say 'uneducated' instead of 'unintelligent'. (Laughter and applause.) You must not think I am going to back out from my colours in any respect. I think the natural intelligence of the Boer in this country is very greatly to be respected, and his inability to grasp the questions of the day is simply owing to the circumstances under which he has grown up. (Hear, hear.) It is our duty to educate him up to a knowledge of these duties. (Laughter.) I have many firm friends amongst the Dutchmen in this country. I am a South African born, and my parents were born here, and I claim to be as good a South African as any of them. I yield to no man in my admiration of the good qualities which the Dutch population undoubtedly possess. The Boer is prejudiced, and has not had the opportunity for the wider culture which many of us have enjoyed, and we should assist him and not blackguard him too heartily.

I have heard it stated in Pretoria that this meeting is froth and mere indisposition, which would be cured in a week. I ask the meeting to say 'Yes' or 'No' to that. (Cries of 'No.')

I have also seen newspaper paragraphs which have dared to say to the intelligent population of Johannesburg that to speak out as men was rebellion. (Hooting.)

I have also heard it said that those men who last Saturday night pleaded for the feeling that was in their hearts would hang separately someday. I ask you whether these people are the exponents of our opinions. (Cries of 'No.')

In dealing with the present state of things it is necessary to go back somewhat in the history of the Transvaal. Fifty years ago a number of people, moved by diverse considerations, no doubt nomadic instincts, a rooted objection to any settled form of Government, and a terrible objection to taxation (Laughter), came across into the Transvaal. That objection to taxation is present still. (Laughter.) They came across the river which now forms the boundary of an independent State; they cleared a few niggers out, shot a few lions, about which they boast a great deal, like Lord Randolph Churchill (Laughter), they obtained a great quantity of land for nothing; and claim, because they were immigrants a few years before the Uitlanders were, that they have the right to rule our destinies for ever.

I will say that for the original body of trekkers they had very sound ideas of what a Republic was. (Laughter.) They formulated what are now

Chapter 6

known as the 33 Articles, and I find upon looking at that Constitution that there is nowhere a qualification with regard to immigration, and that every white man in the country at the time was a burgher. (Applause.) We shall see how far they have departed from that right of equality. Later on, in 1855, they passed a law by which any foreigner could become a full citizen upon payment of £25, but in 1874 the franchise qualification was again changed. Holding land or real estate in this country entitled a man to burgher rights, and, if he did not hold land, residence for one year was sufficient to entitle him to all rights of citizenship. In 1882 the law was again changed, and it was prescribed by the Volksraad that foreigners had to reside for five years in this State, but after that they had every right the original trekker had. In 1892 another change was made in the franchise law. There was a great deal of feeling against the Government about two years ago, and the result of that feeling was that we had the Second Chamber given us. The Volksraad of this country decided on giving us a sop, in granting us the Second Chamber. Those who had been two years on the Field-Cornet's list, and who had taken the oath of allegiance and paid a sum of £5, were naturalised.

Now, gentlemen, the meaning of that was that, although they gave us the Second Chamber, we had no control over the purse-strings of this country. When we were getting that sop they were giving us the shadow and took away the substance. I will ask you to compare the 33 Articles with the law of 1893, which was so altered to our detriment that you had to be on the Field-Cornet's list for ten years before you could have the right to vote for a Member of Parliament, and fourteen years before you are eligible to become a Member of Parliament. I am justified in saying they have given us a shadow and taken away the substance. (Hear, hear.)

I don't doubt there are many present here to-night who, moved by the spirit of obedience to the laws, and desiring to become citizens, availed themselves of the privilege of naturalisation. Men thought – and the Volksraad Act leads to that assumption – that, if they complied with the conditions, and paid their £5, they were entitled to the full rights of citizenship. They were told now that it was not so. This session of the Volksraad a Member of the Raad has said: 'We never intended to give you those privileges when we took your £5; it was only a sham; and if we did not make it clear then we will do so now.' (A voice: 'Shame!') Is that the thing to say to men I see around me? ('No!') What is naturalisation? To an ordinary man it conveys the idea that you become a citizen of this country. Has the Volksraad not admitted, by giving us the Second

Chamber, that we are peaceable citizens, and that we should get what we are asking for? ('Yes!') There are some extraordinary minds in this country. (Laughter.) When we are peaceable and orderly citizens, and trusted to a certain extent with the management of local affairs, why should they now, when they have already admitted our claims, deprive us of them? Why do they refuse us full rights? What can be the object of this distrust but a selfish desire to retain the power which they have?

Prior to the breaking out of the goldfields what was the position of the Transvaal? They were in a position of abject poverty, and a Transvaaler who fought in the War of Independence said that with another six months of it he would have struck out for a change of Government. He had no money, no food, no markets for his produce, and no means of feeding his children. That may have been an isolated case. Still, the Transvaal was in a very poverty-stricken state. We have, however, a fact, that the Government had to borrow £5000 from a person in the State at 12 per cent., and to pledge as security a large amount of ground for the debt. That money was wanted to pay the salary of the officials.

Contrast that to the condition of things today. Wealth came upon them beyond the wildest dreams of men. Taxes had to be imposed, and nobody here objected to the taxes because there could be no Government without money. (Hear, hear.) But we do object to taxes when we have no voice in the spending of them. (Applause.) Taxation comes with representation. (Applause and cheers.)

Upon whom were the taxes imposed to produce this sudden wealth? (Shouts of 'Uitlander!') Yes, it was upon the Uitlanders. The Boers object to taxation, and it was their reluctance to pay taxes that brought them across the Vaal River in 1839. The same spirit characterised him in 1880, and with the influx of people subsequently to the Gold Fields, he said, 'We have the voting power, we will put on the taxes and keep these Johnnies in their place.' (Laughter.) It always has been the fault with the Dutch of giving too little and asking too much. They have not lost that qualification yet. (Laughter.)

They were always hearing talk about the political independence of this State being threatened. Now, I ask you, gentlemen, to say whether it is the intention of any one to interfere with it. (Cries of 'No!') They simply said this in order to save themselves from burdens, and to put them on us. (Hear, hear.) None were desirous of interfering with the form of the Government in the State, and I believe many here would go

Chapter 6

further and resent it in a practical way. We want a Republic in truth and not in name. (Hear, hear.)

What is the condition of things in the Cape Colony? The newcomer or the Uitlander arrives in Cape Town and states he would like to settle in the country and become a citizen. Well, then, he is asked to sign a document, pays his half-crown, and it is published once or twice in the Gazette, and he is a full-blown citizen. (Laughter.) Now I ask you, has that broad system endangered in any respect the Cape Colony? (Voices: 'No.') I think the Cape Colony an infinitely truer Republic than this. (Hear, hear.) If a similar condition had existed here, would we not have been a truer Republic?

Speaking of the Free State, a certain Act has been established between the Free State and this country by which the inhabitants of the Free State and the Transvaal have equal rights in the other's State, but we, who contribute the revenue of the country, are excluded from those rights. Is that just and fair? (A voice: 'No!') Why should the Free State alone participate in these privileges when we and others are excluded? We don't seek to go upon racial lines[211]; the racial distinction is brought about by the Government of this country; we seek to obviate this distinction. (Hear, hear.)

Who has made the Transvaal? We came here and found the original burghers settled upon farms; they had no markets; no means; their only means of living was to contract their wants. (Loud and continued applause.) Who enabled them to live, who made markets for them? We! Yet we are told we are mere birds of passage, and that, because they were here before us, we have no right. Have we not obeyed the laws of the country? We have given hostages to fortune. Our wives, our children, our homes are here, and most of us are likely to live, and a great many to die, here. Gentlemen, I appeal to the town of Johannesburg, to the public men, for the sake of the thousands of children growing up, I appeal to the permanent character of the town buildings, and I say the very stones of Johannesburg plead eloquently for the cause and justice of our case.

What has been our attitude during all this time? We have paid the taxes, hoping for better things; we have been waiting patiently for five years. Hope deferred makes the heart sick, and I believe we are all getting very sick. I say a wave is coming. The time is come when we have to

---

[211] Here, he refers to those of British and Dutch origin.

stand up as men for our rights. I believe the Boers will see the justice of our cause, and respond to our demands. When once the paths diverge, how difficult it may be to remove misconception and bring peace again! I say with the words of the resolution: 'There is reason to fear that exclusion from political rights may develop into a source of weakness and danger to the State.' These words speak for themselves, and it is unnecessary for me to add to them. A house divided against itself cannot stand. We want to be friends and brothers of the farmers; a perpetual sore of irritation and discontent can lead to no good. Nobody is more anxious than we to avoid friction and discontent. I say what is in my heart. I believe I echo the feeling of this meeting when I say we want to be friends and brothers. (Applause.) Why should they display this feeling of hostile legislation? Everything is put upon us. 'Things are not what they seem.'

Now, gentlemen, I am not here to stir you up to any sudden flood of mutinous rage. This meeting itself shows that we mean business, that we want reform, and that we will not relax our efforts until it is conceded. (Applause.) There are a number of other speakers to follow, and I will not keep you any longer, but I wish also to show [that] the matter lies deep in my heart, and I do not speak in any light spirit. I am not a public man, and do not seek notoriety [*sic*]. I should like best to live in obscurity, and if we get our rights I shall not be seen on any public platform again. I ask you to make it clear that this movement is in earnest and not nonsense, as the *Diggers' News* would make out.

There is one other thing: Deputations are about played out. We may send our best men to Pretoria and let them plead their best only to be snubbed. Memorials are sent to the Volksraad and referred to a Committee, and thereafter they are never heard of again. Unless we rise as one man and tell our feelings, we shall never be understood and listened to. This has never been done yet, but I hope that this meeting will do it. I do not think there can be any doubt that we are unanimous there must be a change. Reform there must be, and reform we will have. (Applause.) ...

As the fruit of tonight's meeting, I expect a better political understanding in this State (long and loud applause) and I hope that the establishment of the Transvaal National Union will contribute to destroy all racial prejudices, and that this country will become the most prosperous and one of the greatest, as it certainly will if we only act in unity. (Loud and prolonged cheers.)

Chapter 6

As Charles returned to his seat, he must have felt immensely gratified at the reception he had received. In fact, the men of Johannesburg thereafter called him 'Charlie', a sign of affection and a token of their sense that he spoke for them; that he was, in the words of the reporter, a 'Pleader for the People'.

James Hay, who seconded the resolution proposed by Charles, then gave a short speech, after which the resolution was submitted to the meeting and passed unanimously.

In the light of later developments, there are a few important points to note regarding Charles's speech. The most crucial is that at the outset he and his comrades had no intention of overthrowing Paul Kruger's government; all they wanted was reform. Charles repeatedly makes this point, saying that the Union aims 'to maintain the independence of the State'; 'not to go against the laws of the country'; 'we are peaceable and orderly citizens'; 'we want to be friends and brothers of the farmers'; 'I am not here to stir you up to any sudden flood of mutinous rage'; 'Reform there must be, and reform we will have'.

The second important point is that he and his comrades were committed to a shared future in the Transvaal. They had no intention of leaving: 'we are told we are mere birds of passage'; 'our wives, our children, our homes are here, and most of us are likely to live, and a great many to die, here'; 'I appeal to the permanent character of the town buildings'; 'this country will become the most prosperous and one of the greatest…if we only act in unity'.

The third important point is that he was reluctant to court publicity or seek public office, in spite of later claims to the contrary: 'I am not a public man, and do not seek notoriety [sic]. I should like best to live in obscurity, and if we get our rights I shall not be seen on any public platform again.'

Sadly, these wishes were not to be fulfilled for some time to come, but in the meantime, Charles Leonard had established himself as one of the leading political figures in the Reform Movement.

Four mass meetings were convened in the two months immediately following the formation of the National Union, but thereafter the leaders appear to have been content to let agitation rest for a while, and to devote themselves to the business of 'getting at the people' in other parts of the country. Charles Leonard prepared a manifesto and by the middle of November 1892, it was being circulated to 'every homestead in the Republic'. The manifesto took the form of 'a statement, in the language of the land, of the inception, growth and purposes of the Transvaal National Union', and was clearly intended as a piece of propaganda to win over supporters in the outlying districts of the Republic.

At the same time, the business of forming branch unions in other centres of the country proceeded apace. Members of the committee visited various centres, public meetings were held, the objects of the Union explained, and in several cases, branches were formed. By the end of the year, Potchefstroom, Klerksdorp, Rustenburg, Pretoria, Boksburg, Germiston, Krugersdorp, Heidelberg and Nigel had all been included within the ambit of the Union.[212]

---

[212] Webb, C. *op. cit.*, 24.

Chapter 6

President Paul Kruger

Cecil John Rhodes

John Hays Hammond

Dr Leander Jameson

Col. Francis Rhodes

Lionel Phillips

President Kruger (seated right) gives audience to a deputation in Pretoria

A political cartoon by J.M. Staniforth, satirising the slow pace of franchise law reform. It depicts an Uitlander miner and President Paul Kruger. The shadowy figure in the background is the British Secretary of State for the Colonies, Joseph Chamberlain, who secretly exploited the crisis for his own ends.

CHAPTER 7 : BETWEEN A ROCK AND A HARD PLACE (1892-1894)

I have taken a man into my coach, and as a passenger he is welcome; but now he says, Give me the reins; and that I cannot do, for I know not where he will drive me.

– President Paul Kruger

President Kruger was no fool, although he may have appeared so. He was a shrewd politician who had already faced a challenge to his leadership from the Progressives in his Volksraad and had succeeded in holding them at bay through a combination of bluster and cunning.

Born in the Cradock district of the Eastern Cape a few months after Charles Leonard's grandparents had left the district to settle in Somerset East, Stephanus Johannes Paulus Kruger was still a boy when he took part in the Great Trek. He and his fellow trekkers learned how to survive against tremendous odds as they ventured into the unknown interior. If even a few of the many legends about his courage are based on fact, there were times when he fearlessly faced down danger, from both wild animals and assegai-wielding warriors. But he also learned the traditional Boer defensive manoeuvre of withdrawing into a *laager*.[213] This tactic may have been effective in the wilds, but it was a suicidal strategy against the forces of progress.

To understand Kruger's reluctance to extend the franchise to the Uitlanders, it is necessary to consider the predicament in which he found himself. For a number of years, the Transvaal Boers had been facing

---

[213] A defensive arrangement of wagons formed into a circle to protect those within.

mounting pressure.

A primitive pastoral people, they found themselves isolated, surrounded – 'shut in a kraal for ever', as Kruger is reported to have said… Expansion of territory, once the dream of the Transvaal Boers, as their incursions into Bechuanaland, into Zululand, and the attempted trek into Rhodesia, all testify, was becoming daily less practicable. One thing remained – to accept their isolation and strengthen it.[214]

Yet this proved to be extremely difficult as they lacked markets for their agricultural produce, and there was very little other economic activity. Their Republic was in dire financial straits. Then, in the blink of an eye, the Uitlanders flocked to their land and brought it great wealth – by developing its resources, paying nine-tenths of its revenue, and providing a market for the farmers' produce – but now they wanted a say in how the country was governed. This the Boers could not allow. But how to prevent it? That was the vexing question.

On 1 September 1892, a deputation from the National Union was invited to Pretoria for an interview with President Kruger and his Vice-President. A report of that interview was read to a meeting of the National Union afterwards. This is how the *Standard and Diggers' News* reported that meeting:[215]

SEPTEMBER 12TH, 1892.

'CIVIS ROMANUS SUM'

TRANSVAAL NATIONAL UNION.

FROM STRENGTH TO STRENGTH.

THAT INTERVIEW.

HIS HONOUR'S MESSAGE.

REJECTED AND DESPISED.

'WE WON'T WAIT.'

A GREAT GATHERING.

WE GO TO THE BURGHERS.

---

[214] Hillier, Alfred P. *Raid and Reform*, 25.
[215] *Standard and Diggers' News*, 12 September 1892.

Chapter 7

From out of the cold wind of Saturday night the members of the Transvaal National Union congregated in their beloved Circus once more. The Tree in Hyde Park and the Lions in Trafalgar Square have perhaps gathered around them larger numbers, but never men more determined in will and more stentorian in voice than the Unionists that assembled in the local Acropolis on Saturday night. The clamorous enthusiasm evinced at the previous three meetings was completely outdone by the peaceful uproar of this last assembly. There were many things which evoked the sturdy shout. Hitherto the Uitlanders' wail had not officially or formally reached the Government ear; but last week it was carried to the Capital by the most popular of the People's advocates, Mr Tudhope, only, however, to be slighted. The pettish rebuff and angry, arbitrary attitude of the governors upon that occasion formed matter for the-always-legally-and-constitutionally-expressed indignation of the governed.

...

Mr Tudhope, on rising, was greeted with loud applause. He said: Citizens of Johannesburg, it is gratifying to see another large assemblage here tonight to carry on the business put into our hands to do. I do not propose to occupy your time at great length this evening, but will just briefly indicate the programme advised by the Committee for this evening. Now, with regard to the proceedings, we shall first read an abbreviated narrative of what occurred between the deputation which went to interview his Honour the President in Pretoria. We shall afterwards read a message from his Honour the President to the people of Johannesburg…

REPORT OF DEPUTATION.

The interview took place in Pretoria on Friday, 2nd September, 1892. The deputation consisted of Messrs John Tudhope, James Hay, W.H. Rogers, J.G. Auret, J.F.E. Pistorius, James W. Leonard, and Charles Leonard. The President, after shaking hands with the deputation, indicated that he wished them to proceed. He stated that he was speaking unofficially. Mr Tudhope thereupon stated that those present had come as a deputation to discuss questions which were agitating the general public in Johannesburg, and briefly reviewed the question of the franchise rights and the incidence of taxation, illustrating the fairness and justice of the proposition that the new-comers, who would give their certain guarantee for obedience to the law, and all who had a stake in the country were entitled to have a vote. He pointed out that this would be a source of strength to the Republic... He briefly touched upon the administration of justice and a municipal government.

The President thereupon apparently thought he was going to close the interview and addressed the deputation, informing them that it had always been his policy to unite the two sections of the people, and that he would continue in this policy; that the Presidential election was now pending in which there were three candidates, and that any one of these three candidates who should give a pledge for the granting of the franchise would be rejected by the people. He stated that what was sought for in the franchise would, if granted, deprive his people of their sole privilege; he claimed that in granting the Second Chamber he had made a great concession in favour of the new-comers, and that he had reduced the period which must elapse prior to obtaining political rights by the new-comers; he counselled the deputation to go back to Johannesburg, cease to hold public meetings, and be satisfied with his policy of uniting the people.

The President was somewhat excited in speaking [a marvellous example of bathos!].

General Smit thereupon, also being apparently under the impression that the interview was closed, said that it had given him great pleasure to attend this meeting, as meetings of this character could only tend to produce a good understanding.

The deputation, however, not being satisfied with the answer given, Mr J. W. Leonard rose, speaking through the interpreter. Mr Leonard, as Mr Tudhope had done, assured the President that the policy which he announced of uniting the people was the only thing that lay at our hearts; that we could not go away and say we were satisfied; that [it] would be false if we did so.

Mr C. Leonard controverted the proposition that we wished to take away the only right of the President's old burghers, and claimed that a Republican Government could only be carried on by the representation of all classes of the community; that we did not seek to take away the privileges of the old burghers, but only to share them under certain conditions. He pointed out further to the President that the people of Johannesburg felt that the powers of the Second Chamber were so limited as practically to amount to an exclusion from all the more important functions of the Government; that it would be wiser to go

Chapter 7

back to the old Grondwet, and in any case the representation which had been asked for was a representation in all the functions of Government. He also pointed out that, when the Second Chamber was established, the Volksraad in the same year increased the period of probation to ten years for the right to vote for a member of the First Chamber, and fourteen years for the right to sit in the First Chamber, and that this, practically, amounted to exclusion for life of all the businessmen who were now established in the country. This was felt as a great grievance. He respectfully assured the President that the desire was only for union, and to be law-abiding subjects of the Republic, and that while the method of those represented was to remove distrust and discontent, his method of depriving the new-comers of the vote would perpetuate their discontent.

The President during these statements got very excited several times, and on one occasion said: 'Well, why didn't they then leave the country?'

To this Mr Leonard replied that they could not be expected to do so, as everything they had in the wide world was vested here.

During one of his agitated moments the President said: 'Well, why don't they say at once that they reject my proposition?'

Mr Leonard pointed out that there was no proposition before them; he had merely requested them to go home and be satisfied, and hold no more meetings…

The above section of the report sheds light on both Charles Leonard's leadership abilities and his courage. When other members of the deputation appeared to be politely trying to appease the excitable President, Charles decided to take the lead and speak truth to power. He was also prepared to take the President on, fearlessly challenging 'Oom Paul' on a number of points and refusing to be intimidated by the old man's notorious bluster. The report continues:

Then ensued an irregular conversation between General Smit and Mr Charles Leonard, also between the President and several members of the deputation, in which both the President and Vice-President became very much excited.

There is, however, no reason to report on this occasion what passed then, the foregoing being a fair narrative of the most important points which were discussed.

The Chairman (continuing) said: You have heard read what has occurred between the deputation and the President and Vice-President. We went there at the invitation of these gentlemen and for the express purpose of interchanging our views. You see what the result of the interchange of views has been. (Laughter.) It is quite evident that our deputation made a great and strong impression upon the mind of his Honour the President. Not only did he speak of it to gentlemen who interviewed him after our departure, but on the following day he met one of our Committee, who was there on other business, and he desired to use him as a medium of sending a message in reply to the people of Johannesburg. The message is as follows:

MESSAGE FROM HIS HONOUR THE PRESIDENT TO THE PEOPLE OF JOHANNESBURG.

1. In view of the forthcoming elections, the claim made by the deputation for the extension of the franchise to the new population is untimely. No candidate for the Presidency can raise the issue with any hope of success, and if raised then such candidate would thereby forfeit all chance of being elected by the burghers.

2. His Honour has always kept in view the blending of the two people into an [*sic*] united race, but this must of a necessity be a somewhat slow process. To open the door unreservedly for the admission of the new population would mean the abolition of the rights of the old burghers in the country, inasmuch as the new-comers are in the majority. In America the liberal provision for the admission to the full political rights of new-comers is not attended by the same dangers, the thousands who enter that country having no influence to disturb the rights of the old residents, who are numbered in millions; whereas here, the old burghers, being numbered in hundreds, at once become the minority, and lose all their political power. To obviate this the admission of the new-comers to full burgher rights must be regulated with great care; but in view of meeting the exigencies of the case, as far as it may be done with safety to the rights of the old burghers of the country, the President would be in favour of a plan

> that would during the course of law, which is fixed at ten years, within that period from time to time admit of the names of trustworthy burghers being laid before the Volksraad with the view to such being admitted to the qualifications required for membership in the First Volksraad.

Mr John Tudhope, continuing, said: This message was received with the respect which I trust we shall always show to utterances from the head of the State. (Hear, hear.) It was most carefully considered, and a copy of it was sent to his Honour to ascertain if it properly expressed his views, and it came back with his approval, and was now read to the people of Johannesburg. I will now call upon Mr Charles Leonard to address you upon it. (Applause.)

Mr Charles Leonard (who was received with loud cheers) said: Mr Chairman and Gentlemen, I think it is a wise thing to change your speakers as much as possible, and I should not have appeared before you tonight had it not been for the fact that I was one of the deputation to Pretoria. I have consented to speak simply because I was one of the deputation... The resolution which I have to submit arises partly out of the visit of the deputation to his Honour the President, and I will read it to you:

> That, while recognising with satisfaction the recognition by his Honour the President, in his message to the people of Johannesburg, of the fact that the new population are in the majority in the State, and of the principle that they are entitled to electoral rights, this Union regards the proposal to admit only some of these citizens to burgher rights by a slow process of selection as contrary to sound Republican principles, impracticable in working, and as failing to satisfy the reasonable requirements of the people.

If you will pardon me for a moment diverging, I would say a word as to what fell from General Smit in Pretoria, when he was in an excited state. In anger sometimes the truth comes out. In conversation with the General, he said that behind this movement was political intrigue... (Cries of 'No.') I gave him my assurance and my word of honour that there was nothing of the kind. I ask you to say no. We are not traitors to the flag of this country, and are not conspiring against it, but seek to strengthen the republican institutions of this country. (Applause.)

I shall now proceed to deal with the matter of the resolution. The President, in speaking, said…that no candidate for the Presidency would dare to promise the franchise, that it would endanger his chance of re-election. I pointed out that this re-election was in the hands of the burghers of this country, and had nothing to do with it, that there was no desire to take away the rights of the burghers, but that we simply desired to share those rights upon true republican principles. I may state that what struck me here was that nothing was said or urged by his Honour the President on the ground of our not being entitled to the franchise, but that we, getting those rights and being in the majority, would take away their privileges. I pointed out that instead of being a source of weakness, we should be a source of strength; pointed out that, whilst perhaps it might be unwise to ask for a vote for the Presidential election, with regard to the First Chamber we wanted a vote; that we did not want dummy votes, but we wanted a part in everything coming under the science of Government. I pointed out that, according to the distribution at present in force, we would send only a fourth of the members to the Volksraad, that the old members would still be in the vast majority, but we would be there with our representatives to imbue the Volksraad with the true sentiments of the community. I ask you whether those views were sound or not. (Applause.)

Let us now analyse the President's proposal. I think, in the message to the people of Johannesburg, the President has admitted two great principles, principles which fully justify the support of the National Union. He admitted we were in the majority, and admitted by his proposition of selection that we are entitled to some alterations in the present law of the franchise. The question before us is whether we as a Union can accept the President's proposals. ('No, no,' and loud applause.) I say it is a proposition that cannot obtain a hearing in a republic, where the people are imbued with republican sentiment, and is opposed to the true principles of republicanism. It is one which, if accepted, would paralyse the highest and best interests in us, and it is probably intended to lead to disunion amongst ourselves. I say, No, we will not have it, and intend standing shoulder to shoulder. (Loud applause.) If this process of selection were accepted, it would be found that sycophant jellyfishes and hunters after concessions will be selected, and thus the very thing held out as a lure to cease agitating would be the very thing to put new chains upon us and our liberties. (Cheers.) I say that if we were to take the proposal seriously, the last state would be worse than the first. We are suffering under two things today. The political disability under the circumstances as altered by the present Government is rankling deeply in our hearts, and then the sins of administration, but I had better say no more. (A voice: 'Speak out,' and laughter.)

I think, gentlemen, it is our business to attack incompetent administration and its abuses. It is our duty to teach the burghers of this country that the iniquities of which we complain are suffered by them as well. I decline to accept the Government as representing either the burghers or ourselves. (Loud cheers.) The reason why I say that is, that it is five years since the burghers were called upon to elect a Government, and in these five years changes have taken place which fully justify our demands. Government persistently ignores these demands, but it would be a very poor compliment to the burghers generally to say that they supported the Government in this. No, gentlemen, I believe strongly in the sense of justice and the common sense of the burghers. It is to this sense of justice that we must appeal, and this can only be done by the widest publication of our wants and wishes. (Loud applause.)

Mr W.H. Rogers, who seconded the resolution, said: You have all heard of the interview which the deputation of this Union had with his Honour the President and with the Vice-President. My impression of that interview amounts to this: 'I am very pleased to see you; go back to Johannesburg and be very good boys; wait till I have been re-elected, and then I will see what I can do for you.' (Laughter)…

The Chairman then put the first resolution, which was carried unanimously.

Not included in the report of the deputation's interview with the President was Kruger's unofficial angry response to Charles Leonard, which he later revealed. It was: 'Go back and tell your people that I shall never give them anything. I shall never change my policy. And now let the storm burst.'[216]

But the storm did not burst – at least not for the next three years. Another mass meeting was held on the night of 23 September at which Charles Leonard outlined a programme for making the National Union 'a force in the politics of the country'. Henceforth, no election was to go

---

[216] Leonard, Charles. *op. cit.*, 44.

uncontested, and all the funds which Johannesburg could muster were to go to the assistance of 'progressive' candidates. Finally, it was resolved to 'renew and continue agitation in order to secure reform in the Government of the country'.[217]

However, during the first few months of 1893, the Union maintained a policy of total quiescence. Presidential and Volksraad elections were pending, and the leaders of the Union appear to have been wary of conducting any agitation which might arouse fears and suspicions amongst the electorate and jeopardise the chances of 'progressive' candidates.[218]

In May, the new session of the Volksraad having been opened without any reference to the reforms desired by the Uitlanders, the Transvaal National Union decided to revert to active agitation, and it was announced that a mass meeting was to be convened 'to lend all the moral weight and support which such a gathering carries' to the petitions of the Union.

> Petitions to the Government were sent in year after year. Resolutions calling for some amelioration in the conditions of the franchise law, the dynamite trade, education, and the courts of justice were passed both by the National Union meetings and by other public bodies – but all to no avail.[219]

In January 1895, John Tudhope resigned his position as chairman of the National Union and Charles Leonard was elected his replacement. He is on record as having responded to his election thus: 'If I am deeply sensible of the honour conferred upon me by being elected Chairman of the National Union, I am profoundly impressed with the responsibilities attached to the position... The issues to be faced in this country are ...momentous in character.'[220]

At this pivotal point in the National Union's history, Charles took his family on their first overseas holiday 'for a change'.[221] It seems likely that he had bowed to pressure from Catherine because he would hardly have voluntarily left Johannesburg at such a critical juncture. Jim's wife, Catharina (or Kate, as she was now known), accompanied them, so perhaps she and her sister-in-law had colluded. In mid-May, they boarded the train to Cape Town, where they spent a few days buying new outfits and visiting Catherine's family

---

[217] Webb, C. *op. cit.*, 26-27.
[218] *Ibid.*, 25.
[219] Hillier, Alfred P. *op. cit.*, 34.
[220] Leonard, Charles. *op. cit.*, 23.
[221] *Leonard Papers*, 79.

before boarding the mail ship on 28 May 1894 and sailing for England.[222] One can imagine their excitement. After enduring the boredom and extreme vicissitudes of nature on the Transvaal Highveld, they were to experience an English summer, with regattas at Henley, concerts in Hyde Park, cricket at Lord's, the theatre in Covent Garden, racing at Royal Ascot, and innumerable garden parties and 'At-homes'.

They returned to South Africa as the English winter started setting in, sailing from Southampton aboard the *Norham Castle* on 1 November. Catharina (Kate) had evidently returned earlier or was staying longer as she is not listed as a passenger.[223]

Back in Johannesburg, Charles found the National Union in despair. In May, 13,000 Uitlanders had petitioned the Volksraad for the rights of the franchise, and it is on record in the minutes of that legislative body that this petition was received with jeers and laughter. Then in July, they had sent another petition, signed this time by 32,500 inhabitants,[224] but it had been received by the Volksraad in the same manner, with one of its members (C.B. Otto) going so far as to rise and say, 'I am tired of all these threats. I say, Come on and fight, if you want a fight. Come on!'[225] This was the death knell for the Reform Movement. The men of Johannesburg realised once and for all that, whatever else might come, to look for redress of their grievances by constitutional means was hopeless.

It is only fair to acknowledge that in the Volksraad itself and amongst the Boers in general, there was a small minority of men who held enlightened views and a more far-seeing patriotism. Carl Jeppe, Richard Loveday, Lucas Meyer, Eugène Marais, Lodewyk and Gert de Jager and Ewald Esselen are some of those whom Charles Leonard later identified as 'Progressives'. Ewald Esselen began his political career as a prominent member of the Afrikander Bond in the Cape House of Assembly. He was then made a Judge in the High Court in the Transvaal, and having resigned that position, took an active part in the politics of the country. In 1892, he addressed a meeting of the National Union with these words:

> I may tell you I am in entire accord with the movement of the National Union, and I am proud to be asked to say a few words. I wish to ask you

---

[222] www.ancestorsonboard.com
[223] *Ibid.*
[224] Webb, C. *op. cit.*, 37. Other sources place the number of signatories at 38,500.
[225] Crisp, Robert. *op. cit.*, 190.

whether you can give any credence to the statement of a man [President Kruger] who says he is going to unite two people, when the whole of his acts for the last ten years show it is absolutely untrue. I do not speak without knowing what I am talking about – I say you have been kept out of your political privileges, not because the people have kept you out from fear that your being granted these privileges would wreck or endanger the independence of this country, but to enable a few, and a greedy few, to rule the country for their ends.[226]

Another to warn his compatriots of the impending storm was the Chief Justice of the Republic, John Gilbert Kotzé. In October 1894, he delivered an address at Rustenburg, in which he said:

No-one who for a moment considers the condition of things in the State will deny that the country is at present in a very critical position. The unmistakable signs of an approaching change are apparent on every side. It entirely depends upon the people whether the impending change is to take place peaceably, or to be accomplished with violence. Do not let us close our eyes and ears to the truth. The people should thoroughly understand the true position of things. I repeat what I have just said – the non-observance of and departure from the Grondwet menaces the independence of the State… The trek spirit has well-nigh become extinct; the Republic has its beacons and boundaries, which, with the exception of our eastern border, can no longer be extended. In the wise dispensation of Providence everything has its proper season. It is remarkable that, although our mineral treasures have for ages existed in the country, they have only recently been discovered and developed (by the Uitlander)… There is but one safe course to follow in dealing with public matters under the altered conditions – the country must be ruled in accordance with the recognised rules of constitutional Government.[227]

Unfortunately, Kruger and his allies in the Volksraad not only refused to heed these warnings, but made two major political blunders, both of which, in the words of the Chief Justice, further menaced the independence of the State.

---

[226] Hillier, Alfred P. *op. cit.*, 37-8.
[227] Leonard, Charles. *op. cit.*, 345-7.

Chapter 7

George Farrar — Joseph Chamberlain — Mohandas Gandhi

Charles Leonard met Rhodes at Groote Schuur, his stately home in Rondebosch

CHAPTER 8 : KRUGER MUST FALL
(1894-1895)

Johannesburg is ready...[this is] the big idea which makes England dominant in Africa, in fact gives England the African continent.

– Rhodes in a secret letter to Alfred Beit, August 1895

In June 1894, the Transvaal Republic engaged in a war with a recalcitrant African chief, Malaboch, and decided to conscript a group of Englishmen to serve in the campaign. Five of the Pretoria conscripts refused to go and were imprisoned. They appealed to the High Court, but their liability to service was upheld. They were then taken under compulsion to the front. This caused the greatest indignation throughout the Uitlander community and induced the National Union to appeal to the British Government. Sir Henry Loch, the Governor of the Cape and British High Commissioner, was despatched to Pretoria, and, after making the views of Her Majesty's Government known to the President, extracted from him a pledge that no further commandeering of British subjects would occur. While Loch was in Pretoria, he met a delegation from the National Union, excluding Charles Leonard, who was holidaying in England. They informed him of their grievances and of the dismissive responses to their petitions. The High Commissioner is reputed to have asked how many rifles the Uitlanders could muster.

Upon his return to Cape Town, the High Commissioner discussed conditions on the Rand with the Prime Minister, Cecil John Rhodes. It was either during or soon after this meeting that Loch conceived of a plan for intervention in the affairs of the Transvaal and submitted it to the British Secretary of State for the Colonies for consideration. It involved having a force held in readiness at Mafeking so that in the event of an insurrection in the Transvaal this force could be despatched to lend assistance. His superiors rejected his proposal out of hand and Loch was recalled to face the music.[228]

The second of Kruger's blunders was the Drifts Crisis of September and October 1895. In order to divert freight traffic from entering the Transvaal via the railway from the Cape to that from Delagoa Bay, which would be more lucrative for the Netherlands Railway Company operating that line, the Volksraad increased tariffs on the route from the Cape. Rather than pay these exorbitant tariffs or make use of the cheaper rail link from Delagoa Bay, importers still used the comparatively inexpensive railway from Cape Town to Kimberley, but then unloaded their freight there and transported it the rest of the way by ox-wagon. The Volksraad responded by arbitrarily closing the drifts (fords) over the Vaal River to all goods traffic. These drifts were on the main wagon roads between the Cape and the Transvaal. The Cape Colonial Government issued an ultimatum to the Volksraad to reopen the drifts and privately came to an arrangement with the British Government that in the event of this ultimatum not attaining its end, the two Governments would share the expenses of a joint military expedition to the Transvaal. The ultimatum did attain its end, and the drifts were reopened, but this incident was significant in showing how close the two Governments had come to resorting to military intervention.

In 1895, Cecil John Rhodes turned forty-two and was at the height of his power. Not only was he Prime Minister of Cape Colony, but he was also Managing Director of the British South Africa Company (BSA Company) with an almost free hand to safeguard the interests and, where possible, expand the dominions of the British Empire in southern Africa. He was also an extremely wealthy man: he was Chairman of the De Beers Consolidated Mining Company, which had monopolised diamond mining in Kimberley, and Managing Director of Goldfields South Africa in Johannesburg.

Rhodes had been slow to risk involvement in gold mining in case it should prove a costly but futile investment. However, in 1894, he secured the services of a leading American mining engineer, John Hays Hammond, who later wrote:

> I went out to South Africa in 1893 as consulting engineer to the firm of Barnato Brothers, one of the largest mine-owners in the Transvaal; but within a year Mr Cecil Rhodes, at that time Prime Minister of Cape

---

[228] Meredith, Martin. *Diamonds, Gold and War: The Making of South Africa*, 309.

Colony, offered me a position of wider scope and interest in connection with the general development of the mineral deposits in Rhodesia controlled by the British South Africa Company, and the mines at Johannesburg of the Goldfields of South Africa, of which he was the Managing Director and the moving spirit. This offer I was glad to accept, as I knew Rhodes to be a man of large views and progressive methods; and his reputation, great as it was throughout the British Empire, was in nothing greater than in the staunch backing he afforded to men who earned his confidence.[229]

Hammond, Rhodes and Dr Leander Starr Jameson, who was not only Rhodes's physician and close friend but also his right-hand man in the BSA Company, made a tour of inspection of Matabeleland and Mashonaland in September 1894 to ascertain whether the region had any significant mineral potential. However, while out riding or while gathered around the campfire in the evenings, talk usually turned to the fraught situation in the Transvaal and the grievances of the Uitlanders. 'Mr Hammond assert[ed] that … unless a radical change was made there would be a rising by the people in Johannesburg.'[230] 'Let's hope old Kruger'll see sense,' Hammond said. 'Otherwise he'll have to have some sense knocked into him.'[231]

Rhodes sent Jameson to Johannesburg in October 1894 and again in March 1895, where Hammond (who had become a prominent member of the National Union) introduced him to the leaders. Jameson became convinced that Johannesburg was ripe for rebellion, even though he was warned that heated words do not necessarily lead to fiery actions.

In August 1895, Charles Leonard travelled to Cape Town as he was suing Andries van Niekerk of Visserhoek, Durbanville, for breach of contract regarding the purchase of two carriage horses. The case was heard in the Supreme Court on 30 August and Charles argued, via his counsel, for the sale to be rescinded and for repayment of the purchase price of £150, as well as for damages (to be determined by the court) and for the keep of the horses. The court appointed a commissioner to obtain testimonies from witnesses to the sale in Johannesburg and the case was adjourned.[232]

---

[229] Hammond, John Hays and Ireland, Alleyne. *The Truth about the Jameson Raid*, .8-9.
[230] Dr Jameson's testimony, Report of the Select Committee on British South Africa – Evidence. Question No. 4513.
[231] Crisp, Robert. *op. cit.*, 163-8.
[232] KAB, CSC 2/6/1/159, 274. Motion, Charles Henry Brandt Leonard versus Andries Jacobus Bester van Niekerk, 1895.

While Charles was in Cape Town, Rhodes met him informally and sounded him out on the position in Johannesburg. Charles confirmed that a public uprising was likely. Although nothing definite was decided, Rhodes and Jameson privately determined to adopt what was to all intents and purposes Loch's plan. Rhodes next persuaded his brother, Colonel Francis (or Frank) Rhodes, to join the conspiracy as the military adviser. The Prime Minister then sent a secret letter to his wealthy friend Alfred Beit in England, asking him to lend financial support. He wrote: 'Johannesburg is ready… [this is] the big idea which makes England dominant in Africa, in fact gives England the African continent.'[233] Beit was at first reluctant to become involved, but Rhodes's persuasive arguments eventually won him over.

By 1895, Lionel Phillips, the President of the Chamber of Mines in Johannesburg, had become a supporter of the National Union, if only in his personal capacity. The other leading capitalists remained aloof. Charles Leonard now explains how the National Union became embroiled in the plot:

> In October I went to Cape Town with Mr Lionel Phillips. We had given up all hope at that time of getting any redress of the political situation by constitutional means and it had been suggested that it was perfectly clear that disturbances would break out in Johannesburg sooner or later, that the public were getting very excited… It was suggested that Mr Rhodes was willing to help us in this matter; and the result was an interview between Mr Rhodes, Mr Phillips, Mr Hammond, Colonel Rhodes, and myself at Cape Town.[234]

This meeting took place at Groote Schuur, Rhodes's magnificent Cape Dutch homestead in Rondebosch, about five miles to the south of Cape Town.[235] Charles later recalled:

> I hesitated at first but was gradually drawn under by the singular magnetic power of Rhodes … Step by step I was drawn further, and I can now see how skilfully my weaknesses, nay! my strengths – were played upon – how I was *used* – until retract was all but impossible.[236]

---

[233] Pakenham, Thomas. *The Boer War*, 1.
[234] Leonard, Charles. *op. cit.*, 364.
[235] Literally 'Large Barn'. It became the official Cape Town residence of future Prime Ministers and Presidents.
[236] Leonard 'Short Story'.

Chapter 8

Charles later explained:

> I had a[nother] conversation with Rhodes [on 24 October] in Mr Lionel Phillips' presence; and generally the outline of what followed was agreed upon. It was then agreed that I should go away that day and draw up what was called a manifesto, which was to be published throughout the South African States to steady opinion and to show what the reason of our action was and what our objects were.[237]

Charles worked on the manifesto throughout the day and had a draft ready by the evening. The key section of this lengthy document reads as follows:

> I have stated plainly what our grievances are, and I shall answer with equal directness the question, 'What do we want?' We want –
>
> 1. The establishment of this Republic as a true Republic.
> 2. A Grondwet or Constitution, which shall be framed by competent persons selected by representatives of the whole people and framed on lines laid down by them, a Constitution which shall be safeguarded against hasty alteration.
> 3. An equitable Franchise Law and fair representation.
> 4. Equality of the Dutch and English languages.
> 5. Responsibility to the Legislature of the heads of the great departments.
> 6. Removal of religious disabilities.
> 7. Independence of the Courts of Justice, with adequate and secured remuneration of the Judges.
> 8. Liberal and comprehensive education.
> 9. An efficient civil service, with adequate provision for pay and pension.
> 10. Free trade in South African products.
>
> This is what we want.
> There now remains the question which is to be put before you at the meeting of the 6th January, viz., 'How shall we get it?' To this

---

[237] Leonard, Charles. *op. cit.*, 364-5.

question I shall expect from you an answer in plain terms according to your deliberate judgment.

     (Signed)   CHARLES LEONARD,
    Chairman of the Transvaal National Union.[238]

That evening, the meeting resumed at Groote Schuur. Charles recalls it thus:

> We read to him [Rhodes] the draft of our declaration of rights. He was leaning against the mantel-piece smoking a cigarette, and when it came to that part of the document in which we refer to Free Trade in South African products, he turned round suddenly and said: 'That is what I want. That is all I ask of you. The rest will come in time. We must have a beginning, and that will be the beginning.'[239]

This seems an odd response, considering how much importance the National Union placed on the franchise. Perhaps the shrewd politician was covering his back in case he should afterwards be accused of interfering in the internal affairs of an independent state. After all, nobody could blame him for wanting to promote free trade! Yet those in the room were all embroiled in the plot, so why he should have distrusted any of them is a mystery.

> [The National Union's] plan was to declare itself at the public meeting on 6 January. By that time, it hoped to have 5,000 rifles, a sufficient number of Maxim guns, and 1,000,000 cartridges hidden away within the limits of Johannesburg and in the surrounding mines; it also counted, with reason, on having control of the forts which covered the city, and which were at that time guarded by a few Boer soldiers, who could have been driven out by assault. The committee relied confidently on the immediate services of at least 20,000 of the inhabitants of Johannesburg and on the help of many who would join them when they saw that it was safe to do so. With these men fully armed, with the town provisioned for a two-months' siege, they felt they would be in a position by Jan. 6 to send their ultimatum to the Government at Pretoria.
>
> On its being treated with contempt, the revolutionary party was to take possession of Johannesburg one fine night, declare itself the

---

[238] The Johannesburg *Star*, 26 December 1895.
[239] Meredith, Martin. *op. cit.*, 319.

Chapter 8

provisional Government of the country, and the same night pay a surprise visit to Pretoria, seize the State arsenal and the seat of Government, and issue an appeal to South Africa and the world proposing to submit its acts and grievances, and the future of the Transvaal, to a plebiscite of the entire white population of the country.

The moment uproar began, and life and property were in danger, a plausible excuse would be created for the interposition of any organised British force which was within two days of striking distance. The pretext for its action would be the jeopardy of British lives, property and interests, the interregnum of the country, the necessity for the preservation of order, and an emergency of a kind to justify acting first and asking leave afterwards.

...

They had [soon] spent £70,000 in provisions, which they expected would outlast a two-months' siege; they had arranged that the water supply of Johannesburg could not be cut off from the outside, and they had ordered rifles and Maxim guns and were smuggling them across the border.[240]

Over the next few months, with the assistance of the Secretary of State for the Colonies, Joseph Chamberlain, Rhodes succeeded in obtaining a strip of territory just outside the western border of the Transvaal at a place called Pitsani Potlugo, from which Jameson and his force would march on Johannesburg. It was handed over to the BSA Company in October on the pretext that a railway was to be built there. The Company's police were moved into the area almost immediately on the pretext that they were required to guard the railway material.

On 19 November, Jameson once again visited Johannesburg to ensure that all was in readiness. If he had been observant, he would have noticed that the town was experiencing an economic boom and should have realised that men who are making money are not likely to make desperate revolutionaries. In addition, he would have been told that far too few weapons had been smuggled into Johannesburg, with the result that the inhabitants were ill prepared to stage a coup.

He had for some time been pestering Lionel Phillips for a letter, signed by the leaders of the National Union, inviting him to come to their aid, but Charles Leonard had so far declined, seeing no need for it. Now, however,

---

[240] Garrett, Fydell Edmund and Edwards, E.J.. *The Story of an African Crisis*, 38-40.

perhaps sensing that he might need a pretext to come in, Jameson once more asked for the letter. Charles again refused, but after Jameson had assured him that he would use it only to justify his actions to the Directors of the BSA Company afterwards, Charles agreed to sign it, but only in his personal capacity and on condition that Phillips and some of the others co-signed it. The letter was left undated, but Jameson later inserted the date '29th December, 1895', which was, of course, incorrect, but suited his purposes.

The following day, Charles mentioned the letter to Fred Hamilton, the editor of the *Star* and a leading member of the National Union. He was aghast, responding, 'Charlie, are you mad?'[241] With his second thoughts about the wisdom of the letter having been confirmed, Charles hurried round to where Jameson was staying to ask for it back, but the Doctor replied, drily, 'Awfully sorry, old man, but it has gone down to Cape Town by the last train.'[242] This letter, which was soon to be used in a way that Charles and his fellow signatories could least have expected, includes the following key sentences:

> The position of matters in this State has become so critical that we are assured that at no distant period there will be conflict between the Government and the Uitlanders...
>
> Thousands of unarmed men, women and children of our race will be at the mercy of well-armed Boers, while property of enormous value will be in the greatest peril...
>
> Not to go into detail, we may say that the Government has called into existence all the elements necessary for armed conflict...
>
> It is under these circumstances that we feel constrained to call upon you to come to our aid should disturbance arise here...
>
>   [Signed] Charles Leonard
>   [Signed] Lionel Phillips
>   [Signed] Francis Rhodes
>   [Signed] John Hays Hammond

George Farrar later appended his signature.[243] Percy Fitzpatrick, however, refused to do so, describing the letter as 'full of foolish rhetoric'.[244]

---

[241] Harlow, Vincent (April 1957). 'Sir Frederic Hamilton's Narrative of the Events relating to the Jameson Raid', 293-294.
[242] Garrett, Edmund and Edwards, E.J., *op. cit.*, 48.
[243] Meredith, Martin. *op. cit.*, 325.
[244] Rhoodie, Denys (1967). *Conspirators in Conflict*, 39.

Chapter 8

That same day, Lionel Phillips opened the new Chamber of Mines building in Johannesburg and made a last desperate appeal to the Government to try to avert bloodshed. In his speech to the gathered dignitaries (including representatives of the Volksraad, no doubt) he said:

> All we want in this country is purity of administration and an equitable share and voice in its affairs. I hope that wiser counsels may prevail and that the Government of this country may be induced to see that the present policy will not do. Nothing is further from my heart than a desire to see an upheaval which would be disastrous from every point of view and which would probably end in the most horrible of endings – in bloodshed.
>
> But I should say this, that it is a mistake to imagine that this much maligned community, which consists of a majority of men born of free men, will consent indefinitely to remain subordinate to the minority in this country…[245]

Of course, from a modern perspective, those pealing words ring with dramatic irony since they could just as easily have been uttered by a young Nelson Mandela during the early years of apartheid. However, the thought of extending the franchise to black South Africans would not even have crossed Lionel Phillips' mind – and in this he is typical of almost every white South African of his era. It took white South Africans almost a century to extend the franchise to their black compatriots, and then only under duress. Men have ever been slow to grasp the lessons of history and apply them in different contexts.

It would be interesting to know what was going through Charles's mind as things were coming to a head. It was envisaged that he would serve as Provisional President until a plebiscite could determine the way forward, although this was later denied.[246] Edmund Garrett, the editor of the *Cape Times*, certainly had no doubt that Charles was entirely unsuited to this role, writing:

---

[245] *South Africa* magazine, 21 December 1895.
[246] The Reform Committee prepared a draft proclamation identifying Charles Leonard as President of an envisaged provisional government. This is reproduced in Eric Rosenthal's *Today's News Today*, 90-93. However, the Fairbridges Law Letter Supplement of 20 September 2012 states: 'It later leaked out that Lukas Meyer had been selected by the Reformists as the first President of the reconstituted Republic. [Hole, Hugh Marshall. *The Jameson Raid*, 74, Footnote 1.]'

Mr Leonard comes of a stock noted in South Africa for great abilities, great amenities, but not equal strength of character; he was, however, very sincerely liked and respected as a good fellow and an honest, clever, professional man. And as an Afrikander he was a suitable figure-head for the constitutional Uitlander movement. A less apt man to cast for the part of President by force of arms of an insurrectionary Republic, it would be hard to find.[247]

Since Charles never had the opportunity to prove himself in this role, there is no knowing whether Garrett would have been proven right or wrong. However, it needs to be stated – and stated categorically – that Charles would never have agreed to lead the revolutionary party had he been aware of Rhodes's true intentions.

In July 1895, before he had even conceived of his plot, Rhodes had granted an interview to Francis Dormer, former editor of the Johannesburg *Star*. Dormer had urged Rhodes to be patient with the Transvaal Government as there were many progressive members of the Volksraad who were opposed to Kruger and his reactionary supporters. Dormer had said that the reforms they all wanted would surely come if they would only wait a little longer, to which Rhodes had replied:

But I don't want your reforms, or rather your reformed Republic. The ideal system is that of a British colony… I also do not like the idea of British subjects becoming burghers, and that is why I prefer that burghers become British subjects.[248]

Years later, in an interview with the renowned journalist W.T. Stead, Rhodes frankly admitted his true motives:

It seemed to me quite certain that if I did not take a hand in the game the forces on the spot would soon make short work of President Kruger. Then I should be face to face with an American Republic – American in the sense of being intensely hostile to and jealous of Britain – an American Republic largely manned by Americans and *Sydney Bulletin* Australians who cared nothing for the [Union Jack]. They would have all

---

[247] Garrett, Fydell Edmund and Edwards, E.J. *op. cit.*, 48-49.
[248] Meredith, Martin. *op. cit.*, 313.

the Rand at their disposal. The drawing power of the Outlander Republic would have collected round it all the other Colonies. They would have federated with it as a centre, and we[249] should have lost South Africa. To avert this catastrophe, to rope in the Outlanders before it was too late, I did what I did.[250]

Charles Leonard and his confederates were completely oblivious of the fact that Rhodes was exploiting them for his own imperialistic designs. Some may credit Rhodes with being a shrewd politician and canny strategist, but others will regard him as a scheming, manipulative and deceitful opportunist, guided by expedience rather than principle. Charles Leonard, on the other hand, was a man of integrity. At a meeting of the National Union, he had addressed the crowd as follows: 'We are not traitors to the flag of this country, and are not conspiring against it, but seek to strengthen the republican institutions of this country.' He would not have supported (let alone led) the proposed uprising if he had been told that it was an attempt to replace the Vierkleur with the Union Jack and to make the Boer Republic a British Colony, as Rhodes secretly intended. The possibility would not even have crossed his mind, as subsequent events would confirm.

It would be interesting to know whether Charles confided in his wife during these tumultuous days. Catherine would, of course, have known about his frequent trips to Cape Town, but did she know that he was visiting, or even that he was in league with, the Prime Minister? Even though Charles may have wanted to protect her and their daughters from possible implication in the plot, it seems unlikely that he would have been able to keep them entirely in the dark. It would be a cold man indeed who could hide his turbulent emotions from his wife, and Charles was not such a man. We know that Charles had given Jameson the letter with a degree of reluctance, so perhaps it was Catherine who persuaded him to try and retrieve it the following day. We do know that later, when Charles was being sought by the authorities in Cape Town, he confided in Catherine and even asked her to send a telegram on his behalf, and that he continued to confide in her extensively thereafter, so perhaps it is fair to speculate that he did confide in her while in Johannesburg and that she was able to give him the emotional support and sensible advice that only a devoted wife can.

Charles would have neglected his legal practice as his involvement in the

---

[249] Meaning the British.
[250] Stead, W.T. *The Americanization of the World*, 56-57.

plot consumed more and more of his time and energies, so perhaps it is understandable that he chose to leave his firm in the capable hands of his partner, Willem van Hulsteyn, at about this time, and that he and Woodford began assisting their elder brother Jim.[251] From his and Catherine's later correspondence, it appears that Charles had no option but to take Woodie with him since his younger brother required close supervision: he had taken to drink and could not be trusted if left to his own devices. Besides his office in Simmonds Street, Jim also had an office in Pretoria, and it was while he was in the capital that President Kruger gave Jim the nickname *Windhond*, meaning 'Greyhound'.[252] Perhaps, reasons Owen Rogers, this was because a greyhound is given to trembling.[253] It could, alternatively, have been a polite variation of *Windgat*, meaning a person who boasts a lot, talks too much or has opinions on every subject!

It was also in Pretoria, in 1893, that Jim made the acquaintance of a 24-year-old Indian lawyer who had recently arrived in the country. That lawyer was none other than Mohandas Gandhi. In his autobiography, Gandhi calls Jim 'that famous barrister of South Africa' and recalls how Jim helped him:

> In a certain case in my charge I saw that, though justice was on the side of my client, the law seemed to be against him. In despair I approached Mr Leonard for help. He also felt that the facts of the case were very strong. He exclaimed, 'Gandhi, I have learnt one thing, and it is this, that if we take care of the facts of a case, the law will take care of itself. Let us dive deeper into the facts of this case.' With these words he asked me to study the case further and then see him again. On a re-examination of the facts I saw them in an entirely new light, and I also hit on an old South African case bearing on the point. I was delighted and went to see Mr Leonard and told him everything. 'Right,' he said, 'we shall win the case.'[254]

---

[251] In Longland's 1894 Johannesburg Alphabetical Street Directory, Charles Leonard's business address is given as Fraser's Building, Commissioner Street, where his firm had its offices, but by 1895, Longland gave his business address as the Mercantile Building in Simmonds Street, which is where Jim's firm was located. http://archiver.rootsweb.ancestry.com/th/read/SOUTH-AFRICA/2014-02/1392824828 Retrieved 17 February 2014.
[252] McMagh, Kathleen. *op. cit.*, 70.
[253] Rogers, Owen. *op. cit.*, 282.
[254] Gandhi, M.K. *An Autobiography*, 96.

In fact, so helpful did Gandhi find Jim's advice that it shaped not only his legal career, but his whole philosophy of life. He writes:

> That year's stay in Pretoria was a valuable experience in my life. Here it was that I …acquired a true knowledge of legal practice. Here I learnt the things that a junior barrister learns in a senior barrister's chamber, and here I also gained confidence that I should not after all fail as a lawyer. It was likewise here that I learnt the secret of success as a lawyer…I had not fully realised this paramount importance of facts. Facts mean truth, and once we adhere to truth, the law comes to our aid naturally.[255]

> As a result of this realisation of the paramount importance of facts…, Gandhiji was never known afterwards to brush aside or slur over a fact, however inconvenient or prejudicial it might be… The Mahatma was an ardent and inveterate votary of truth. Truth, like nonviolence, was the first article of his faith and the last article of his creed.[256]

Gandhi came to respect Jim immensely, particularly as he represented the Indian cause on many occasions over the next fifteen years.[257] He also sought Jim's legal opinion in December 1907 when the Transvaal colonial government sought to register 'Asiatics', with Jim advising that no colony possessed any power to act beyond its own borders, but the court upheld the right of the government and sentenced Gandhi and other so-called ringleaders of the defiance campaign to lengthy terms of imprisonment early in 1908.[258] However, when Gandhi tried to retain Jim to represent the Indians before the Supreme Court later that year, he was unavailable (for personal reasons which will be revealed later), forcing Gandhi to go with his second choice, whom he described as a 'very able barrister, though not of the same calibre as Mr Leonard'.[259]

---

[255] *Ibid.*, 100.
[256] Kher, S.B. (ed.) *Gandhi, M.K.: The Law and the Lawyers*, 3-4.
[257] For example, 'The Licencing Case in the Transvaal', July 5, 1904, *Collected Works of Mahatma Gandhi*, Vol. 4, 182 (1960 edition) and 'Legalised Robbery', *Collected Works of Mahatma Gandhi*, Vol. 5, 231 (1961 edition).
[258] *The Transvaal Leader*, 31 December 1907: 'Asiatic Crisis: The Legal Position – What Counsel Advise'; *The Transvaal Leader*, 11 January 1908: 'Ringleaders Sentenced: Heavy Terms of Imprisonment'.
[259] 'Johannesburg Letter', June 14, 1908, *Collected Works of Mahatma Gandhi*, Vol. 8, 297 (December 1962 edition).

It seems likely that Charles would also have met Gandhi while working with Jim in Pretoria. They would not have known at the time just how much they would soon have in common, for Gandhi was shortly to lead the Natal Indian Congress campaign against the Government of Natal for wanting to introduce legislation that would deny Indians the right to vote. But while the Indian lawyer was beginning to formulate his methodology of *Satyagraha* (devotion to truth), or nonviolent protest, the South African lawyer was leading a plot to overthrow the Transvaal Government (for denying Uitlanders the right to vote) by means of armed insurrection.

Chapter 8

The library at Groote Schuur, where Cecil Rhodes met the conspirators

The British South Africa Company, leaving no doubt as to where their allegiance lies. Rhodes is seated in the centre with Dr Jameson (in the dark jacket) at his right hand. Dr Frederick Rutherfoord Harris is standing on the far left.

CHAPTER 9 : CONSTERNATION (DECEMBER 1895)

There seems to be a fiasco at Johannesburg…

– Secretary of State for the Colonies, Joseph Chamberlain

The scene now shifts to the Leonards' Johannesburg home on the morning of Christmas Day, 1896. Dawn had no sooner dispelled the darkness than there were excited squeals as Daisy and Violet tore open their presents. One can picture their parents looking on happily, and possibly opening their gifts too.

Suddenly, there was an urgent knocking at the door. Catherine, still in her nightgown, ushered the girls from the room while Charles tightened his robe and went to see who was there. Standing on the front porch was George Farrar, a leading member of the National Union. He was clearly agitated as he forgot to wish Charles 'Merry Christmas', but started blurting out his news. Charles had to quieten him and lead him into the garden, out of earshot of his family. This is how Charles later recalled their conversation:

> I will tell you exactly what happened. Mr George Farrar came to me at seven o'clock in the morning, and he was very much disturbed. He said to me, 'I hear, if Jameson comes in, he is going to hoist the Union Jack.' He said, 'I have induced every man who has joined me, and who is helping me in this business, to go in on the basis that we want a reformed republic.' I remember his very words were: 'This is the Boer country; it would be absolutely morally wrong to do anything else, and I will not go a yard further in this business unless that basis is maintained.' I had never heard any question about a doubt as to the basis before, and I was astonished. I asked him where the news came from, but I could

not get to learn from him where it came from; it seemed to be in the air somehow (I knew later in the day where it came from) [an unguarded remark by Dr Rutherfoord Harris, Rhodes's secretary in the BSA Company]. I scouted the whole thing, and told him not to be distressed, and told him of…my conversation with Mr Rhodes, and said I did not believe there was the slightest reason for his distress. He went away satisfied.[260]

Although Farrar would not have known it, he had good reason to be concerned. The Secretary of State for the Colonies, Joseph Chamberlain, knew of the plot (he had arranged the transfer of the strip of territory to the BSA Company only weeks before) and privately enquired of the Company officials in London whether Jameson was going in under the British flag. They confirmed this, but Harris, who was in London at the time, sent a coded telegram to Rhodes to make sure. It read: 'We have stated positive that results of Dr Jameson's plans include British flag. Is this correct?' Rhodes responded, also in a coded telegram: 'As to English flag they must very much misunderstand me at home. I of course would not risk everything as I am doing excepting for British flag.'[261]

After attending Christmas mass with his family, Charles popped in at the Rand Club. He now takes up the story:

Later in the day, about half-past eleven, I went to the club, and there I met an American, Captain Mein, and he started the same thing. His words were: 'If this is a case of England gobbling this country up, I am not in it; otherwise I am up to my neck in it.' I tried to soothe him. I could not find out where it came from. However, I did not take any further notice of it.

I had some friends to lunch, and at about a quarter to three, or three o'clock, as I was sitting at table, I got a message to come to a meeting. When I went down to this meeting at Colonel Rhodes' house I met assembled there practically the whole of the men who knew anything about this business at the time. They had unanimously passed a resolution affirming that they would not consent to any such action on

---

[260] Leonard, Charles. *op. cit.*, 379.
[261] Report of the Select Committee of the House of Commons inquiry into the origin and circumstances of the incursion into the South African Republic of an armed force (hereafter, House of Commons Report), Appendix 14, No. 9.

the part of Jameson if he came in; that they deemed themselves bound to the men who were behind them, and who were following them, and that the thing must be set straight. They had passed that resolution when I got there. I only got up and said I could not agree to the alteration of the basis, supposing it had been made; and that it would be morally wrong in trying to steal the Boer country, and that we were morally in the right in going for reform. I sat down; and they then decided to send me to Cape Town to get this matter cleared up.[262]

This was disastrous! As Charles recalls, 'I saw in the room in a minute what was going to happen outside: dissention and disunion at the very eve of action.' Rhodes had decided only two days earlier that Jameson should set off on the evening of Saturday 28 December and that the uprising would commence in Johannesburg at midnight.

If Charles's thoughts were in turmoil, imagine what Catherine and the girls must have been going through. Their Christmas morning had been rudely interrupted by Farrar's intrusion. Then Charles had gone to his club straight after church. Then he had suddenly excused himself from the Christmas meal and left Catherine to entertain the guests while he rushed off to an emergency meeting. And now in her husband storms, saying that he must pack and be off to Cape Town on the next train! Catherine must have pleaded with him to tell her what on earth was afoot. As he had done with the agitated men, perhaps all he did was try to mollify her. For her own sake, it is unlikely that he would have let her in on what had transpired. He and Fred Hamilton boarded the train at Park Station that very evening and set off for the Cape.

Charles later wrote that he had left his private affairs 'absolutely uncared for, as the most casual inspection of my banking account and the state of my property in the Transvaal will show.'[263]

While he and Hamilton were on their way to the Cape, numerous encrypted telegrams were exchanged between Johannesburg, Cape Town and Mafeking. The first, sent by Colonel Rhodes to Jameson, stated: 'It is absolutely necessary to postpone flotation. Charles Leonard left last night for Cape Town.'[264] Messages to the same effect were sent from Sam Jameson (also a leader of the National Union) to his brother, explaining that any

---

[262] Leonard, Charles. *op. cit.*, 379-80.
[263] *Leonard Collection* M3002.
[264] Hole, Hugh Marshall. *op. cit.*, 132. The conspirators made use of code names and ciphers to refer to their enterprise.

movement had to be postponed 'until we have C.J. Rhodes' absolute pledge that authority of Imperial Government will not be insisted on.'[265] Harris, acting on instructions from Rhodes, also sent a cable to Dr Jameson, concluding: 'You must not move till you hear from us again. Too awful. Very sorry.'[266] In addition to these urgent telegrams, two messengers were also dispatched from Johannesburg to impress on Jameson the necessity for delay.[267]

The following day, as the train carrying Charles and Hamilton trundled across the Orange Free State, Jameson telegraphed Harris: 'I am afraid of Bechuanaland Police for cutting wire [telegraph wires]. They have now all gone forward, but will endeavour to put a stop to it. Therefore expect to receive telegram from you nine tomorrow morning authorizing movements. Surely Col. F.W. Rhodes advisable to come to terms at once. Give guarantee, or you can telegraph before Charles Leonard arrived.'[268]

Two hours later on the same day, Jameson sent another telegram to Harris: 'If I cannot, as I expect, communicate with Bechuanaland Police cutting, then we must carry into effect original plans. They have then two days for flotation. If they do not, we will make our own flotation with help of letter, which I will publish.'[269] On the same day, Jameson telegraphed his brother in Johannesburg: 'Guarantee already given, therefore let J.H. Hammond telegraph instantly all right.'[270]

To this Hammond sent a clear reply condemning Jameson's proposed action: 'Wire just received. Experts' reports decidedly adverse. I absolutely condemn further developments at present.'[271] At this point, Jameson ought to have accepted, albeit reluctantly, that the raid was off, or at least postponed. Eight days earlier he had received a message from the National Union leaders instructing him to wait until they gave him the go-ahead. Charles Leonard explains:

On the 19th December...we sent a message to [Jameson], not from

---

[265] *Ibid.*, 132.
[266] Cape House of Assembly Majority Report of the Select Committee on the Jameson Raid into the Territory of the South African Republic (hereafter, Cape Report), Appendix, ccxxxiv, No. 73.
[267] Hole, Hugh Marshall. *op. cit.*, 134.
[268] Cape Report, Appendix, ccxxxvii.
[269] *Ibid.*, Appendix, ccxxxvii.
[270] *Ibid.*, Appendix, ccxxxviii.
[271] *Ibid.*, Appendix, ccxxxviii, No. 76.

Johannesburg direct, but by Cape Town, with a message to be conveyed to him stating in emphatic terms (we heard he was getting impatient) that he was not to forget he was auxiliary to us; that we were in the major position; and that under no circumstances was he to move until we had notified we were ready; that our arms were not reaching us; that we were not ready, and that we were the only judges of the time to strike.'[272]

As dawn broke on Saturday 28 December, Charles Leonard and Fred Hamilton reached Cape Town. They quickly made their way to the Chartered Company's offices in town, where they met Rhodes. Charles recalls what transpired there: 'I told Mr Rhodes what had happened, and he gave me assurances that the basis had not been altered. Mr Hamilton was with me, and a telegram was sent from us…, saying that Mr Rhodes had given us satisfactory assurances [that the flag question might be left to a plebiscite of the inhabitants of the Transvaal].' The telegram ended with the reassuring words: 'In our opinion continue with preparations, but carefully and without any sort of hurry, as entirely fresh departure will be necessary. In view of changed conditions Jameson has been advised accordingly.'[273]

While their meeting with Rhodes was in progress, Jameson sent the following petulant telegram to Harris: 'There will be no flotation if left to themselves… All mean fear. You had better go as quickly as possible and report fully, or tell Hon. C.J. Rhodes to allow me.'[274]

Harris replied: 'It is all right if you will only wait. Captain Maurice Heany comes to you from Col. F.W. Rhodes by special train today.'[275] Then, two hours later, he sent another telegram on behalf of Rhodes: 'Heany, I think, arrives tonight; after seeing him, you and we must judge regarding flotation, but all our foreign friends are now dead against it and say public will not subscribe one penny towards even with you as a director – Ichabod.'[276] Two further telegrams were sent to Jameson from Cape Town soon afterwards, almost together, one of them concluding, 'we cannot have a fiasco'[277] and the other informing Jameson that Lionel Phillips anticipated a complete failure of any premature action.

After the meeting, Harris sent Colonel Rhodes a telegram: 'Charles

---

[272] Leonard, Charles. *op. cit.*, 386-7.
[273] Fitzpatrick, J. Percy. *The Transvaal from Within*, 104.
[274] Cape Report, Appendix, ccxxxvii.
[275] *Ibid.*, Appendix, ccxxxix, No. 81.
[276] *Ibid.*, Appendix, ccxi, No. 82. Ichabod was the code name for C.J. Rhodes.
[277] *Ibid.*, Appendix, ccxl, No. 79.

Leonard says flotation not popular, and England's bunting will be resisted by public. Is it true? Consult all our friends and let me know, as Dr Jameson is quite ready to move resolution and is only waiting for Captain Heany's arrival.'[278]

A few hours later, Jameson telegraphed Rhodes, via Harris: 'Received your telegram Ichabod re Capt. Maurice Heany. Have no further news. I require to know. Unless I hear definitely to the contrary, shall leave tomorrow evening and carry into effect my second telegram of yesterday to you, and it will be all right.'[279] By the time this telegram reached Cape Town, the telegraph office was shut, so it remained undelivered overnight.

After dinner that evening, Charles and Hamilton visited Rhodes at Groote Schuur, as he had requested. After their morning meeting, their minds were 'more at rest than for many weeks past', according to Hamilton. They found Rhodes in his study, 'looking rather like a Roman emperor in a rumpled shirt and an ill-fitting dinner jacket'.[280] Beit dozed quietly in a corner.

> Hamilton told Rhodes that the intervention of the Chartered Company, unless as a last resort, would antagonize the Dutch and many of the English. He suggested that Johannesburg should now arm and organize 'without the pretence of secrecy, which was merely hampering'. Once rifles were in the right hands, a monster petition could be sent to Pretoria. 'Boer feeling was so divided that it was improbable that Kruger dared shoot.' There was, he said, 'a great body of sympathetic Dutch' behind them. Jameson was 'a trump card as long as he was in the background – once over the border he became a liability'.[281]

Charles had the following recollection of the meeting:

> On the evening of the Saturday, by arrangement, we met Mr Rhodes again at his house, and there, I believe, almost at the instance of Mr Rhodes, it was finally agreed that there was to be no overt action then. I had pointed out to Mr Rhodes the absolute absurdity of Johannesburg going into an armed revolution at a time when they had not got a thousand rifles in the place. One of the bases of our action was that we

---

[278] *Ibid.*, Appendix, ccxl.
[279] *Ibid.*, Appendix, ccxlii.
[280] Harlow, Vincent. *op. cit.*, 298.
[281] Rogers, Owen. *op. cit.*, 131. He quotes from Harlow.

Chapter 9

should rush Pretoria Arsenal, take the Boer artillery away from them, and arm ourselves from their arsenal; we expected to get eight or ten thousand rifles from there, and we were to get 4,500 rifles from Cape Town and a million rounds of ammunition and three Maxims. At the time I left Johannesburg, we were absolutely unprepared for a revolution. It was not our fault that the arms had not reached us. [It was the fault of Rhodes's representative, John Hays Hammond, who was in charge of the arms smuggling.] I pointed out to Mr Rhodes that everything was misfitting. Success could only come if everything dovetailed. We had to strike in Johannesburg and to strike in Pretoria on the same night, and Jameson was to come in from the west. There was disunion in the town itself; we could not organize the men in the town. But the question of the arms was the main thing; we had not got the arms that had been promised; as a matter of fact, I believe out of the 2,500 rifles, eventually 1,500 reached Johannesburg on the Tuesday after Jameson had crossed the border. The final arrangement with Mr Rhodes was this. He said: 'I will keep Jameson six months or nine months, or longer, on the border as a moral support to you. We will get these arms in to put you on a more level basis with the Boers. Go on with your meeting on the 6th January, and await the development of events.'[282]

During this meeting, Hamilton took the liberty of asking Rhodes why he had involved himself in the conspiracy.

'You may well ask,' replied Rhodes, breaking into his characteristic high falsetto. He had, he acknowledged, all the money a man could want, he was prime minister of the Cape and a privy councillor. So why run the risk? The answer, he said, was his dream of a united South Africa. He longed to see the Transvaal take its place as 'a friendly member of a community of South African states'. … And – what was perhaps most relevant to the question Hamilton had asked – he wanted men to associate his name with the union, but knew – on account of his failing health – that time was not on his side.[283]

Hamilton described it as a 'memorable evening'; it went on until about two o'clock in the morning. He and Charles left the prime minister's home

---

[282] Leonard, Charles. *op. cit.*, 381.
[283] Rogers, Owen. *op. cit.*, 132.

greatly relieved, and no doubt slept soundly before spending a pleasant summer Sunday relaxing with friends in Cape Town. They were not to know that Rhodes would vacillate and not inform Jameson of their decision, at least until it was too late.

Having had a special train arranged for him, Captain Heany reached Jameson at about eight o'clock on Sunday morning (29 December). He was later asked to recount how he had been received:

> I read the message from my note-book absolutely accurately to Dr Jameson…he went outside and walked up and down for about twenty minutes, and then he came in and announced his determination [to move].'[284]

At five past nine, Jameson telegraphed Harris: 'Shall leave tonight for the Transvaal. My reason is the final arrangement with writers of letter was that, without further reference to them, in case I should hear at some future time that suspicions have been aroused as to their intentions among the Transvaal authorities, I was to start immediately to protect loss of life, as letter states. Reuter only just received. Even without my own information of meeting in Transvaal, compel immediate move to fulfil promise made. We are simply going to protect everybody, while they change the present Government and take vote from the whole country as to form of Government required by the whole.'[285]

Harris picked up both telegrams at about eleven o'clock and took them to Rhodes, who dithered for several hours before deciding to reply. He later claimed to have told Jameson: 'On no account must you move, I most strongly object to such a course.' But Jameson never received this telegram (if it was ever sent) because the lines had been cut by then.[286]

Addressing a parade of his men later that afternoon, before crossing the border that night, Jameson read out to them parts of the letter which he had obtained from the Reformers: '…thousands of unarmed men, women and children at the mercy of Boers…'

The men gave him a hearty cheer. 'We would have followed the Doctor to hell,' said one afterwards.[287]

---

[284] Fitzpatrick, J. Percy. *op. cit.*, 175 footnote.
[285] Cape Report, Appendix, ccxiii.
[286] Meredith, Martin. *op. cit.*, 332.
[287] *Ibid.*, 334.

Chapter 9

It needs to be emphasised that 'before Jameson left Pitsani...he had received two special messages from his friends, telling him that he was not wanted, and a telegram from a man who was to give him the signal to start, ordering him to stay where he was. In spite of this, on Sunday Dec. 29th, Dr Jameson started on his ride to Johannesburg against the wishes of Cecil Rhodes and against the entreaties of the National Union, and instead of bringing with him the 1,500 men and the 1,500 extra rifles agreed upon, he came with only 500 men and carried no extra arms.'[288]

Before setting off, Jameson sent some troopers to cut the telegraph wires. The southward wire to the Colony was cut south of Pitsani, and again south of Mafeking, but the really important wire, running to Pretoria by way of Zeerust and Rustenburg, was not cut because the trooper entrusted with the task was drunk and painstakingly cut and buried a farmer's fence![289]

Unlike the drunken trooper, Jameson certainly knew what he was doing, but it was a foolhardy gamble. Afterwards lauded as a hero by the British public, Jameson has since had less-flattering epithets conferred on him, being called an impetuous and headstrong bungler. Jan Smuts went so far as to claim that 'the Jameson Raid was the real declaration of war... And that is so in spite of the four years of truce that followed', and modern historians agree with him. Sir Winston Churchill even went so far as to say, 'I date the beginning of these violent times in our country from the Jameson Raid.'[290] With no military experience and no knowledge of the terrain, Jameson ought never to have been entrusted with leading the Raid in the first place. As *The Times* correspondent Francis Younghusband pithily commented, 'The great mistake made was trying to run races with cart-horses.'[291] But Jameson had full confidence in his own capabilities. A month before he set off, he had remarked to Fred Hamilton of the *Star*, 'I shall get through as easily as a knife cuts butter... I shall draw a zone of lead a mile each side of my column and no Boer will be able to live in it.'[292]

On that fateful Sunday afternoon, the Secretary of State for the Colonies, Joseph Chamberlain – who had all along unofficially backed the Raid – got wind of Jameson's intentions, even before his Colonial Office counterparts in Cape Town. Sensing that it might ruin his career, he sent a confidential

---

[288] Davis, Richard Harding. *Dr. Jameson's Raiders*, 20.
[289] Garrett, Fydell Edmund and Edwards, E.J. *op. cit.*, 90.
[290] Churchill, Sir W.S., cited in Longford, Elizabeth: *Jameson's Raid: The Prelude to the Boer War*, 5
[291] Meredith, Martin. *op. cit.*, 326.
[292] *Ibid.*, 326.

telegram to the British High Commissioner to South Africa, Sir Hercules Robinson:

> There seems to be a fiasco at Johannesburg owing probably to Rhodes having misjudged the balance of opinion there.
>
> It has been suggested, although I do not think it possible, that he and Jameson might endeavour to force matters at Johannesburg to a head by Jameson or someone else in the service of the Company advancing from the Bechuanaland Protectorate with police.
>
> In view of Articles nos. 22 and 8 of the Charter I could not remain passive were this to be done. Therefore, if necessary, but not otherwise, remind Rhodes of these Articles, and intimate to him that, in your opinion, he would not have my support, and point out the consequences which would follow to his schemes were I to repudiate his action.[293]

Robinson, to his later embarrassment, immediately replied:

> I learn on good authority movement at Johannesburg has collapsed; internal divisions have led to complete collapse of the movement, and leaders of the National Union will now probably make the best terms they can with President Kruger.[294]

On Monday morning, in response to this telegram, Chamberlain asked: 'Are you sure Jameson has not moved in consequence of collapse? See my telegram of yesterday.'[295]

The previous evening, William Schreiner, the Attorney-General in Rhodes' Cabinet and a leading member of the Afrikander Bond, had gone to see the Prime Minister for a few minutes. He had heard a rumour that Charles had been to see Rhodes but wanted to check for himself.

He came straight out with it, asking, 'Have you seen Charlie Leonard?'

'Yes,' said Rhodes indifferently, 'I have seen him.'

'For goodness' sake,' said Schreiner, 'keep yourself clear from that entanglement at Johannesburg. If there is any disturbance, they are sure to try and mix you up with it.'

---

[293] Cape Report, C7933, No. 2.
[294] *Ibid.*, C7933, No. 3.
[295] *Ibid.*, C7933, No. 4.

Chapter 9

Rhodes merely shrugged his shoulders and said, 'Oh, that is all right.'[296]

After Schreiner had left, Rhodes became increasingly anxious. At a very late hour, he summoned Robinson's private secretary, Sir Graham Bower, to Groote Schuur, where he found Rhodes in an agitated state of mind.

> Holding Jameson's last telegram in his hand, his face ashen, he told Bower that Jameson had invaded the Transvaal, though he had sent word to try to stop him. 'It may yet come all right,' he said. Sitting on the bed, he was clearly distressed, full of self-pity. 'I know I must go,' he said. 'I will resign tomorrow. But I know what this means. It means war. I am a ruined man. But there must be no recrimination. I will take the blame.'

Bower was staggered by the news, but, with the telegraph office closed, considered there was nothing more to be done immediately and left at midnight. Early the following morning, he sent his gardener to deliver a note to Robinson:

> My dear Sir Hercules,
> I hope you will come to town early. There is, I fear, bad news from Jameson. He seems to have disobeyed Rhodes, and to have taken the bit between his teeth.

When Robinson arrived at his office at about ten o'clock, Bower told him of his conversation with Rhodes. 'But, good God,' exclaimed Robinson, 'he has not gone in without a rising? If so, you never told me.'[297]

Like Chamberlain, Robinson's first instinct was to cover his tracks. Indeed, from that moment, he consistently maintained that he had had no foreknowledge of the plot, even repeating this to those who knew that he had. By doing so, he placed his subordinate Bower in an extremely compromised position.

In the meanwhile, Charles Leonard was blissfully unaware of the drama unfolding behind the scenes. He and Hamilton were staying at the Civil Service Club in Queen Victoria Street and were all set to return to Johannesburg when, at about midday on Monday, they received a message from Rhodes that he wanted to see them. Rhodes told them that Jameson had

---

[296] Garrett, Fydell Edmund and Edwards, E.J. *op. cit.*, 155.
[297] Meredith, Martin. *op. cit.*, 336.

crossed the border. One can only imagine the shock with which they received this news. When asked about it later, Charles simply said: 'It staggered me, of course. I knew he had wrecked everything at once.'[298]

His initial impulse was to return to Johannesburg as soon as possible. He told Rhodes that he would be heading back that night (he had the train ticket in his pocket), but Rhodes implored both Charles and Hamilton to stay. He pointed out that they could not possibly reach Johannesburg until Thursday morning; that they would be of the greatest possible assistance at Cape Town at that stage; and he implored them, 'almost on his bended knees, to stop there and help him'.[299] Rhodes said, 'We are 24 hours in front of public opinion. And you must go round to the papers and get them to prepare the mind of the public.'[300] Charles and Hamilton discussed their predicament and reluctantly agreed with Rhodes that it made sense for them to stay, at least for a few days.

When asked at a later date to elaborate on how he had helped Rhodes while in Cape Town, Charles said, 'The Dutch newspapers and the other newspapers had to be influenced.' He and Hamilton visited Edmund Powell, editor of the *Cape Argus*, and François Malan, editor of *Ons Land*, and impressed upon them the need to report on the raid with moderation, since sensational accounts might inflame public opinion and jeopardise any remaining prospects of a peaceful resolution to the crisis. These meetings, to a large extent, had the desired result.[301]

Despite Charles's constructive engagements in Cape Town, of which more will be revealed in the next chapter, it was not a good time for the National Union Chairman to be a thousand miles away from his comrades (and his family) in Johannesburg.

He was later cross-examined in relation to his dealings with Rhodes at this time:

> 8135. Do you happen to have any written documents from Mr Rhodes, or any letter from him, touching upon any of these points? – No public communication.
>
> 8136. I do not wish you to go into any private letter. – The only letter that I have from Mr Rhodes is a private letter.

---

[298] Leonard, Charles. *op. cit.*, 385.
[299] *Ibid.*, 382.
[300] Garrett, Fydell Edmund; Shaw, Gerald (ed.). *The Garrett Papers*, 23.
[301] *Ibid.*, 23.

8137. Would you rather not state what it is? – It is simply a letter in which he says: 'I asked you with Hamilton to stay and help me. You could do no good in a train; you could do great good here. I know you fought for going, but it was nonsense, and too late. Afterwards blame me, but I was thoroughly right.' That is the only letter I have from him.

8138. That letter, I take it, was written after the Monday? – Yes, this letter, I think, was written on the Wednesday night when I was rather bitter about it, everything having gone wrong, and I wished to goodness I was in Johannesburg.

8139. So that in addition to verbal requests, you had written requests from Mr Rhodes that you would not return to Johannesburg? – Yes.[302]

One might have expected Rhodes to have done all in his power to stop Jameson, but he did nothing. The following anecdote sheds light on what he was thinking:

> That evening [Monday], Mr Schreiner hurried out to Groote Schuur with the amazing telegrams from Bechuanaland. Mr Rhodes was still on the mountain side. Mr Schreiner left an urgent message asking to see him, and after supper, Mr Rhodes' confidential man went across and asked him to come over at once. Schreiner hurried through the wood in the dark – he lived on the edge of Rhodes' grounds – Rhodes' man lighting the way with a lantern. For three hours the two colleagues were closeted in the library. It was a significant, and in a sense a memorable interview, because it typified the great struggle between Afrikander sympathies with the Transvaal and Afrikander devotion to Rhodes.
>
> Nothing could be more dramatic, nor more expressively accurate, than Schreiner's own account of their talk:
>
>> I went into his study with the telegrams in my hand. The moment I saw him I saw a man I had never seen before. His appearance was utterly dejected and different.
>>
>> Before I could say a word, he said: 'Yes, yes, it is true. Old Jameson has upset my apple-cart. It is all true.'
>>
>> I said I had some telegrams.
>>
>> He said, 'Never mind. It is all true. Old Jameson has upset my

---

[302] Leonard, Charles. *op. cit.*, 410.

apple-cart,' reiterating in the way he does when he is moved.

I was staggered. I said, 'What do you mean, what can you mean?'

He said, 'Yes, it is quite true, he has ridden in. Go and write out your resignation. Go, I know you will.'

And so I said, 'It is not a question of my going to write out my resignation'; but I elicited from him a good many facts in relation to this matter, and I told him that it was his duty to convene a Cabinet meeting at once.

During this entire interview Mr Rhodes was really broken down. He was broken down. He was not the man who could he playing that part. Whatever the reason may have been, when I spoke to him he was broken down. If it were unfair I would not say it, but it is true. He could not have acted that part; if he did he is the best actor I have ever seen. He was absolutely broken down in spirit; ruined.

I said, 'Why do you not stop him? Although he has ridden in, you can still stop him.'

He said, 'Poor old Jameson. Twenty years we have been friends, and now he goes in and ruins me. I cannot hinder him. I cannot go and destroy him.'

That was how he put it. That was the attitude he assumed to me. Much took place between us. I do not want to go into that. I left in very great distress. It was impossible to do anything on that night, and I left with the understanding that the first thing in the morning he would convene the Cabinet.

...

You would ask me for my theory why Mr Rhodes did not use more energy and vigour in stopping Dr Jameson. I have given you all that I could gather from him when he, in a heart-broken way, said, 'Poor old Jameson, poor old Jameson, we have been friends twenty years, he is ruining me now, but I cannot go and pull him back.'[303]

---

[303] Garrett, Fydell Edmund and Edwards, E.J. *op. cit.*, 155-7.

Chapter 9

Dr Jameson and his column come under fire from the Boers near Doornkop

Dr Jameson and his officers in captivity after the Battle of Doornkop

CHAPTER 10 : COOL HEADS AND HOTHEADS (DECEMBER 1895 – JANUARY 1896)

You must give the tortoise time to put out its head before you can catch hold of it.

— President Kruger, addressing a meeting at Bronkhorstspruit[304]

The executive council of the Volksraad was meeting in Pretoria on Monday, 30 December when General Joubert, the commandant-general, interrupted proceedings to hand over a telegram which had just arrived from Zeerust. It was from an official at the nearby settlement of Malmani, close to the Bechuanaland border, who informed the Government that a force of 800 troops, armed with Maxim guns, had passed through at five o'clock that morning, heading in the direction of Johannesburg. They were bearing the flag of the British South Africa Company.[305] Joubert was told to mobilise a commando to intercept the column, and hundreds of armed burghers were soon in the saddle.

Shortly after this, Jameson received a protest from the Commandant of the Marico district against his invasion of the State, to which he sent the following reply:

December 30th, 1895.

Sir,

I am in receipt of your protest of the above date, and have to inform

---

[304] Cape Report C 7933, No. 6.
[305] W P Schreiner's evidence. House of Commons Report, No. 4117.

you that I intend proceeding with my original plans, which have no hostile intention against the people of the Transvaal; but we are here in reply to an invitation from the principal residents of the Rand to assist them in their demand for justice and the ordinary rights of every citizen of a civilised State.

Yours faithfully,
L.S. Jameson[306]

While the Boers were preparing to repel the invasion, the Colonial authorities were desperately trying to convince Jameson to turn back. At about one o'clock that afternoon, Frank Newton, resident commissioner at Mafeking, received the following telegram from the High Commissioner, Sir Hercules Robinson:

It is rumoured that Dr Jameson has entered the Transvaal with an armed force. Is this so? If so, send special messenger on fast horse directing him to return immediately. A copy of this telegram should be sent to the officers with him, and they should be told that this violation of the territory of a friendly State is repudiated by Her Majesty's Government, and that they are rendering themselves liable to severe penalties.[307]

Newton at once addressed letters to Jameson and each of his chief officers with him, stating: 'I have the honour to enclose a copy of a telegram which I have received from His Excellency the High Commissioner, and I have accordingly to request that you will immediately comply with His Excellency's instructions.'[308]

Early the following morning (Tuesday), two despatch riders, who had been sent by Sir Jacobus de Wet, resident British agent in Pretoria, reached Jameson's column and delivered their letters, informing Jameson that they were to take back a reply from him as soon as possible. They had brought a more peremptory message from Robinson:

Her Majesty's Government entirely disapprove your conduct in invading Transvaal with armed force; your action has been repudiated. You are ordered to retire at once from country, and will he held personally

---

[306] *Cape Report*, Appendix, lxix, No. 88.
[307] *Ibid.*, C 8063, Part II, No. 13.
[308] *Ibid.*, C 8063, Part II, No. 13.

Chapter 10

responsible for the consequences of your unauthorized and most improper proceeding.[309]

Jameson told them, 'All right; I'll give you a reply' and within a few minutes handed them the following letter:

> Dear Sir,
> I am in receipt of the message you sent from His Excellency the High Commissioner, and beg to reply, for His Excellency's information, that I should, of course, desire to obey his instructions, but, as I have a very large force of both men and horses to feed, and having finished all my supplies in the rear, must perforce proceed to Krugersdorp or Johannesburg in the morning for this purpose. At the same time I must acknowledge I am anxious to fulfil my promise on the petition of the principal residents of the Rand, to come to the aid of my fellow-men in their extremity. I have molested no one, and have explained to all Dutchmen met that the above is my sole object, and that I shall desire to return at once to the Protectorate.
> I am, etc.
> (signed) L.S. Jameson[310]

A mounted trooper caught up with Jameson's column at about eleven o'clock that morning, having ridden through the night, and delivered the letters from Newton at Mafeking. At first, the officers refused to take them, but eventually Sir John Willoughby sent a message by him stating that the despatches would be attended to. Jameson did not respond.

He had clearly made up his mind to proceed and nothing except force could deter him. He therefore left the Colonial authorities no alternative but to publicly repudiate him and distance themselves from his incursion. On the instructions of Chamberlain, Robinson issued a proclamation, part of which reads as follows:

> Whereas it has come to my knowledge that certain British subjects, said to be under the leadership of Dr Jameson, have violated the territory of the South African Republic, and have cut telegraph-wires, and done various other illegal acts; and whereas the South African Republic is a

---

[309] *Ibid.*, C 7933, No. 8.
[310] *Ibid.*, C 7933, No. 29.

friendly state, in amity with Her Majesty's Government; and whereas it is my desire to respect the independence of the said State;

Now, therefore, I hereby command the said Dr Jameson and all persons accompanying him to immediately retire from the territory of the South African Republic, on pain of the penalties attached to their illegal proceedings; and I do further hereby call upon all British subjects in the South African Republic to abstain from giving the said Dr Jameson any countenance or assistance in his armed violation of the territory of a friendly State.[311]

Once he learned of this proclamation, Rhodes rushed to Robinson and asked him to retract it, saying that it made an outlaw of Jameson, but Robinson refused to do so.[312] Rhodes was even more upset when he was informed of the following telegram from Chamberlain to Robinson, sent the next day (Wednesday):

You should represent to Mr Rhodes the true character of Dr Jameson's action in breaking into a foreign state, which is in friendly treaty relations with Her Majesty, in time of peace. It is an act of war, or rather of filibustering. If the Government of the South African Republic had been overthrown, or had there been anarchy at Johannesburg, there might have been some shadow of excuse for this unprecedented act. If it can be proved that the British South Africa Company set Dr Jameson in motion, or were privy to his marauding action, Her Majesty's government would have to at once face a demand that the charter should be revoked and the corporation dissolved.[313]

In a fit of pique, Rhodes sent a slightly modified version of the 'women and children' letter to Flora Shaw, correspondent for *The Times* in London, who had acted as confidential go-between for him and Chamberlain, asking her to publish it in order to portray Jameson in a more favourable light. He even presumed to rebuke Chamberlain. He still hoped that Jameson would reach Johannesburg, even at this late hour:

Inform Chamberlain that I shall get through all right if he supports me,

---

[311] *Ibid.*, C 8063, Part II, No. 13.
[312] Garrett, Fydell Edmund and Edwards, E.J. *op. cit.*, 191-2.
[313] Davis, Richard Harding. *op. cit.*, 31.

but he must not send cable like he sent the High Commissioner in South Africa. Today the crux is, I will win and South Africa will belong to England.[314]

We now need to turn our attention to Johannesburg, where the Reformists had been relieved to receive Charles Leonard's telegram from Cape Town informing them that the raid was to be postponed. But then, between four and half-past four on Monday 29 December, Arthur Lawley, a member of the 'inner ring', rushed into the room at the Goldfields Building where some of the leaders were meeting, saying, 'It is all up, boys. He has started in spite of everything. Read this!' He threw a telegram from Mafeking on to the table. It read: 'The contractor has started on the earthworks with seven hundred boys. Hopes to reach terminus on Wednesday.'[315] They soon learned that the Boers were aware of Jameson's intentions and were mustering a commando to mount a defence.

> The effect of this news on the Johannesburg leaders and the few others who were cognisant of the Jameson plan was one, to use no stronger term, of astonishment. They saw their plans blown to the winds – themselves discredited and apparently distrusted by their ally – the worst possible hour for action forced upon them; and to what end, for what reason? Whether Dr Jameson reached Johannesburg or not, would not this premature movement prejudice the whole cause?[316]

Fortunately, the Reformists kept their heads and enlisted the services of a large body of men to take control of the town. Initially numbering sixty-four, they called themselves the Reform Committee and in Charles Leonard's absence, Lionel Phillips was elected Chairman. Jim Leonard was one of their number. Unprepared as they were, they determined first and foremost to demonstrate their allegiance to the Transvaal Republic by hoisting the *Vierkleur* above their headquarters in the Goldfields Building.

> The Committee then...formally repudiated Jameson. Through their unofficial organ, the *Star*, they disavowed 'any knowledge of, or sympathy with, the entry into the Republic of an armed force from the

---

[314] House of Commons Report, Appendix 16, No. 1556.
[315] Fitzpatrick, James Percy, *op. cit.*, 109.
[316] Hillier, Alfred P. *op. cit.*, 59.

Bechuanaland side', and denied having been 'in any way privy to the lamentable step.'[317]

This was not entirely true, at least for those members of the Reform Committee who had led the National Union. They then turned their attention to defending Johannesburg against a possible surprise attack. The guns which had been smuggled into Johannesburg were unpacked and distributed, defensive earthworks were thrown up, and volunteers drilled on the Wanderers' Ground.[318]

The following official notice was posted on the doors of the Goldfields Building shortly after noon on Tuesday 31 December:

> Notice is hereby given that this Reform Committee adheres to the National Union Manifesto and reiterates its desire to maintain the independence of the Republic. The fact that rumours are in course of circulation to the effect that a force has crossed the Bechuanaland border, renders it necessary to take active steps for the defence of Johannesburg and preservation of order. The Committee earnestly desire that the inhabitants should refrain from taking any action which can be construed as an overt act of hostility against the Government.
> By order of the Committee,
> J. Percy Fitzpatrick,
> Secretary.[319]

The editor of the *Cape Times*, Edmund Garrett, alerted by Charles Leonard and Hamilton, sent his Assistant Editor, E. J. Edwards, to Johannesburg to report on the crisis. He wrote:

> With the growing tension of feeling in the streets as the day wore on, a crowd of men, estimated at ten thousand, assembled in the neighbourhood of the Goldfields, and anxiously awaited some sign from the Committee. A new fear was in the air. The distribution of arms had been suspended, and rumour got abroad that the Reform Committee was not so well prepared after all. The thought was maddening, and there were

---

[317] Garrett, Fydell Edmund and Edwards, E.J. *op. cit.*, 161.
[318] Gutsche, Thelma. *op. cit.*, Ch. 5, 21.
[319] Garrett, Fydell Edmund and Edwards, E.J. *op. cit.*, 163.

loud and persistent calls for some one or other of the leaders to come out and explain.

'Make J.W. Leonard speak,' Jameson had remarked in one of the cipher telegrams; and the eloquent Q.C., brother of the National Union Chairman, now stepped into the breach. Addressing the multitude from horseback, Mr Leonard declared that every precaution that prudence combined with capital military knowledge and political sagacity could take had been taken to ensure the safety of the town. There were, he declared, sufficient organized, armed, and equipped men ready to cope with any force the Boers might send against them. There would be a satisfactory settlement of the difficulty before long. There was a Reform Committee, which was practically a Provisional Government, consisting of the best and strongest men that could be found in the place, who were taking charge of affairs. The constitution of such a committee was inevitable. It was, however, only provisional, and there was no intention to go back on the feelings of the people of this place or to impose upon them anything of which they might not ultimately approve. Needless to say, these sentiments were cheered to the echo.[320]

An unsavoury corollary is recorded by Sir Graham Bower: 'In speaking of this gentleman's speech, I said to Sir Hercules: "If it came to fighting that fellow would be found under the bed." Sir Hercules replied: "Yes, and there would be a prostitute in the bed."'[321] Bower had little confidence in the Reformists as revolutionaries, writing, 'Orators and phrasemakers are not fighters, and I know most of the orators.'[322] Sir Hercules had no doubt heard the scandalous gossip doing the rounds in Cape social circles that Jim Leonard had deserted his wife and moved in with an actress almost half his age.[323] A member of Lockwood's Company, Emma Blanche Beresford Whyte[324] was no temporary dalliance, however, and we shall have cause to return to her later.

The Reform Committee may have succeeded in averting a riot outside the Goldfields Building, but they were unable to prevent scenes of

---

[320] Ibid, 167-8.
[321] Schreuder, Deryck and Butler, Jeffrey (eds). *Sir Graham Bower's Secret History of the Jameson Raid and the South African Crisis, 1895-1902*, 61.
[322] Garrett, Fydell Edmund and Edwards, E.J. *op. cit.*, 61.
[323] *Ibid.*, 61.
[324] Her full names were Blanche Marie Augusta Diendonne Beresford Whyte. www.1820settlers.com/genealogy/getperson.php?personID=l152037&tree=master

pandemonium at the railway stations.

The effect of this tumult and excitement was shown in the growing activity of the Cape Government Railway Offices on Market Square. From early morning the offices were besieged by panic-stricken people, anxious to escape from what they regarded as a doomed city. They cared not whither they went, provided only they crossed the Vaal in safety. Those who had friends in the Cape Colony booked through; others betook themselves to Kroonstad, Bloemfontein, and other places in the Free State.

By three o'clock in the afternoon, eight hours before the time of departure, people boarded the train as it stood in the station yard at Braamfontein, preferring the discomforts of a stuffy compartment on a sweltering summer's day, to the risk of losing their seats when the rush set in at night. Anticipation was realized. When the train drew up at ten p.m. at the Braamfontein Station, where the trains are 'made up', a mile or so from town, a crowd of more than a thousand persons seized it, and scrambled into such compartments as had not been already taken.

But the most maddening scene of all was that which took place at the town (or Park) station. Four or five thousand people greeted its approach, and then there was such a fight for seats as never before was witnessed. People who had booked first-class, and had anticipated a clean and comfortable bed for the night, found themselves glad enough to sit in second-class compartments four and five in a row. Wealthy gold-bugs disguised themselves and hid under the seats and behind the petticoats of their womenkind from the jeers of the men who stood on the platform. The women and children were cheered and wished God-speed on their journey. At midnight the train of carriages, twenty-two in number, steamed away towards the border – and safety. And thus the Great Exodus commenced.[325]

Catherine Leonard and her daughters were amongst those who managed to secure seats on the packed train to Cape Town. It must have been extremely uncomfortable, but they could count themselves fortunate that they were not aboard the train bound for Port Natal: it derailed near Glencoe, injuring thirty-one and killing twenty-one of the fugitives, men, women, and children. 'Distraught relatives were naturally inclined to hold the Reform

---

[325] *Ibid.*, 131-2.

leaders vaguely responsible, though the accident was more directly traceable to the deficiencies of the Netherlands' cars—and therefore to a characteristic feature of the Unreformed Transvaal.'[326]

Catherine and the girls arrived in Cape Town on the morning of Friday 3 January and went to stay with relatives or friends named Dot and Eric in Sea Point. They were able to spend only a few hours with Charles before he headed back to the Transvaal, but before we deal with that, let us return to a promising development in Johannesburg.

It was late on Tuesday afternoon that Eugène Marais and Abraham Malan (both members of the Volksraad) arrived at the Goldfields Building. They had come to invite a deputation of the Reform Committee to attend a meeting in Pretoria the following morning at which they could present their demands. The leaders of the Committee assured them that those who had taken up arms in Johannesburg had done so as a last resort and that all they wanted was fair treatment. They said that they stood by the Manifesto that Charles Leonard had published, but that they would accept as sufficient for the time being any reasonable proportion of the redress demanded. The Volksraad members then informed the leaders of the Committee that they would be proceeding with the commando to intercept Jameson, should he fail to obey the High Commissioner's order, and added that in the Government ranks would be found many of those who had supported the National Union.

Before setting off for Pretoria early the next morning, the leaders of the Committee sent the following telegram to the High Commissioner in Cape Town:

> Rumour prevalent that Doctor Jameson has crossed the border; we know nothing of this. The result of this report is massing of Boers, who are threatening Johannesburg. We presume, if Dr Jameson has left, that it is on behalf of Imperial Government to avert bloodshed here. We invoke your immediate assistance to prevent civil war, and urge you to come up at once and establish peace.[327]

No reply was received to this, so a telegram was sent to Charles Leonard, asking him to try to persuade Robinson to intervene as best he could.

The deputation met the Government Commission in Pretoria at noon. They had been given an unambiguous mandate:

---

[326] *Ibid.*, 138.
[327] *Ibid.*, 180.

'[They were] to negotiate with the Government for a peaceful settlement on the basis of the Manifesto, accepting what they might consider to be a reasonable instalment of the reforms demanded. They were to deal with the Government in a conciliatory spirit and to avoid all provocation to civil strife, but at the same time to insist upon the recognition of rights and the redress of the grievances, to avow the association with Dr Jameson's forces so far as it had existed, and to include him in any settlement that might be made. ... However awkward a predicament he had placed the Johannesburg people in, they accepted a certain moral responsibility for him and his actions and decided to make his safety the first consideration.'[328]

The delegation was not to know that the Government Commission would not negotiate in good faith. When Executive Member Jan Kock remarked that the deputation spoke as though they represented Johannesburg, whereas for all the Government knew the Reform Committee might be but a few individuals of no influence, they denied this. He then asked them to provide him with names, which they did from memory and offered to telegraph for a full list. The reply came in time to be handed to the Government. This telegram was later used as evidence against those listed. The Chief Justice then informed the deputation that the Commission was not empowered to arrange terms but was merely authorized to hear what the deputation had to say, to ascertain their grievances and the proposed remedies, and to report back to the Executive Committee. After further discussion, the meeting was adjourned at noon until five o'clock to allow the Commission time to consult with the Government's Executive Committee.[329]

During the adjournment, a telegram arrived from Charles Leonard and Fred Hamilton, informing the Reform Committee that the former had seen the High Commissioner, who had declined to move unless invited by the other side; that they were using every effort to induce him to move, but no reliance could be placed upon him. They further advised that in their strong opinion a reasonable compromise should be effected, and that it was most vital to avoid offence.[330] At this point, finding that there was nothing more to be done and feeling that his proper place was with his comrades, Fred Hamilton returned to Johannesburg.

---

[328] Fitzpatrick, James Percy. *op. cit.*, 151-2.
[329] *Ibid.*, 157.
[330] *Ibid.*, 154.

Chapter 10

Charles did not accompany Hamilton as he wanted to try one last throw of the dice. He asked his good friend, David de Villiers Graaff, then an M.P. in the Cape Parliament and a prominent member of the Afrikander Bond, to help him persuade the Cape leader of the Bond, 'Onze Jan' Hendrik Hofmeyr, to go to Pretoria and use his influence to persuade Kruger to address the grievances of the Uitlanders so that there would no longer be any need for an uprising. Charles later recalled that '[Hofmeyr] promised me virtually to do so, and then withdrew from that promise.'[331] However, Hofmeyr did succeed in persuading President Kruger to invite Sir Hercules Robinson to Pretoria to mediate in the crisis, and the High Commissioner, prompted by Chamberlain, accepted the invitation. Charles must have been elated to discover that his efforts in this regard had borne fruit.

When the meeting in Pretoria reconvened, the Chief Justice informed the deputation of the Executive Committee's response, which was in the form of a written resolution, the substance of which was:

> The High Commissioner has offered his services with a view to a peaceful settlement. The Government of the South African Republic have accepted the offer. Pending his arrival, no hostile step will be taken against Johannesburg provided Johannesburg takes no hostile step against the Government. In terms of a certain proclamation recently issued by the State President the grievances will be earnestly considered.[332]

On receipt of this resolution, the deputation enquired whether the Government's offer was intended to include Dr Jameson. The Chief Justice replied that the Government declined to include him in their negotiations as he was a foreign invader and would have to be turned out of the country.

The deputation returned to Johannesburg fully convinced that the Uitlanders' grievances would be redressed, that a peaceful settlement would be arrived at through the mediation of the High Commissioner, and that Dr Jameson would inevitably obey the latter's proclamation and leave the country peacefully on ascertaining that there was no necessity for his intervention on behalf of the Uitlanders. Sadly, they were to be proven wrong on all three counts.

---

[331] Leonard, Charles. *op. cit.*, 389.
[332] Fitzpatrick, James Percy. *op. cit.*, 158.

Sir Hercules Robinson

Sir Graham Bower

David P. de V. Graaff

Bordeaux, the Graaffs' home in Sea Point, where Charles Leonard recuperated

Chapter 10

Prisoners playing marbles inside the Pretoria gaol

The crowd outside the Goldfields Building

The Reform Committee, Johannesburg, 1896.
Men mentioned in this biography are circled (l. to r.): William Henry Somerset Bell; Captain Mein; Henri Bettelheim; Sam Jameson; and Fred Hamilton.

CHAPTER 11 : UP, DOWN AND AWAY
(JANUARY 1896)

If you can keep your head while all about you
Are losing theirs and blaming it on you…

– Rudyard Kipling, *If*

While Sir Hercules Robinson was seated in his carriage, waiting for the special train to steam out of Salt River station on its way to Johannesburg at nine o'clock in the evening of Thursday, 2 January 1896, Charles Leonard, accompanied by David de Villiers Graaff, boarded the train to petition him. The High Commissioner was not relishing the prospect of a thousand-mile journey and then having to mediate in a mounting crisis, particularly as he was unwell: he was suffering from heart trouble and his legs were swollen with dropsy. It is unlikely that he took kindly to being disturbed. Charles and Graaff had hurried to the station in order to try to persuade Robinson to take Hofmeyr with him, declaring that the Bond leader would yield to pressure. Charles still felt that the highly respected Hofmeyr would have more influence with Kruger than would the rather pompous and feeble Englishman.

Robinson did send a telegram to Hofmeyr, *en route*, inviting him to come up by the next night's mail train, remarking that he had never doubted the loyalty and peaceful co-operation of the Afrikander population, and adding that his own desire from the first to have Hofmeyr's help was strengthened by finding that he enjoyed the confidence of the Chairman of the National Union. Hofmeyr responded: 'Thanks kind wire. Owing to physical complaint

I shall go only when supreme necessity arises, which is not yet.'[333]

Earlier that day, Jameson and his column had found themselves surrounded by a superior force of 500 Boers near a hill called Doornkop, just outside Krugersdorp and about eighteen miles from Johannesburg. They had put up a brief and courageous fight, but with casualties mounting, they had had no option but to surrender. Jameson and about 400 of his raiders had been taken to the Pretoria gaol, and the wounded to a hospital in Krugersdorp. Amongst those taken to Pretoria was Frederick Liesching, who had married Charles Leonard's sister Gertie. Liesching had joined Dr Jameson somewhere along the route. He had driven a buggy drawn by two horses and Jameson had actually driven with him for some miles. He was fortunately able to send a message to his brother William, who was then practising as an attorney in Middelberg, only a few hours away. William immediately went to see General Joubert, the Commandant General of the Boer forces and a close personal friend and pleaded his brother's case. Learning that Frederick was a non-combatant, General Joubert generously agreed to release him. Fred never spoke of this episode in later life.[334]

The Poet Laureatte, Alfred Austin, wrote a poem commemorating the Raid:

> Right sweet is the marksman's rattle
> And sweeter is the cannon's roar,
> But 'tis bitterly bad to battle,
> Beleaguered, and one to four,
> I can tell you it wasn't a trifle
> To swarm over Krugersdorp glen,
> As they plied us with round and rifle,
> And ploughed us, again – and again.
> …
>
> Not a soul had supped or slumbered
> Since the Borderland stream was cleft;
> But we fought, ever more outnumbered,
> Till we had not a cartridge left.
> We're not very soft or tender,

---

[333] Garrett, Fydell Edmund and Edwards, E.J. *op. cit.*, 200.
[334] McMagh, Kathleen. *op. cit.*, 71-3.

Chapter 11

> Or given to weep for woe,
> But it breaks one to have to render
> One's sword to the strongest foe.[335]

When news of Jameson's surrender reached Johannesburg, angry crowds gathered outside the Goldfields Building, hurling abuse at the Reform Committee. Percy Fitzpatrick wrote a letter to his wife, describing his feelings that evening:

> Tonight we are hooted and howled at by the crowd because they say we have deserted Jameson. We have done nothing of the sort but he has failed to reach [us] and, as far as we can learn, he has had to surrender to the Boers. It is the blackest and most cruel game of treachery ever played. Chamberlain sold Jameson and the High Commissioner or Rhodes sold us both.[336]

> Throughout the troubles which followed the invasion it was not the personal suffering or loss which fell to the lot of the Johannesburg people that touched them so nearly as the taunts which were unjustly levelled at them for not rendering assistance to Dr Jameson. The terms 'cowards', 'poltroons', and 'traitors', and the name of 'Judasberg', absolutely undeserved as they were known to be, rankled in the hearts of all, and it was only by the exercise of much self-denial and restraint that it was possible for men to remain silent during the period preceding Dr Jameson's trial.[337]

Should Johannesburg not have made some effort to assist Dr Jameson even with the inadequate means at their command and in the circumstances as they then stood? On this question Lionel Phillips wrote in *Nineteenth Century* as follows:

> I think today, as I thought at the time, that it would have been an act of the grossest folly to send out a force on foot to meet an ally whom we had not the slightest ground for believing was in any need of our aid, in direct opposition to the commands of the High Commissioner, and

---

[335] Austin, Alfred. *Jameson's Raid*, Stanzas 5 and 7.
[336] Meredith, Martin. *op. cit.*, 347.
[337] Fitzpatrick, J. Percy. *op. cit.*, 166.

moreover, as a declaration of hostilities against the Government which we were unprepared to fight. The mere fact of the invasion having occurred prior to the internal rising put us hopelessly in the wrong.[338]

Colonel Rhodes presented a slightly different defence in his later testimony at the official inquiry:

> 5405. Were you in a military position to enable you to send out anything in the nature of a force? – If one had thought they were in difficulties, of course one would have sent out a force. But I do not think we were in a position to send them anything that would have been of very much service to them.
>
> 5406. And in your opinion I understand you to say you were clear in your mind that Dr Jameson would get in without any difficulties? – Certainly, I always thought so.[339]

To their credit, despite the public backlash, the members of the Reform Committee continued to take their responsibilities extremely seriously:

> The Reform Committee…remained in perpetual session day and night throughout the crisis. Whatever more this well-abused Committee might have done, they at any rate preserved perfect order among an excited community, both white and black; they enrolled a police force and closed the canteens; they provided food and shelter for numbers of men, women, and children who flocked into the town from the outlying mines…[340]

By the time that the High Commissioner's train steamed into Johannesburg that Saturday night, he was so weak that he had to lie down during the sensitive negotiations. Desperate to counter negative publicity and opportunistic German propaganda, Chamberlain had sent a stream of telegrams demanding the most unreasonable terms from the settlement: the franchise after five years' residence; English-medium schools; full municipal powers for Johannesburg; tax cuts; and acceptance of the Reform Committee's manifesto. The Transvaal Government, said Chamberlain, was to

---

[338] Hillier, Alfred P. *op. cit.*, 63.
[339] *Ibid.*, 65.
[340] *Ibid.*, 59, 62.

Chapter 11

be reminded that 'the danger from which they have escaped' might recur if they were obdurate.[341]

Robinson, however, understood that Kruger held all the aces. He gratefully accepted Kruger's proposal to hand the raiders over to Britain so that they might be tried there. Kruger also demanded the unconditional surrender of Johannesburg within twenty-four hours. When Robinson tried to raise the issue of the Uitlanders' grievances, Kruger merely said that he would deal with the grievances after the surrender. As for the Reformers, he would deal with them too. Robinson felt powerless to do more, except to send a telegram to the Reform Committee advising them to surrender unconditionally and warning them that, should they refuse, they would 'forfeit all claim to sympathy from Her Majesty's Government and from British subjects throughout the world as the lives of Jameson and the prisoners are now practically in their hands'. The Reform Committee felt cornered and reluctantly replied that they would lay down their arms and place themselves and their interests in the hands of the High Commissioner.[342]

In the meanwhile, Charles Leonard had decided to head back to the Transvaal, despite the protestations of Catherine and his friends. Charles takes up the story:

> On the Friday I started to get back to Johannesburg. On the way I got a telegram from a Mr Stewart [*sic*], the editor of a newspaper,[343] saying that the position of things was very critical, and was becoming more critical every minute; that the Boers had taken possession of the bridge on the railway at Vereeniging, and were examining every passenger, and had made five arrests already. I went on to Victoria West, which is a couple of hundred miles further. At Victoria West I got a telegram from a friend of mine[344] who had begged me to be guided by him on my northward journey, and had given me his solemn word that he would not interfere with me unless it was hopeless for me to get through the Boer lines. I got a telegram from him telling me to stop. I hesitated as to what I should do, but I thought to myself it is only a matter of the next train, he will

---

[341] Meredith, Martin. *op. cit.*, 346.
[342] Crisp, Robert. *op. cit.*, 281-3.
[343] This should read 'Mr Stuart'. John Stuart was editor of the *South African Telegraph*, a Cape Town morning newspaper owned by the Randlord J. B. Robinson and published from August 1895 to September 1896, according to Garrett, Fydell Edmund; Shaw, Gerald (ed.). *The Garrett Papers*, 46, Footnote 19.
[344] David de Villiers Graaff.

telegraph to the station; he has given me his solemn pledge not to interfere unless it is hopeless for me to get through: I had better stay.

The next news I got was a telegram from the same man to this effect: 'Come back; passports have been established in Free State; Boers are on the line and are looking out for you, and you will never get there.' At the station the news that reached me was that Sir Hercules Robinson had been grossly insulted by the Boers on his arrival at Pretoria; that he had broken off diplomatic relations, that he was on the way down, and the Black Watch was on the way up… Under those circumstances I returned to Cape Town, as I deemed it hopeless to get through the lines; and I am satisfied, from information now, that I would never have got through. I had no passport, among other things, and could not get through the Free State; the Free State was in arms in aid of the Transvaal. I had therefore got to travel through a hostile territory for 300 miles, and then run into the net at this railway bridge, which was in the hands of these infuriated people. I [therefore] returned to Cape Town.[345]

Charles was picked up at the station and taken directly to Bordeaux, the imposing home of the Graaff brothers in Sea Point. He was in a bad way and was immediately confined to bed. David Graaff's personal physician, Dr Manikus, examined him and wrote out a certificate stating that Charles was not to be disturbed as he was suffering from 'congestion of the brain and nervous prostration'.[346] Charles later said, 'When I got back to Cape Town I was broken down. I could see the wreck of everything, and for many days I was very ill; in fact, I was kept quiet by constant administration of morphia. I intended to go back to the Transvaal the moment I should be fit to travel.'[347]

Catherine remained at Charles's bedside throughout his state of enervation. One can imagine the anguish she must have endured seeing her husband laid low like that.

On Monday 6 January, Rhodes resigned as Prime Minister of Cape Colony and the following day, the Reform Committee surrendered and laid down their arms in Johannesburg. Two days later, in a surprise move, 25 of the by now 78 members of the Reform Committee were arrested, most at the Rand Club. Jim Leonard was one of them. The prisoners spent the night in the Doornfontein gaol. In a bizarre sequel, some of the prisoners had to

---

[345] Leonard, Charles. *op. cit.*, 382-3.
[346] Dommisse, Ebbe. *op. cit.*, 80.
[347] Leonard, Charles. *op. cit.*, 390.

arrange for their own vehicles to take them to the gaol in Pretoria since the Boers had made insufficient provision in this regard. The following day, the Boers made 29 more arrests and warrants were issued for those still at large. 12 more were arrested thereafter, bringing the total to 66. Many of those arrested had played no part in the plot; they had joined the Reform Committee in order to help manage the resultant crisis. On 10 January, Jim Leonard wrote to Charles to inform him that he would be in prison from the following day for an indefinite period.[348] As the prisoners made their way from the Pretoria station to the gaol, they were verbally and physically abused by the burghers. Once there, they were kept separate from Jameson and his troopers.

> The four leaders [Lionel Phillips, Colonel Rhodes, John Hays Hammond and George Farrar] were put in a cell 11 feet by 11 feet, which was closed in by an inner court. There was no window, only a narrow grille over the door. The floor was of earth and overrun by vermin. Of the four canvas cots two were blood-stained, and hideously dirty. They were locked in at six o'clock – one of them [Hammond] ill with dysentery – and there they remained sweltering and gasping through the tropical night until six of the morning. For two weeks they remained in this cell.[349]

While Charles was lying ill at Sea Point, Catherine wrote a note to Dr Manikus, asking him to send a telegram to Jim Leonard at the Rand Club, informing him that Charles was unfit for business. Once he had recovered sufficiently, Charles himself managed to cable notes to his brother and Hamilton on 9 January. To the former he wrote:

> Tell Hamilton and friends I am ill in bed ... I was stopped on the way to Rand by wire which made it clear I could not get through. I waited day and a half without news and broke down under strain. Was then positively recalled ... I scarcely think anything can matter to me again but I cannot travel now and men must say what they please until I can.[350]

On 13 January, a telegram arrived from Ewald Esselen, the former Attorney-General of the Transvaal Republic and a man sympathetic to the

---

[348] Hagley Hall Archives 201/1/1a.
[349] Hammond, Mrs Natalie Harris. *A Woman's Part in a Revolution*, 47-8.
[350] NASA TAB FK 2115 p. 79; NASA TAB SP Vol 82 (1896) (SPR 113/96).

grievances of the Uitlanders. He had been asked to enquire as to Charles's intentions on behalf of the Government, who had issued a warrant for his arrest. It was published in the *Staatscourant* (Government Gazette) and read: 'There is reasonable ground to believe that Charles Leonard has committed the offence of sedition, or high treason.'

Charles was later cross-examined about the warrant and the telegram at the official inquiry. He was grilled by the Liberal Party M.P., Henry Labouchère, who was a most unpleasant man. Besides being sneeringly sarcastic towards Charles, he was openly opposed to feminism and homosexuality, and was an anti-Semite. To his credit, he was a long-time foe of chartered companies and a vehement anti-imperialist. Charles's answers clearly reveal his irritation with the man and his insinuations:

> 8020. A warrant was issued against you? – No, I do not think so.
>
> 8021. Do you deny it? – An application was made by the State Attorney of the Transvaal for a warrant, which, of course, was a ridiculous thing, because I was not liable to arrest in Cape Town.
>
> 8022. Then you deny, so far as your knowledge goes, that a warrant was submitted to the State authorities to be used against you by the Transvaal? – Absolutely; I never heard of it before.
>
> 8023. You never heard of it before? – No, I never heard of any warrant at all being applied for.
>
> 8024. There were two other gentlemen with you; what were their names, do you remember them? – Do you mean Mr Bettelheim and Mr Joel?[351] They were not with me; they had joined the Reform party after I had left Johannesburg. I was the leader of the National Union; I never was the chairman of the Reform Committee, because I was not there.
>
> 8025. They were brought back under arrest? – No, they were not brought back under arrest; they were arrested, and I believe they agreed to go.
>
> 8026. Was there any communication between you and Mr Esselen[352] on the subject? – Yes.
>
> 8027. Would you state the nature of it? Mr Esselen was, I think, ex-Attorney-General of the Transvaal? – I have stated that up to the 16th or

---

[351] Captain Henri Bettelheim was the Turkish Consul in Pretoria and Solly B. Joel was the nephew of the Randlord Barney Barnato and the resident partner in the firm of Barnato Brothers.

[352] The official report incorrectly spells his surname 'Esselin' throughout. I have corrected this error.

17th January it was my firm intention to return to the Transvaal.

8028. I am asking about Mr Esselen. – But I wanted to say that in absolute sincerity, in pursuance of that intention, I had telegraphed. The fact was, as I have told you, I was lying down ill there and a telegram came to me: 'Where is Leonard; will he come up?' and, in a fit of pique, I said to my wife, 'Telegraph to Mr Esselen to make it public I am coming up,' and I telegraphed to my own partner in the same sense. That was the only meaning of it; I really wanted more to let my friends know I was coming up, and I believe I added afterwards, as an afterthought, 'and to the authorities of the Republic' or something of that sort. I cannot remember the date.[353]

Charles was well enough to be taken to Muizenberg on 13 January, where the *Cape Times* of the following day reported him to be. When he thought it was too unsafe to remain with the Graaff brothers at Bordeaux, he hid in the stables at Fresnaye Villa (Catherine's uncle's home).[354] Afterwards, Charles insisted that it had always been his intention to return to the Transvaal to stand trial with his confederates, but before leaving, he wanted certain assurances from Rhodes:

He [Rhodes] came down on the morning of the 15th from Kimberley, and I had drafted him a letter that morning in which I said, 'You have been absent and I have been very ill; I am going back to stand my trial with my friends, but I want so-and-so.' [Charles asked Rhodes to supply him with copies of the telegrams Rhodes had sent Jameson over the period 27-29 December, declaring that Rhodes owed this to him and to the other four men who had signed the letter of invitation.] Before that letter could reach Mr Rhodes, he had sailed for England that afternoon.[355]

Rhodes sailed for England to try to save his position as Chairman of the BSA Company and to negotiate on behalf of his friend, Jameson. Before leaving, he made a parting speech, in which he said, 'I am going home to face the unctuous rectitude of my countrymen.'[356] Charles was disappointed to learn that Rhodes had left the country before his letter could be delivered, but

---

[353] Leonard, Charles. *op. cit.*, 396-8. Charles's letter was dated 18 January.
[354] Murray, Marischal. *op. cit.*, 139.
[355] *Ibid.*, 390. Charles Leonard to Rhodes, 15 January 1896, NASA TAB FK 2115 pp. 65-73 (handwritten) and *Leonard Collection* M3002 (typed).
[356] Meredith, Martin. *op. cit.*, 349.

worse news was to follow:

> The next day I got a collection of the news, and I saw the position taken up by the press, and this was the general spirit of it: that the Johannesburg men were a lot of cowards, and this was a dirty stock-jobbing transaction; that the Cape politicians were raging against us, they were all crawling on their stomachs to the Boers; the Governor had been bowed out of the country after the redress of grievances or the consideration of grievances was practically understood to have been promised; and Jameson was defending himself on that letter, and the whole world was against us.[357]

It was at this point that Charles decided to flee South Africa, but he claimed not to have been motivated by self-interest:

> When I saw that that was the position of things, I then, for the first time, contemplated coming to England, but not before the 16th or 17th of January. I said: 'Good Heavens, I am the only man free who knows these facts, and every engine of calumny and misrepresentation is being used against us; I am going to England as the one solitary man free (I can come back and go to gaol afterwards) to try to represent my friends' case.'[358]

Once Charles had decided to skip the country, he hurriedly made the necessary arrangements, all the while maintaining the strictest secrecy. It seems likely that an urgent message was conveyed to the Dock Superintendent of the Union Steam Ship Company, Mr F. Bishop, who lived at Rose Villa in Sea Point,[359] and that he pulled strings to have Charles booked on the next mail ship leaving Cape Town harbour. By a stroke of luck, Charles had a valid passport, having taken his family to England in 1894.

Charles did not even confide in David Graaff, who was a leading member of the Afrikaner Bond, which vehemently condemned the invasion of the Boer Republic and turned its anger on Rhodes. It is a tribute to Graaff's high principles that he put loyalty to his friend before political considerations. He certainly had to endure a great deal of derogatory speculation as a result.

Many years later, the editor of the *Cape Times* wrote:

---

[357] Leonard, Charles. *op. cit.*, 390-1.
[358] *Ibid.*, 391.
[359] Murray, Marischal. *op. cit.*, 148.

Chapter 11

The full story of that exciting episode has never been told, but rumours of it were current at the time… There is no doubt that Sir David's part in the escapade was gratefully remembered by the Reformer to whose assistance he came, and it was quite in keeping with Sir David's sporting instincts.[360]

Graaff wrote a letter to Charles, dated 15 July, which confirms his lack of involvement in his friend's escape. There is no reason to doubt his word in private correspondence:

> As you know, I knew absolutely nothing at all about your going away, but somehow or other the *Times* has been putting two and two together with the result that instead of making four, it turns out to be half a dozen. The editor is altogether out in his method of reckoning. … Everyone knows and the editor of the *Cape Times* should also know that you and I have been on terms of very great friendship for many years past; and however much I may personally regret your unfortunate connection with the Reform Movement I shall never allow it to interfere with my personal feelings towards yourself. So don't fear anything on that score. Newspapers however are sometimes in want of copy and it appears that the *Cape Times* has determined upon getting as much excitement as possible worked into the public for the purpose of selling their papers.[361]

---

[360] *Cape Times*, 14 April 1931, 7.
[361] NASA TAB FK 2115 pp. 88-90. See also Graaff's letter to Leonard of 6 January 1897 in *Leonard Collection* M3002.

CHAPTER 12 : AT SEA AND AT THE GRAND (JANUARY – FEBRUARY 1896)

Some work of noble note may yet be done…

– Alfred Lord Tennyson, *Ulysses*

So it was that sometime after midnight on Sunday, 19 January 1896, Charles Leonard slipped out of the stables at Fresnaye Villa and made his way undetected to the Alfred Docks in Cape Town, where he boarded the Union Steamship Company's intermediate liner, *Guelph*, and sailed away to England and to safety.[362]

He must have had mixed feelings as the *Guelph* steamed out of Table Bay at ten o'clock the following morning and passed Sea Point, where his family and friends were no doubt following the ship's progress and bidding him *bon voyage*. On the one hand, he must have been relieved to have been escaping, but on the other he must have been disconsolate at having to leave his family behind. One can imagine him standing at the rail until Table Mountain disappeared from view. According to the ship's physician, Dr Frank Scorer, Charles was still gravely ill when he left Cape Town and continued in a poor way until shortly before his arrival in England.[363]

Once again, let us pause to consider Catherine and the girls. They might also have been relieved to know that Charles would be safe (or at least, comparatively so), but they must also have been upset to be parted from him

---

[362] Murray, Marischal. *op. cit.*, 139-40.
[363] Rogers, Owen. *op. cit.*, 143.

once again and anxious about his health. We know from their correspondence that it was a trying time for them. The more personal excerpts of their correspondence are presented in the next chapter, but Catherine did try to keep Charles informed of political developments as well. In her letter of 29 January, we hear Catherine's authentic 'voice' for the first time:

> The news of your escape, as the papers put it, caused no end of consternation in Upingtonian circles.[364] I believe Dr Manikus has been partially blamed for helping to get you away. Above saying you escaped, the papers have made next to no comment. Some people say Pretoria was not anxious to have you; others again think you are better in England where you may possibly be of some assistance to the cause.
> …
> I have written to Mr van Hulsteyn[365] in answer to a letter he wrote to me, which I enclose. I was very much pleased with the general tone of it as it shows your own people still put implicit faith & confidence in you. When writing to him I explained to him the motive for your sudden departure, which I sincerely trust everybody will understand & see in a true light. So far it is people's impression that your mental aberration was out of order & your health generally had suffered & they also say you no doubt will return for the trial in April. I tell them I cannot enlighten them as I don't know until I hear from you.
> …
> I see by the papers the Boers are continuing their insults in the J.B.[366] streets to ladies. I am posting some cuttings for you to read & to show Englishmen.[367]

Catherine completed this letter the following day, but as it deals with a development still to be revealed, the remainder will have to be quoted then. Of course, her letters would not have reached Charles until he arrived in England, but he would nonetheless have been aware of and concerned about her feelings.

It must, therefore, have come as a pleasant surprise and welcome distraction to find that amongst his fellow First Class passengers was an old

---

[364] Sir Thomas Upington was Attorney-General at the Cape.
[365] Willem van Hulsteyn was Charles's partner in his Johannesburg law firm.
[366] Johannesburg.
[367] Hagley Hall Archives 201/1/8.

acquaintance from Johannesburg, Augustus Bernard Tancred.[368] Known as A.B., he was also a lawyer who had been born in the Eastern Cape, but he achieved lasting fame as a cricketer. He represented his country in the first Test match ever played against an English touring team and also become the first South African to score a century in a First-Class match. *Wisden Cricketers' Almanack* called him 'undoubtedly the finest batsman in South Africa'.[369] Besides their mutual interest in law and cricket, he and Charles would also have shared perspectives on the political crisis in the Transvaal because 'Captain' Tancred, as he was known, had helped guard the road from Pretoria to Johannesburg when it was feared that the Boers might attack the town.[370]

After his arrival in England, Tancred became an honorary member of the Marylebone Cricket Club and was also made an honorary member of the Surrey County Cricket Club. After returning to South Africa, he played his last First-Class match against Lord Hawke's touring English team. During the Second South African War, he worked for British Intelligence and then as legal adviser to the Military Governor in Bloemfontein. After the war, he moved to Salisbury in Southern Rhodesia to open a law firm in partnership with Charles Coghlan (later to be knighted for his services as Premier of Southern Rhodesia). Tancred fell seriously ill in 1911 and was brought to Cape Town *en route* to England to receive specialised treatment, but his condition deteriorated, and, after emergency surgery, he died in Cape Town at the age of 46.[371] Charles must have befriended Tancred and maintained contact with him, for after the latter's untimely death, Charles arranged for his widow to receive a monthly allowance of £4, 3/- and 4d.[372]

Another First-Class passenger, travelling under a false name, was Dr Wolff, one of inner circle of the National Union conspirators, who had managed to escape from Johannesburg. The three men soon became acquainted with another First-Class passenger, Henry Byron Reed, Conservative Party M.P. for Bradford East, who was returning to England after a short holiday at the Cape.[373] He maintained contact with Charles after

---

[368] www.ancestorsonboard.com
[369] *Wisden Cricketers' Almanack* 1912, 'Obituaries'.
http://content-eap.cricinfo.com/southafrica/content/player/47521.html Retrieved 25 September 2015.
[370] www.remembered.co.za/augustus-bernard-tancred-6733 Retrieved 25 September 2015.
[371] https://en.wikipedia.org›wiki›Bernard_Tancred Retrieved 26 February 2016.
[372] KAB, MOOC 13/1/4558, 264. Leonard, Charles Henry Brandt, Liquidation and Distribution Account, 1922.
[373] www.ancestorsonboard.com

their arrival in England, dining with him at least once.[374] Sadly, he died in October that year, at the age of 41, two days after his pony trap had overturned near his home on the Isle of Wight.[375]

While Charles was setting off on his voyage, Jameson and his troopers were placed on a train and transported under armed guard from the Transvaal to Port Natal, where they were to board ships bound for England. Chamberlain and Kruger had negotiated their handover to Britain.

Then, on 22 January, the new Attorney-General at the Cape, Sir Thomas Upington, 'prostituted his office', as Charles later described his action. Upington was asked to arrest Charles and extradite him to the Transvaal to stand trial, but to his dismay he was informed that Charles had given him the slip. In a disgraceful attempt to appease the Boers, Upington sent telegrams to the Portuguese and Spanish governments, asking them to arrest Charles when the *Guelph* entered their territorial waters and to extradite him to South Africa. The islands of Madeira (Portuguese) and Teneriffe (Spanish) were scheduled ports of call on the mail ship's voyage. It was this development that so distressed Catherine and which she mentioned in the concluding section of her letter dated 29 January:

> Wednesday morning.
> Since writing the letter, I have been most terribly upset by a paragraph in the papers which contains a telegram from J.B. saying authorities had issued instructions to have you arrested at Teneriffe. I am nearly at my wits' end to know what to do; one's troubles seem to increase instead of to diminish every month. What must I do? It is too dreadful to think of all this misery.[376]

To their credit, both European countries refused to comply with Upington's unprecedented request, but Charles was understandably furious when he discovered what had happened, as is evident from his responses to questions under cross-examination by Henry Labouchère:

> 8040. There is this distinction, is there not, between the Extradition Treaty between Great Britain and the Continental States and the Extradition Treaty between the Cape Colony and the Transvaal, that

---

[374] Hagley Hall Archives 201/2/20, 201/2/27 and 201/6/7.
[375] *The Times*, 6 October 1896, p. 4.
[376] Hagley Hall Archives 201/1/8.

persons guilty of political disturbances may be extradited? – No.

8041. Not? – No; there is no extradition at the Cape Colony for a political offence; absolutely none. That is the whole point of the thing.

8042. Then I understand from you that you have no knowledge that the Cape Government did actually act upon this warrant, and sought to give effect to it? – I have this knowledge, that the Cape Attorney-General prostituted his office, and telegraphed to Spain and Portugal, and asked them to arrest me at the instance of a third nation, when the original request to him was utterly invalid.

8043. That was the Cape Attorney-General? – Yes.

8044. Then I understand that the Cape Attorney-General and you do not entertain quite the same views as to the scope of the Extradition Treaty? – I am absolutely convinced in my own mind of the real scope of the Extradition Treaty; it was the one word 'violent', and I had been guilty of no violent action.[377]

There were also significant developments in Pretoria at this time. Jim's wife, Kate, as the daughter of a well-known Dutch family, was considered to have such influence with the Republican Government that she was specially selected to act as an intermediary between the Reform Committee prisoners and President Kruger. She was granted a private audience with the President and informed him that the prisoners, who included her husband and son-in-law, were being held in deplorable conditions in Pretoria Gaol. As a fellow Christian, she appealed to him to grant them some relief. Despite giving her a courteous hearing, Kruger failed to intervene.[378] A few days later, on 25 January, one of the prisoners committed suicide, prompting Kruger to release the rest on bail of ten thousand rix dollars each, with the exception of the five leaders (Percy Fitzpatrick by now being regarded as the fifth). Those released on bail were not permitted to leave Pretoria. Then, after repeated expressions of concern about John Hays Hammond's declining health, the five leaders were moved to a cottage in Pretoria, where they were kept under round-the-clock armed guard.

Late in January, Jameson and thirteen of his officers set sail for England aboard H.M.T. *Victoria*, still under armed guard. They sailed up the east coast of Africa, through the Suez Canal and across the Mediterranean. This means that, for approximately a week, Rhodes and his entourage, Jameson and his

---

[377] Leonard, Charles. *op. cit.*, 399-400.
[378] *South Africa* magazine, Vol. CXL, 16 November 1923, 307.

officers, and Charles Leonard – all leading players in the Jameson Raid – were simultaneously at sea, all bound for England.

The remaining Raid prisoners – 26 officers and 399 other ranks – embarked on a specially chartered mail steamer, the S.S. *Harlech Castle*, and set sail from Port Natal a few days later. Those with homes in South Africa were permitted to land at Cape ports, the remainder being conveyed to England. Captains Coventry and Barry, together with 19 other rank and file under treatment for wounds, were left in hospitals at Krugersdorp and Pretoria, and, with the exception of Barry, who died of his wounds, were handed over to the British authorities later.[379]

On 3 February, after the unconditional release of another of their number on the grounds of ill health, the preliminary examination of the remaining 64 Reform Committee prisoners began in the Second Raadsaal in Pretoria. However, as the proceedings were conducted in Dutch, most of the prisoners were unable to follow them. This hearing ended a week later, with all the prisoners being committed to stand trial on charges still to be determined.[380]

On the day that this hearing began, Rhodes and his entourage arrived in London. He immediately consulted his attorney, Bouchier Hawksley, who had compiled a dossier of fifty-nine telegrams, many of which implicated the Secretary of State for the Colonies, Joseph Chamberlain, in the plot, contrary to his public assertions that he had had no foreknowledge of the Raid. Rhodes clearly intended negotiating with a gun to Chamberlain's head. 'Pushful Joe', however, was ready with his own gun. As things turned out, neither of these shrewd politicians had to produce his weapon. They emerged from their private meeting on 6 February having settled on a *quid pro quo*: if Rhodes withheld the most damaging of the telegrams, Chamberlain would see that Rhodes maintained control of the BSA Company.[381]

On 12 February, the *Guelph* docked at Southampton, whence Charles travelled to London, where he booked into the Grand Hotel, Trafalgar Square, and immediately launched a campaign on behalf of his imprisoned colleagues. Unfortunately, he was up against public opinion, which was firmly behind Jameson. In addition, Charles came in for a great deal of criticism, in both England and South Africa, for seemingly having deserted his colleagues in their hour of need.

On 19 February, a week after his arrival in England, Charles wrote to

---

[379] Cape Report, C 7933, No. 209, and 8063, Part II, No. 17.
[380] Garrett, Fydell Edmund and Edwards, E.J. *op. cit.*, 261.
[381] Meredith, Martin. *op. cit.*, 349.

Chapter 12

Catherine from his hotel, expressing his feelings and confiding in her:

> My dear Tommy,
>
> I have just had a letter from Woodie[382] which makes me mad. He says I am being abused for 'leaving' the Rand; that my friends (he calls it 'the crowd here') have neglected to protect my honour and that he advises me not to consider them in any respect, and 'told them go to the devil'.
>
> It is too bad of the Rand people not to have made it public that I left Johannesburg at the unanimous request of a meeting of leaders, on *their* mission – a mission which they had decided on before I got to the meeting which resolved it, and which I accepted with great reluctance only because I felt I was perhaps the best man in the room to fulfil it.
>
> However, everybody here to whom I have told the facts thinks that I acted rightly in not going back to be arrested when there was no chance of my doing any good, and I am certain that it was the right thing to do. I must simply be content to let the truth come out later on, and in the meantime a clear conscience is my strength. If anything should happen to me before the whole truth comes out it will be your task to protect my honour from the aspersion of having left Johannesburg to escape the trouble. The mischief is largely done already unfortunately and one will never quite get over it. You know how I tried to get back to the Rand as soon as possible – though all chance of success and all possibility of a fight were over – and how I was recalled.
>
> I know Sir Hercules Robinson telegraphed to Kruger expressing his regret that I had 'escaped'. This is the sort of conduct to strengthen one's love for England and to encourage one to sacrifice oneself for principle. [Note the bitter sarcasm.]
>
> You may take it as certain that when this business is concluded my connection with politics or public affairs will be severed forever, and I shall in future live my own life with you and my children. There has been an amount of 'using' and 'giving away' of people in this affair which has made me distrustful of human nature and human motives; and has taught me how little the subordinate is considered when bigger men consider he should be sacrificed.
>
> However, an end to this, but never forget what I have said.
>
> The fools in the Transvaal little know how I have been working for them here; and I suppose I shall go on doing so for the sake of James and

---

[382] Charles's younger brother, Woodford.

a few other staunch friends who have *not* allowed me to suffer wrong.

I am spending all my time, and a good deal of money, in this cause. I have seen most influential people and can get access to very good channels in the Press for anything I may write. So far I have confined myself (with two exceptions) to influencing, by interviews, strong people.

The position is extremely delicate. England has asserted a 'moral' right to see the Uitlanders' grievances remedied; Kruger denies her right to interfere in the internal affairs of the Republic; will England, if he refuses to admit their right to claim the introduction of reforms, go further?

Germany is still menacing in tone, and there is no doubt that for the last 8 weeks Leyds has been carrying on a 'branch of the Govt. of the South African Republic in Britain'.[383]

War is the last thing we want. If Kruger refuses reforms nothing but war can save our last state from being worse than the first; and from strengthening the Hollander and German influences in the Transvaal.

Naturally I have refused to discuss with anyone the events immediately connected with the outbreak, but the question I have had to consider is whether it was wise (in view of our friends' trouble) to educate public opinion here on the *causes* which led to the outbreak. I have consulted many wise heads, and they all think it is desirable to do so. Of course my name would not appear, but there is a danger of my hand being traced. The argument is that Kruger will not be lenient to his prisoners from any sense of mercy or justice; but that he may deem it policy [*sic*] to be clement if he finds a strong public opinion formed here, & holding him responsible for the outbreak.

I think this is the right line to take – especially as Leyds & Lippert[384] and others are now working the English Press to prove that there *are no grievances* for the Uitlanders to complain of, and that the outbreak occurred simply as the result of a conspiracy among a small group of capitalists for their own selfish ends. If this view were to prevail there would be no opinion here to back up the English Govt. in protecting the prisoners. I had a long cable from James on the subject of a permanent settlement on an Africander [*sic*] basis, and am keeping it in view, but am compelled to

---

[383] Dr Willem Leyds was born in Holland and held the office of State Secretary in Kruger's Cabinet. He was serving as ambassador extraordinary and minister plenipotentiary of the Republic in Europe at the time of Charles's writing.

[384] Edouard Lippert was a German who held the controversial dynamite and other concessions in the Transvaal at that time. He was known to favour German interests in the Transvaal.

Chapter 12

go very slowly, and am now awaiting the development of correspondence between Chamberlain and Kruger. If the latter comes to England there may be a permanent settlement arrived at, – though I have no shadow of a doubt Kruger not only will not give anything if he can help it, but will want to receive something.

I also had a telegram from Weinkal, Editor of the *Press*, saying much good was expected to result from my sojourn in England and that my work here might produce best results to all friends concerned. Now the *Press* is a supporter of the [Transvaal] Govt., and this message struck me as intended to convey either a bribe or a menace. Thus translated: – If you act favourably to the Republic, your friends may get off lightly; if you oppose its interests, vengeance will be wreaked on them.

Now as I have never had any desire to injure the Republic, but have wanted to save it from destruction I can have no difficulty in supporting its true interests. But I cannot swallow all my public utterances, and my convictions, I cannot, even to save my friends, say pretty things about Kruger and his Govt., whose policy I consider fraught with danger to public interests and with the certainty of another revolution. I can, and most certainly shall, advocate steadily the recognition and maintenance of the independence of the Republic side by side with internal reforms which shall remove discontent, provide equality, and secure good Govt. But as I have said the matter is in bigger hands than mine, and I can only do all in my power to influence sentiment here so that there shall be no rabid views against the Boers, that their just rights shall be safeguarded, and that our own legitimate demands shall be satisfied.

This, however, is not the game of Kruger and his foreign friends, and the hope of a satisfactory settlement is justly dashed by doubts. Enough of politics. I have endeavoured merely to give you a clear picture of how matters stand today. I got a private note from the Colonial Office last night announcing that the four prisoners are to be moved from the gaol to a private house. I have worked every source I know to get them released, and am thankful for this relief at least. I think I told you that I had seen Mrs Phillips & dined with her. I went up, too, the night Chamberlain announced that he had asked for the release of the prisoners, & not finding her in I left a note to tell her. I have written to George Farrar's mother trying to cheer her up.

...

This morning I breakfasted with the Bayers who were *very* kind. Tonight I dine at St Stephen's Club & meet several members; tomorrow night I am to meet another lot of members, and through them hope to get the ear of the Duke of Devonshire. On Friday I meet another lot of members at dinner at the House of Commons.

You will say this is very good fun. I say it is terribly hard work, & I feel very tired, but I feel I must go on and on in this work – for all my social engagements are made in view only of the one thing. I have not been to a single theatre yet, and cannot divest myself of the one absorbing idea.

Now I have got a private room in an office[385] where I can work quietly, and I intend writing a powerful article for the *New Review*, which comes out next month, and also a series of separate articles which will probably appear in *The Times*. Do not say anything about this. It is better not.[386]

The letter continues with references to family life in South Africa, to which we shall turn our attention in the next chapter. Before doing so, however, it is important to pause and pay tribute to Charles's untiring efforts on behalf of the Pretoria prisoners and in trying to help resolve the crisis in South Africa. His intentions should by now be beyond dispute.

Sadly, at the time, this was far from being the case, as is evident from the following bristling exchange between Henry Labouchère and Charles during his testimony before the House Select Committee later that year:

8048. And you somehow came to England? – No, I came to England by sea.

8049. From what port? – In the *Guelph*.

8050. From what port? – From Cape Town.

8051. Then you came to England because you had come to the conclusion that it would be more desirable, in the interests of the Transvaal, that you should not surrender yourself to justice? – I did not consider the interests of the Transvaal at all; I considered the interests of my comrades who were in gaol.

8052. I will say, more to the interests of your comrades who were in gaol, that you should not join them and be put on your trial, but that you should come back to England a free man? – Yes.

8053. In order that you might represent their case in England? – Yes.

---

[385] In the office of Wernher, Beit & Co.
[386] Hagley Hall Archives 201/2/30.

Chapter 12

> 8054. That I gather? – Yes.
>
> 8055. When you came to England did you represent their case? – Yes.
>
> 8056. Where? – Privately and publicly. I wrote an article in the *New Review* in March over my name. I wrote an article in an American newspaper, which was very widely commented on, and I venture to think had some slight influence in moulding public opinion. I, in season and out of season, did this. I may add that I got nothing, no communication at all, except letter after letter from these men in Johannesburg. 'For goodness' sake stop free and help us to fight our case.' I looked upon it as a mandate that I was their only representative, and fought for them here.
>
> 8057. You came here before the mandate was issued? – Yes, I came here before the mandate was issued, and they have ratified it.[387]

Labouchère would not let this go, however, and soon returned to this line of questioning:

> 8093. Then who authorizes you to represent them here? – I have never said that anybody authorised me to represent them here. I feel that I have a right to state the case, because I was concerned in this movement; but as a matter of fact, all my old friends who were on the Reform Committee, and who are in London now, have been in constant communication with me, and I have been told by letter from Johannesburg that they look to me to put the case. But I speak apart from any mandate.
>
> 8094. You put it to the Committee that these gentlemen look to you to put the case? – Yes.[388]

We can understand why these questions particularly irked Charles because he had answered similar questions put to him by John Ellis only a few minutes earlier:

> 7980. Then do you come before us in any representative capacity at this moment? – I am in touch with the whole of the reform leaders who were in gaol.
>
> 7981. Perhaps you do not understand my question. Have you been selected or appointed in any formal or official manner to come before this Committee? – Oh, no; but I think it is generally expected by the

---

[387] Leonard, Charles. *op. cit.*, 400-1.
[388] Ibid, 404.

Johannesburg men that I should state their case for them.

7982. Yes; but you have no representative capacity? – I have no power of attorney from them.

7983. You have no representative character? – No.[389]

It is clear from this line of questioning that the two Committee members were trying to discredit Charles as a witness by getting him to admit that he had been given no formal mandate to testify on behalf of his fellow reformists and, in this way, to cast aspersions on his integrity by insinuating that he had fled South Africa to avoid standing trial rather than to represent his comrades' interests, as he claimed. It was against such snide insinuations that Charles was having to defend himself.

Fortunately, we do not have to rely solely on Charles's defence of his actions:

> But speaking of Mr Charles Leonard, there is no doubt that he did yeoman service to the cause by indefatigably educating colonial opinion and gaining colonial sympathy for it during his absence; and he should not be hastily judged yet, nor until all the facts are known, for his apparent desertion of his post of leader.[390]

Alfred Hillier, a member of the Reform Committee who was imprisoned at Pretoria, and therefore one of those who might be considered to have had most reason to harbour resentment towards Charles for 'deserting' them, was another who defended him against allegations of cowardice:

> With reference to Mr Charles Leonard a good many hard things have been said, because he did not return from Cape Town after his interview with Mr Rhodes. The period of the 'Armed Incursion' was, it was felt, rather an unfortunate one for the Chairman of the National Union to be absent; and in deference to Mr Leonard it is only fair to notice the explanation which he at least has been at no great pains to make public. He had intended to return with his colleague Mr Hamilton, when he received an urgent message from Mr Rhodes to remain and render him what assistance he could with Mr Hofmeyr and the Imperial authorities at Cape Town… It is

---

[389] Ibid, 391.
[390] *Oamaru Mail*, Vol. XXI, Issue 6502, 11 March 1896, under the heading 'South African News', 4.

Chapter 12

thus clear that if Mr Leonard has erred, it was an error of judgment; and personally now that all the circumstances are known, I do not consider him even to have erred in that. To have returned at a later stage after the warrant for his arrest was made public would not have served any useful purpose; whereas it is clear from the unremitting attention which he devoted to the matter in England that he used his liberty to better purpose in the Uitlander cause than any that could have been served by his imprisonment at Pretoria.

The action of the Cape Government in first arresting Messrs Joel and Bettelheim and subsequently in endeavouring to arrest Mr Charles Leonard, pursuing him with that end to a Portuguese port, will ever remain a stain on this page of the history of the Cape Colony…

To Mr Leonard it was left to find on the shores of England that protection which even a Portuguese port would not withhold from him, but which was denied him in the land of his birth, a British colony. Well might he exclaim in the bitterness of his heart that Cape politicians, during this crisis in Africa, thought of nothing but 'crawling on their stomachs before the Boers'.[391]

If further evidence were needed that Charles was a man of integrity and determined to do the right thing, it is provided in the following testimony, again in response to questions from Labouchère, about the unforeseen consequences of his having sent that telegram to Ewald Esselen while lying ill in Cape Town:

> 8032. Subsequently you wrote letters to Mr Esselen, did you not? – I subsequently wrote to him. When this startling combination of things made me decide that my duty to my own friends was to come to England, I wrote to him and said: 'I regret that circumstances have changed' (I have not a copy of the letter), 'and that I cannot come to the Transvaal at the present moment.'
>
> 8033. Was it borne in upon you that Mr Esselen had somewhat complained of your having compromised him with the Government? – Yes, afterwards; it was not present to my mind then. Perhaps you will allow me to explain what was in my mind. I looked upon myself as an absolutely free agent at the Cape. I maintain today, sitting here as a lawyer, that I am as free in the Cape as I am in England; that it was a purely

---

[391] Hillier, Alfred P. *op. cit.*, 72-4.

voluntary act, an act that could not be compelled in any way by the Kruger Government, that I should go to the Transvaal; that I merely announced my intention of going back as a voluntary act, and that I was perfectly free to alter that intention; in other words, that the Transvaal Government was not prejudiced in any way by it. That was the aspect in my mind at the time. When I decided to come to England, that was the impression on my mind.

In England, in March, shortly after I arrived here, Mr Hamilton saw me, and he told me that I had prejudiced Mr Esselen; I said, 'Well, it is a mere matter of sentiment.' As a matter of fact, I regret very much that I should ever have used Mr Esselen as a medium of making a statement voluntarily like this; and I wrote to him accordingly a fresh statement, and asked him to make it known. I said: 'You can use my letter as you like.' I wanted to clear up the point in my own mind that by communicating to Mr Esselen – this was borne in upon me in March – I might have suggested some implication with my own affairs in Johannesburg, and that was the reason why I regretted sending him the telegram.[392]

Besides his concern about the political crisis and its fallout, Charles was also concerned about his family back home in South Africa, and it is to this that we now need to turn our attention.

---

[392] Leonard, Charles. *op. cit.*, 388-9.

Chapter 12

Preliminary examination of the Reform Committee prisoners begins in the Second Raadsaal, Pretoria, on 3 February 1896.

The trial of the Reform Committee begins before Judge Gregorowski in the Market Hall, Pretoria, on 24 April 1896. He sentenced the four leaders to death.

The Grand Hotel, Trafalgar Square, London, c. 1896

CHAPTER 13 : HOME AND ABROAD
(JANUARY – FEBRUARY 1896)

Oh, to be in England…

– Robert Browning

Catherine Leonard missed Charles dreadfully and was initially in a state of shock at how suddenly and quickly her family's life had been turned upside down. Her letters to Charles, dated 22 and 29 January and 5 February, all mention how difficult it was to cope without him. Daisy and Violet also wrote a number of letters, saying how much they missed him and that they wanted to be with him.[393]

Besides the political news in her letter of 29 January, Catherine also opened her heart to Charles about their home life:

> My dear Daddie [*sic*],
> You will be pleased to hear that we are keeping well. I am still suffering from insomnia & when I do get any rest I keep dreaming over & over again all the events of the past few weeks, waking up with a start which sends my old heart thumping like fury.
> …
> Woodie left by the mail train for Pretoria. Up to now I have not heard from him. He has got a good many instructions from me; whether they can be carried out or not remains to be proved.

---

[393] Hagley Hall Archives 201/1/6, 201/1/8, 201/2/2, 201/2/4, 201/2/7, 201/2/8, 201/2/9 and 201/2/18.

...

I have not heard from Susie[394] again; the last I heard was Professor MacWilliam had Typhoid in her house & she was in a dreadful state about your health, as I believe the wildest rumours were in circulation. When I last wrote to her I did not actually tell where you had gone.

I do miss you so fearful much. I feel quite ill at times with longing just for a hug & a kiss. You must keep your promise & never go in for politics again as you have had quite enough of that lately. One is only watching now to see how everything will end. Dear old sweetheart, what a bad time you have had & all through no fault of your own.

...

Woodie is wanting to hurry me on, but I will wait & see what course events take as I believe it is very cold & dull in London at this time of the year; not only that, but as I am no lover of hotels I should prefer to wait.

You might just cable to me come or wait, but don't let me come only to pamper you when you will probably have a good deal of business to transact & have no time for poor me & the babies. It seems so hard just to have given up everything in such a hurry. I cannot yet owe it; I am just constantly haunted. You will remember what fears I had about it long before things actually came to a crisis.

...

Eric[395] I believe is sending your clothes by this mail care Wernher etc.[396] I have asked Woodie to get your London clothes sent without delay. I trust he will act promptly as I don't know what you will do. I have been to the bank to sign my name & get a cheque book. The General Manager very friendly attended to me; he made out cheques for me for the Grand Hotel £30 something. £35 I owed Miss Pearce. £50 Woodie asked me for expenses to J.B. £7.5.9 for Markham & I see there is another £15 owing for goods Eric got for you. £10 I drew for myself. I feel quite strange at having to make out my own cheques. I don't quite like it & am afraid I will be frightened to spend [illegible].

The children are enjoying themselves very much. They both swim beautifully. Violet has learnt to dive; she is almost too fearless. Mrs Thirkmans [?] also taught Daisy. She ties a rope round in case she remains

---

[394] Charles's younger sister, Susannah Marx, who lived in Johannesburg.
[395] Eric and Dot were the couple who had taken Catherine and the girls into their home in Sea Point.
[396] Wernher, Beit & Co., London.

Chapter 13

under water too long. I have, however, forbidden her to do it again. Daisy is benefitting by the exercise; she is getting much thinner & more active already. She misses you as much as I do & is constantly urging me to go to you. Violet I think is too young & very differently constituted; she says she misses you, but she won't worry mother so much. I feel quite sorry for the poor things.

…

Goodbye, sweetheart. Much love & oceans of kisses from your anxious & troubled wife & kiddies. A fond old hug.

From your devoted

Tommie.[397]

Charles responded to this letter on 19 February, a week after arriving in London, from his room at the Grand Hotel. The lengthy first part has already been quoted, but he continued:

Now sweetheart, I have told you about myself. Let me turn to your dear letter and that of sweet Daisy. I am astonished at the letter she writes, and proud of her. She is worth cultivating and I intend to devote a good part of my time in future for the leading out of her mind. She is original, shrewd, happy in expression, and withal so fresh and childlike that I read and re-read her letter with never failing delight. Tell Tobbie[398] I missed my budget of kisses this mail, but considered they were wafted across the sea to me. I am glad they have learned to swim. It is useful, and very healthy exercise. Daisy tells me you are getting the dogs down. I don't know what you are going to do with Lucy. Let Bobbie or Maclean take her or decide what to do with her. I feel I shall never care to live in the Transvaal again, and therefore the dogs must go. I shall be glad to learn what has been done about closing up what Daisy calls our Johannesburg Estate, but at present I think it best for you to stay at Cape Town as my movements are uncertain. I cannot see any sense in putting myself in Kruger's clutches, but have not altogether put away the idea of going back. Be sure, however, that I shall do nothing rash. My letters are longer than ever they were before, but then sweetheart! I have never been so situated before, & I feel the necessity of speaking out my heart to you, and I know you won't mind but rather welcome a talk on paper – though it is so poor a substitute even

---

[397] This was evidently Catherine's pet name. Hagley Hall Archives 201/1/8.
[398] This was evidently Violet's pet name.

for one hug or one loving word from your dear old lips.

It is nearly time for me to go to St Stephen's Club, so I shall not write much more tonight, but resume later. I fear the postage on this letter will be a somewhat severe drain on my attenuated purse. By the way, I have asked Beit to invest £20,000 in 5% debentures. This will commence bringing in an income of £1,000 a year, which will keep us from starving. When the other things are realised I shall invest the money too, and eventually may decide on starting an office here, in the hope of becoming, as Daisy puts it, a 'rising junior' in about 30 years. Thank God, however, that, in addition to all this misery, we are not burdened with pecuniary cares. Even if we had nothing besides the wreckage of our fortune we need never starve, and I know you would be content to live our lives out, caring for our children, heedless of the world and its hollowness, happy in our own unalterable love.

Goodnight darling.[399]

On that same day, Catherine also wrote to Charles. It provides such a privileged insight into her thoughts and feelings that it is worth quoting virtually in its entirety:

My own old Hubbie [*sic*]

I am still patiently waiting for my first letter from you. The cable you sent from London satisfied me in some ways but in other ways only made me more sad [*sic*] than before. I just yearn for a look at your dear old face & a hug. Daisy tries to fill your place by making me sleep in her arms. The child misses you terribly too. She is always asking me to follow you soon. I am waiting to hear from you just what your plans are for the future.

Things are going on in much the same way as before. Our people are all out on bail & allowed to go to Johannesburg with the exception of the four, who have been let out on bail to the amount of £10,000 each on condition that they remain in Pretoria & are carefully watched. I don't think they will agree to it. I have not heard from J.B. again. Harry wished to know whether I would sell the carriage & horses etc. for £300, but I don't know what to do. It seems so hard to be so absolutely helpless, & have to give up all one loved & cherished in this world. I sometimes think my brain is giving way. I wish we had never seen the Transvaal. You remember how much I was against going up there. You have almost killed

---

[399] Hagley Hall Archives 201/2/30.

Chapter 13

yourself with hard work & got practically nothing in return, but abuse from dirty Hollanders. Mr Graaff made me promise not to write grumbling letters to you & not to worry you, but I cannot help it, I do feel so miserable at times, & I want you ever so badly it is a dreadful sort of vacuum to have you so far from us. Who would have thought such a thing even possible a few weeks ago? How changed our lives are now. Where everything was sunshine, there is only darkness & gloom for us.

I saw Lady Scanlen the other day. She asked to be kindly remembered to you & said Sir Thomas would feel so pleased if you would write to him to Salisbury.

...

I gave Bobbie a cheque for £150. £100 he said was for you & £50 for Gertie Liesching.[400] I had a note from Van Hulsteyn asking me whether you had authorised me to give Fred thirty pounds. I wired back that I had no instructions from you. It strikes me people are draining your purse in all directions. Mrs Feethacco [?] sent down some accounts owing in J.B. which I have checked, & sent back as requested. Do write to me fully & tell me what to do about your business matters. Woodie doesn't come out here to see us, so he is of no use to me. Eric however says he is still at the Grand Hotel in Cape Town. I offered to send him cheques, but he told me he did not require any just yet, & meanwhile borrowed from Stephan Cavanagh. He is however I believe behaving fairly, but is very much annoyed with me. I have not had a line from any of our J.B. people. My goods and chattels have arrived. Bobbie is storing the bulk. My silver however is in the Standard Bank. I have no time for more as Mrs de Smidt has called & I must go in at once.

Much love & any amount of kisses & hugs from yours
Tommie[401]

Charles wrote to her again on 28 February and this was a far more emotional letter than the first. It also includes details of his fraught relationship with Woodie, and the cause thereof:

My darling 'Wifie' [*sic*]
I fear you are going to get a very short letter this mail, for I was prevented from writing yesterday as intended and now have only a little

---
[400] Charles's sister.
[401] Hagley Hall Archives 201/2/31.

time before the mail closes.

I wanted you very badly last night and would have gave [*sic*] anything to have put my head on your shoulders, & had a good old talk, and played with your hair. I wanted your loving sympathy dreadfully. I think I had overtired myself and got rather dumpy, for I felt '*dreadful* bad'. However, I went to dine 'tête-a-tête' with Ballance, and felt better when I went to bed. Mrs Ballance has had a bad winter, & is absent from London. Her children look very well & you can scarcely imagine the interest they have all been taking in the Johannesburg developments. I have been terribly hardworking, seeing Members of Parliament and others, dining & lunching with Sir This and Lord That – always pounding away at the same old mill. I have received 'Cards' to several Ladies' at-Homes, but so far have not gone to one of them. The social engagements I have accepted have been entirely connected with the spread of my Gospel – & I cannot tell you how tired I am of it all, – not the Gospel, but the functions. I would give the world to have a quiet chat with my sweetheart! I hate parade of all sorts, & would simply detest being lionised as in a certain way, there seems a desire to do. But you know how little store we have always both set on the cheap and utterly hollow joys for which so many vulgar people set their souls. I want you. I want you! I want you!

I am sorry that I have had no letters from S. Africa to indicate what type of defence the accused intend to take, and nothing to indicate in which way the Press must be worked – so I have been working on lines which I had to lay down after consultation with people here. You will see an article in the *Saturday Review*, I am told, stating that Jameson was told not to come. This has now leaked out; and the Editor here is defending the Johannesburgers against the charge of cowardice. It is the first paper which has seriously done so.

I agree with you about Woodie. It is not fair of him, just at a time when I am heavily burdened, to throw himself on my neck again. In the name of Heaven! When is he going to stand on his own legs? Is he mad to rush to London & what is he going to do here? I only discussed in the most airy fashion the position that in future life in the Transvaal would be unpleasant, and the *probability* that I might start a business in London some day in which case we might arrange [for him] to join me. On the strength of this he wants to rush to London at my expense, & do God knows what. I may never start a business here. Certainly I will not do so for many months. These trials must be over & the air cleared before I can possibly consider ordinary work again; and besides I feel the want of taking a good rest when things are settled. Why! I don't know what my movements are to be & how soon I might go to S. Africa.

I am looking forward to the next letters from you. By the way, I heard on board that W. [Woodie] had not confined himself to tea & coffee. It is hopeless if he goes wrong again, but he does not seem to have any backbone; or in any case takes it quite as a matter of course that I should have spent all the money I have done on him, & now wants to repose on my bosom again.

I am going to a play tonight as I think all work and no 'play' very bad. Have I not been good? I cabled to Graaff that Woodie must wait, and trust that he has communicated my message. What I want him to understand – please tell him so – is that he must not look to me, but must make his own plans and carry them out. I can no longer support him without grave injustice to others & he cannot expect it, – and if I should hereafter start a business & think it feasible he might join me in it. If he is bent on coming to England the Lord only knows what he is going to do by himself & I am terribly worried at having to think of him at this time.

I see the Court has confirmed the intended in the Transvaal.[402] I am anxious to know whether Robins had any trouble about the shares which one transferred to him. Ask him whether the shares are *registered* in his name & everything free from trouble. Tell him the £15,000 Sechelelland [*sic*][403] has been cabled out & he must please get that money sharp from the Syndicate.

Give my love to D. & B.[404] I shall write to both next week. I hope to hear that you have no trouble in your mind about your Johannesburg things. How I wish you could come to me, but I think you understand clearly that to do so might do harm just now. If I should want you to come I shall cable, & then you must simply come on the wings of love. Tell

---

[402] The attachment of Charles Leonard's assets there by a court interdict.
[403] Charles Leonard served as Chairman as well as lead advocate for the Secheleland Syndicate. The Secheleland Concessions granted commercial rights in the tribal land of Kweneng, including monopolies over mining and the potential construction of railways. They were originally registered by a certain Sidney Morris, a clerk in the employ of the infamous "concessions King" Edouard Lippert, with whom Charles and Jim Leonard became partners. 'The private partnership between Lippert and the Leonard brothers is a prime example of the power of money to make bedfellows out of seeming political strangers.' (Mmegi Blogs: The establishment of the protectorate (part 13) – "The syndicate".)
http://www.mmegi.bw/index,php?aid=53546&dir=2015/august/24
[404] Daisy and Baby (Violet).

Daisy and Violet they must accept lots of love from Dad, but go without letters this week. Next week I shall write. Don't trouble your dear heart too much about the future. Now goodbye darling. Love to Dot, Eric & the others. Write to my mother & tell her I am well but have no time to write.

Just think you feel my kisses.

Ever your own

Dad[405]

Charles wrote to Catherine again a few days later, still anxious about Woodie. His letter, dated 4 March, contains a wealth of information about his activities in England and about his sense of betrayal. It reads as follows:

My dear Tommy

I was very much disappointed at getting no letters from you for two days after the other mail letters reached me & I only got my letters this morning. I am very sorry that you have been so worried about Woodie. He ought to be thoroughly ashamed of himself; and he cannot expect me to let him hang on to my coat tails any longer. He accepts as a certainty what I discussed as a possibility – I never promised him a partnership, & could not, on the face of it, have decided to start a business here, seeing the chaos in which everything, including my thoughts, was. I must put up with a certain amount of expense & annoyance, but he must learn to stand on his own legs; I have a long letter from him in which he admits transgressing his promise, but begs forgiveness on the ground of 'the strain' on him. Let us be merciful, but I cannot, dare not, associate myself in business with him, if I am to regard the interests of yourself & others. Alas! That he should be so absolutely limp.

It is too bad to be worried about him at this time when you and I both have had so much trouble. Forget this, now, sweetheart, & let us talk about something else. You must have been very 'down' when you wrote, poor thing, for your letter contains only one thing. Daisy, too, seems to have been just as bad & even Tobbie was bewailing her sad fate at being compelled to accept scoldings from Nurse. I hope things are not unpleasant though in the house. I would rather get you to come to England straight away than be uncomfortable. I know Dot and Eric are all that is good & kind, but in a 'mixed' household trouble might roam, and it would scarcely be worth your while to take a house when the end is likely

---

[405] Hagley Hall Archives 201/2/44.

to be that you will come to this country for a time, if only to get the children settled steadily at education.

If it were not that it might do mischief in other ways I should telegraph to you to come; and even now I am hovering on the brink of sending you a message to do so. After all I can see no sense in going to the Transvaal to be tried before a hostile jury, for offences I never committed, & being perhaps harshly punished. It was my fate, or my luck, to be sent out of the way of the roar, & I am entitled to take the 'benefit' of that as I am compelled to take the very serious loss which has resulted to me from events which were *rushed on me* & others. I have been very hard at work since my arrival, & have been able to do some good, I think. We worked very hard to get them out of the cottage – i.e. released on bail. I am working very hard in other directions which are strictly in accordance with my principles, – the views you know so well. I have met a great number of people, & have dined or lunched every day with strangers who might be useful – in the sense you know. The great thing is to educate public opinion & to guide it in the right direction. I had a letter from Graaff in which he expresses the hope that I will have disavowed Jameson publicly. This would be impossible without telling the whole story & that I dared not do, for it would give our enemies information. It would have been condemned here, too, in no unmeasured terms as being calculated to prejudice Jameson before his trial. I have, I think, acted justly in declining to discuss the Jameson affair at all because of the impending trials and one must wait until after the trials for such vindication as the world may give.

Meantime I have met no end of Lords & Ladies, Members of Parliament, too, and am thoroughly sick of it. I could even enjoy a 'kool breedie [*sic*]'[406] if I could see your dear old face opposite to me, and hear the prattle of the children.

I have longed terribly for you, and look forward like a schoolboy to the day when we shall meet again. I scarcely think I shall go to the Cape soon, & I am very anxious about the children's schooling. Daisy is growing too old to be neglected any longer, & to continue to do so would be a crime. I feel bound to go on with this political business until a settlement is reached & the fate of our friends is determined. After that I shall want a rest & we can then determine whether I shall undertake regular work here. It is a thousand pities that Woodie is so unstable, because he might do good for himself as well as me; – but I fear it is no use. He would keep me

---

[406] Cabbage stew, which Charles clearly found unpalatable.

on perpetual tenterhooks and might ruin us all by some negligence. Why was he born?

I have a letter from Robins in which he says the transfer of certain shares held by him has been interdicted. This will give trouble, but their value amounts to about £5,000 or £6,000, & the trouble must be got over. I don't know the effect of the interdict, which I see has been confirmed, on business moneys, & am very anxious to learn. Anyhow I have sufficient funds clear to support us in comfort even if I never did another stroke of work. Of course, keep this to yourself. If I recover any more of my interests so much the better; but I have paid heavily for political principle, & now feel I must devote myself to my family. Thank Harry heartily for all his care & thought for you. He is a brick, & I shall always look after him as far as possible. What a cur Hancock has shown himself. Fancy trying to prevent the removal of a piano & bedroom suite because he feared Jeppe's rent would not be paid. Carl Jeppe must have known of this. Poor curs some things in the semblance of men are! I am glad you have got your odds and ends sent down. What has been done with the carriage cart horses? Mr Thorpe [says] everything has been disposed of.

Bobbie seems pleased with Pluto, & I am very glad you have got Cottie with you. What a topsy turvy this has been. I daresay we shall smile at many incidents in after life. Alice [his brother Woodie's wife] writes that the *Cape Times* publishes a statement to the effect that 'Charlie' was 'taken in' and 'has sworn to get even with the Giant of Groote Schuur'. Verily people have imaginations. Whatever I may think, I have, as you know, never said anything like this, & have held my tongue. Of course I felt that everything had been precipitated. And if I found treachery – leaving Jameson's mad act out of the question – I should go to great lengths to punish it. But foolish talk must be avoided as well as [illegible] though it is astonishing how trifles travel & influence men, while solid weighty information often goes unnoticed.

I think I told you I had been out to Wernhers – I have not yet seen Hamilton Smith nor his people, but must make an effort to do so soon. I have written an article for the *New Review*, & a series of short articles which will probably appear in *The Times*. I have kept the Press going with letters about the imprisoned men, & also about the disgraceful concealment of the fact that Kruger was bound by the terms of surrender to respect Jameson's life, & the fraudulent use made of the threat to shoot him for the purpose of inducing Johannesburg to lay down its arms. Robinson is catching it hot from everybody here. He did absolutely nothing but get

Chapter 13

Johannesburg to disarm on false representations, and on promises which were never kept, & he will hear a good deal more about this matter. His conduct in telegraphing regrets to Kruger that I had 'escaped' is disgraceful & I could rouse a storm about his conduct if I liked & those men who have heard of it are very indignant.

Upington's conduct, too, is disgraceful. I was never arrested; I certainly did nothing to bring me within the terms of the extradition treaty; I am a British subject – free until arrested legally; and I leave my native soil. A British Governor & a British Attorney-General assume that I am guilty of some offence & express regrets etc. However I care too little for such *canaille*[407] to worry about the personal aspect now, especially as all my time is taken up with the larger issues involved. Britain, however, never gives up anyone charged with political offence, & sentiment here would be very strong if it were generally known that these gentry had sympathised in this manner with a set of tyrants like Kruger's gang, against a man whose only offence has been that he stood up for justice and liberty at the risk of everything in the world. Oh! The pettiness of some of our Cape politicians! It is one of the things that prompts me to turn my back on S. Africa – although it is my own country. Men like Upington for the sake of office, and the Dutch vote, are prepared to oppress their countrymen, and men with characters like Upington's can hold the scales of justice in their hands. Pah! I have no patience with the trickery of politics – while I love the science of politics as dearly as ever. I shall never be any good at S. African politics, I fear, because I could never descend to forswearing my principles for the sake of passing advantage and I am not sure that politics – applied – are not much the same everywhere, – even here in England where I believe you will find the highest standard which is attained in this fraudulent old world. Home, the children's education, books, a little writing, a little travel, and a little sport. How does this picture strike you? My only fear is that an idle man is an unhappy man. Ah! Well! Perhaps one's ideas are a little shaken up just now, and the lapse of a little time may remove some jaundice.

I have not burdened you with the names of the people I have met, as I do not think the record of dinners & luncheons eaten with people who, with perhaps a few exceptions, will pass completely out of my life in a short time would interest you. They have in the meantime been very pleasant – well-bred people who have brains usually are, and I am indebted

---

[407] riffraff (French)

to them for their interest in our cause, as they probably are indebted to me for a passing new sensation. Blessed are the philosophical! I so often thank God I married you. You are a dearie, you know, though I should not tell you so perhaps. I have not seen one face to be compared to yours in my view; – and I know of no heart to compare to yours. God bring us together soon. I am going to stop for tonight. Goodbye, sweetheart. May your dreams be pleasanter than they have been lately & may I soon be able to soothe you to rest. Kiss the babes.[408]

These letters attest to the love that Charles and Catherine felt for each other and for their daughters and reveal how much they longed to be reunited. It was, therefore, entirely predictable that within a week of writing this last letter Charles should have sent a cable asking Catherine and the children to join him in England.

---

[408] Hagley Hall Archives 202/31/1.

Chapter 13

Reform Committee prisoners playing cards in Pretoria gaol

Dr Jameson and his officers appear at the Bow Street court on 25 Feb. 1896

Dr Jameson arrives at Plymouth

Pelham, Manor Park, Chislehurst, Kent

Henry Labouchère

Sir Percy Fitzpatrick

James (Jim) Leonard

Chorus (all except Mr. Blake and Mr. Labouchere): "Well, if we can't safely do anything else, we can all sit on Rhodes. That won't hurt anyone." (Left sitting.) (*Westminster Gazette*, July 15, 1897.)

CHAPTER 14 : IN THE DOCK AND BEFORE THE HOUSE (1896-1897)

From lies of tongue and pen,
From all the easy speeches,
Deliver us, Good Lord.

– G.K. Chesterton

In the early hours of the morning of 23 February, the *Harlech Castle* anchored at Plymouth. The Raid prisoners on board were transferred to H.M.T. *Victoria* and set sail for London. Later that day, she anchored off Gravesend, where the prisoners were transferred to the tug *Corruna* and landed at the Temple Pier. They were immediately arrested and taken to Bow Street police station, amid the cheers of thousands of supporters who lined the route.

The following day, most of the Raiders were released and given railway tickets to go home. Fifteen prisoners were charged under Section 11 of the Foreign Enlistment Act of 1870: 'If any person within the limits of Her Majesty's dominions, and without the licence of Her Majesty, prepares or fits out any naval or military expedition to proceed against the dominions of any friendly State…every person engaged in such preparation or fitting out, or assisting therein, or employed in any capacity in such expedition, shall be guilty of an offence.' The defendants were granted bail of £1,000 each and were accommodated at the Burlington Hotel in Cork Street, where Rhodes maintained a permanent suite. While Jameson and his men were awaiting trial, they dined out in high society and received streams of well-wishers at their hotel. They also held a secret meeting with Chamberlain, striking a deal on an approach to the trial.[409]

Charles Leonard was also extremely busy representing the Pretoria prisoners. He wrote articles to influence public opinion, which were published in the Manchester *Guardian*, the *Pall Mall Magazine*, the *South Africa Journal*, *The Times* of London, the New York *Outlook*, the New York *New Review* and the Johannesburg *Star*.[410] He also met senior Colonial Office personnel, such as Thomas Cochrane and George Fiddes; at least fifteen M.P.s; Bouchier Hawksley, Rhodes's lawyer; and the Prime Minister, Lord Salisbury; as well as the man destined to be his successor, Arthur Balfour.[411]

On 17 March, Jameson and his fourteen co-defendants appeared before Sir John Bridge in the police court in Wellington Street for a preliminary hearing for committal. After the testimony of a few witnesses, the hearing was adjourned until the following week. It resumed on 24 March and the defendants were committed, with bail having been extended.[412]

On 9 April, Catherine Leonard and the girls arrived in England, having sailed from Cape Town aboard the *Norham Castle*, the same ship that had taken them back to South Africa after their holiday eighteen months earlier.[413] Charles had acquired an airy, spacious home in Chislehurst, Kent, and the family moved into Pelham, Manor Park, with their servants.[414] Pelham had been designed by the local architect, George Somers Clarke, and built in 1874 in the Queen Anne style.[415] The Leonards were back together as a family at last and could make the most of the lovely English springtime. Charles was even able to secure some legal work while they were there. A photograph taken of Daisy at this time shows how much she had blossomed since her previous visit to England, when she had still sported the boyish hairstyle that

---

[409] *The Third Keating Lecture – The Trial of Dr Jameson* delivered by the Rt Hon. The Lord Hoffmann of Chadsworth, 6. www.keatingchambers.co.uk/resources/publications/2004/keating_lecture_0610 Retrieved on 2/12/2014.
[410] Hagley Hall Archives 201/2/26, 201/3/37, 201/3/1, 201/4/12, 201/4/20, and 202/31/1.
[411] Hagley Hall Archives 201/2/17, 201/2/29, 201/2/36, 201/2/43, 201/3/4, 201/4/2201/4/19, 201/4/31, 201/6/13 and 201/8/6.
[412] Krout, Mary Hannah (1899). *A Looker on in London*, 236.
[413] www.ancestorsonboard.com
[414] *Cape Times*, 12 September 1896.
[415] www.rightmove.co.uk/property-for-sale/property-35947738.html Retrieved 25 September 2015.

Chapter 14

she had had as a toddler.[416]

Back in South Africa, the trial proper of the Reform Committee began on 24 April in Pretoria's Market Hall, which had been specially converted into a makeshift courtroom, with Justice Reinhold Gregorowski, Chief Justice of the Orange Free State, presiding. He had been specially appointed as he would be regarded as being less partisan than the Transvaal judges, but was also known to impose harsh sentences. He and Charles would have known each other from childhood since Gregorowski had been born in Somerset East in 1856, the same year as Charles, and had graduated top of his class at Gill College.[417] The prisoners were arraigned, after which the court was adjourned for a few days. The case resumed on 27 April, with the four leaders (Lionel Phillips, Colonel Rhodes, George Farrar and John Hays Hammond) pleading guilty to the charge of high treason and to three lesser charges. The remaining sixty accused (now including Percy Fitzpatrick, who had formerly been considered one of the leaders) pleaded guilty to two lesser charges. The following day, the judge sentenced the four leaders to death by hanging. The remaining sixty defendants were each sentenced to two years' imprisonment and a fine of £2,000, with the additional penalty that at the expiration of their term of imprisonment, they were to be banished from the South African Republic for three years.[418]

Charles must have been horrified when news of the death sentences reached him. Had he not escaped, he too would have been in that dock and would have shared the same fate. After all his efforts on behalf of his comrades, he must have been devastated. It is unlikely that he slept that night. It must, therefore, have come as a great relief when, the next day, following both a domestic and international outcry, he learned that Kruger had commuted the death sentences to fines and fifteen years' imprisonment 'as a gesture of magnanimity'.[419]

On the same day that the sentences were handed down in Pretoria, Jameson and his co-defendants appeared at a remand hearing in London. The trial proper was not to begin for another seven weeks, so Jameson, White and Willoughby used the opportunity to go fishing in Norway.[420] One cannot help wondering what the Reform prisoners, languishing in their filthy gaol in Pretoria, would have made of that! On 20 May, Kruger released ten prisoners

---

[416] Hagley Hall Archives. No catalogue number.
[417] *SALJ* 38, 1921, 1. heinonline.org>hol-cgi-bin>get_pdf
[418] Garrett, Fydell Edmund and Edwards, E.J. *op. cit.*, 261.
[419] *Ibid.*, 263.
[420] Krout, Mary Hannah. *op. cit.*, 272.

and commuted the sentences of fifty others: twenty-four had their sentences commuted to three months; eighteen to five months; four to one year; and the four leaders to fifteen years. Because two prisoners had refused to apply for clemency, their sentences remained unchanged. However, the following day, the prisoners were told that they had been misinformed: they would not be released at the end of their new terms of imprisonment; they would, instead, be allowed to submit new appeals for clemency.

Kruger soon changed his mind, however. On 30 May, all but the four leaders and the two who had not applied for clemency were released, on condition that their fines were paid at once and that they refrained from meddling, either directly or indirectly, in the internal or external affairs of the South African Republic for a period of three years. Should there be any breach of the above conditions, the sentence of banishment would come into force. Cecil Rhodes generously paid all the fines, whereupon the prisoners, having accepted the terms, were released.[421] Jim Leonard was one of them. So was his son-in-law, a man named Gordon Sandilands, who had married Jim's stepdaughter, Agnes.[422] Another to be released was William Henry Somerset Bell, who had befriended Charles while they were articled clerks.

After further negotiations, the four leaders were released on 11 June after Cecil Rhodes had paid fines of £25,000 for each of them and they had agreed to abide by the same conditions regarding political meddling as the other prisoners had done, except that, in their case, this condition would apply for a period of fifteen years. Colonel Rhodes refused to accept this condition, however, accepting instead the penalty of fifteen years' banishment. He was escorted out of the Republic the same day.[423] The British Army responded by placing him on the retired list and barring him from further involvement in official military affairs.[424]

While the above negotiations were underway, Charles Leonard once again found his integrity under attack, this time from the editor of the *Cape Times*, Edmund Garrett, who published a defamatory allegation under the name of 'Lobbyist' on 4 July. Charles was later asked about this:

> 8058. Do you remember an article in the *Cape Times* at that time? – Yes; at least when I say 'yes'…

---

[421] Garrett, Fydell Edmund and Edwards, E.J. *op. cit.*, 263-4.
[422] Archiver>SOUTH-AFRICA>2007-01>1169540766 and www.ancestor.co.za/SANDILANDS Retrieved 25 September 2015.
[423] Garrett, Fydell Edmund and Edwards, E.J. *op. cit.*, 266.
[424] *Ibid.*, 260.

Chapter 14

8059. Strongly against you? – On what?

8060. On your not going back to Johannesburg? – I have suffered a great deal of abuse because I have held my tongue over this thing, but the *Cape Times* absolutely went and published a vile slander that I had left Cape Colony in pursuance of a base compact with Kruger, that I should come to England and denounce Rhodes, the benefit of doing so coming to me. A baser lie never was published.[425]

The newspaper published telegrams, ostensibly from a Transvaal official, which seemed to confirm such a compact and claimed that there had been collusion between Charles, David de Villiers Graaff and the Transvaal Government. Graaff issued a categorical denial and Charles himself was quoted in London as saying that it was 'absolutely untrue' that his escape was connected with a supposed Transvaal ploy. He claimed that the delay in the arrest warrant being served had been caused by a legal difficulty and that friendly police had prevented his arrest in Cape Town. The matter was resolved when Jim Leonard wrote to the editor, explaining that he had sent the telegrams in question and that they had no such sinister character as had been imputed. The newspaper had the grace to accept Jim's word and said that it withdrew the assertion.[426]

Privately, however, the editor, Edmund Garrett, was reluctant to let go of the bone. In a letter to his sister, he wrote:

> My Deare [*sic*]
> You will see that we have gone in for the Disclosure business and got a little bitten though obviously on the right track…of course everyone sees that both Leonards were tools and were currying favour with Government, and they *did* wink at his escape and he *did* go home to smash Rhodes, only his heart failed him on the voyage.[427]

This must have been a particularly trying time for Charles because, besides having to contend with Garrett's scurrilous allegations, he was also ill from late June to mid-July, judging from the content of letters which he received during this time.[428] He also decided to cut ties with the ZAR for good by

---

[425] Leonard, Charles. *op. cit.*, 401.
[426] Garrett, Fydell Edmund; Shaw, Gerald (ed.). *op. cit.*, footnote 1, 70; *Cape Times* 3-10 July 1896.
[427] *Ibid.*, 70. Italics and underlining in the original.
[428] Hagley Hall Archives, 201/6/7, for example.

applying to have his name removed from the roll of attorneys there.

His former partner, Willem van Hulsteyn, continued running the Johannesburg law firm with Henry Feltham as his partner, but the adverse effects of their association with Charles Leonard were quickly felt, so the name of the firm was changed to Van Hulsteyn & Feltham. In an unflattering satirical sketch of Van Hulsteyn, the author writes:

> You [Van Hulsteyn] are one of the few who have cause to bless the Jameson Raid ... As a result of that wild incursion, you became possessed of the business of your employer, who wisely, not to say discreetly, put a distance between himself and a too assiduous autocracy – a distance he has not seen fit to retrace ... [T]he business to which you so unexpectedly and opportunely succeeded was able to count amongst its clients some of the most important mining houses here.[429]

In the meanwhile, the Cape House of Assembly had been conducting an official inquiry into the Jameson Raid under the chairmanship of that awful British parliamentarian, Henry Labouchère. It lasted from 29 May to 17 June 1896 and resulted in the publication of its findings in a Blue Book on 19 July. It concluded that the Raid was conducted almost implicitly through the support and encouragement of Rhodes and the mining houses in the Transvaal. Despite this conclusion, the Cape House of Assembly was very lenient with Rhodes. Moving the adoption of the majority report, William Schreiner acquitted Rhodes of anything low or sordid. 'His aim was high,' he said. 'I wish it had been a right one.' This was received with cheers by the House. The Committee found that Jameson was the main culprit, but even here, there was some mitigation, the majority report stating that Jameson wrongly thought himself to be carrying out Rhodes's suppressed wishes.[430] This was bad news for Jameson, though, as he was about to stand trial in England.

The following day, the trial of Jameson and his co-defendants began at the High Court of Judicature before a bench of three judges, with the Lord Chief Justice, Lord Russell of Killowen, presiding. A special jury of men satisfying higher property qualifications than usual was empanelled. However, due to an objection, the court adjourned early. The trial resumed the following morning,

---

[429] Historical Papers Research Archive, University of the Witwatersrand, A127 Van Hulsteyn, pp. 86-88.
[430] *Cape Times*, 1 August 1896.

but after the testimony of a few witnesses, proceedings were again adjourned, this time until the following week. They resumed once more on 27 July and concluded the following day with a unanimous verdict of guilty.

Jameson was sentenced to fifteen months' imprisonment, Willoughby to ten months', and the remaining four defendants to five months', all without hard labour. They were taken to Wormwood Scrubs amid the shouts and cheers of their supporters who had gathered in the Strand. After a public outcry that the Raiders were being held in a gaol for common criminals, they were moved to a separate section at Holloway. The officers lost their commissions, despite assurances that this would not be the case. However, after Willoughby had written to the War Office threatening to reveal what he and his fellow officers had agreed to keep secret regarding Imperial involvement in the plot, their commissions were restored. Willoughby was released after a few weeks because the injury he had sustained near his spine during the fighting at Doornkop was causing him great discomfort. Jameson, too, spent only a few months in gaol. He was released from Holloway on grounds of ill health on 2 December and immediately returned to South Africa.[431]

On 5 February 1897, the House of Commons Select Committee inquiry 'into the origin and circumstances of the incursion into the South African Republic of an armed force' began. The committee comprised nine ministerialists (selected by Chamberlain) and six of the Opposition. Chamberlain himself also took a seat on the bench.[432] In retrospect, as Sir Graham Bower noted, it is obvious that the 'committee was…not only a packed committee. It had a professional, a political and a patriotic interest in giving an unjust judgment for political reasons'.[433] Bower went even further, claiming that 'the opposition leaders had been squared by Chamberlain, and had consented, for political reasons, to take part in a disgraceful and cowardly and unjust farce'.[434]

Rhodes was one of the first to testify, on 16 February. Asked about telegrams which had passed between the Cape and London prior to the Raid, Rhodes, via his solicitor, declared that they were of a confidential nature, and that he objected to their being put in.[435] Despite objections, he was allowed to

---

[431] Garrett, Fydell Edmund and Edwards, E.J. *op. cit.*, 259-60.
[432] Schreuder, Deryck and Butler, Jeffrey (eds). *op. cit.*, 122.
[433] *Ibid.*, 123.
[434] *Ibid.*, 125.
[435] *The Spectator*, 13 March 1897, 10. http://archive.spectator.co.uk/article/13th-march-1897/10/mr-rhodess-evidence. Retrieved 18 November 2014.

get away with this. Sir Graham Bower took the blame for not having informed the High Commissioner, Sir Hercules Robinson, of the plot, even though this was not strictly true: he knew that Rhodes had informed Robinson, and Robinson had discussed it with him (Bower).[436] Flora Shaw, *The Times* correspondent, denied having acted as a go-between for Rhodes and Chamberlain, which was a lie.[437] But the biggest lie of all came from Chamberlain himself when he made the following sworn statement: 'I never had any knowledge, or, until I think it was the day before the actual raid took place, the slightest suspicion, of anything in the nature of a hostile or armed invasion of the Transvaal.'[438]

The facts tell an entirely different story. Chamberlain had sent a private letter to Sir Hercules Robinson late in October or early in November, asking the governor's views on a revolt at Johannesburg, 'with or without assistance from outside'.[439] Sir Hercules had replied, outlining how he intended to respond once the uprising took place, to which Chamberlain had responded via telegram, 'Agree generally with your idea in private letter of Nov. 4th... I take for granted that no movement will take place unless success is certain, a fiasco would be disastrous.'[440] Earl Grey, acting on behalf of Rhodes, had written a private letter to Chamberlain, pressing him for 'an immediate administration of the Bechuanaland Protectorate', not for commercial reasons but for 'political considerations alone' because the [Chartered] Company wanted to place itself 'in a position to help British Interests in the Transvaal in the event of anything taking place there'.[441] On 7 November, immediately after Chamberlain had authorised Robinson to transfer a strip of land in the Protectorate to the Chartered Company, Edward Fairfield of the Colonial Office in London had sent a telegram to Rhodes, stating: 'Secretary of Colonies says you must allow decent interval and delay fireworks for fortnight.'[442] Despite their protestations of ignorance of the plot, Chamberlain

---

[436] Schreuder, Deryck and Butler, Jeffrey. *op. cit.*, 43. Bower recalls how Robinson told him, 'The less you and I have to do with these damned conspiracies of Rhodes and Chamberlain the better.' He continues, 'But he ordered me to allow the troops to come down to Pitsani, and to authorize the contractor to place the forage of our imperial post office relay stations at their service, to facilitate their march.'
[437] Leonard, Charles. *op. cit.*, 454.
[438] *Ibid.*,451.
[439] Schreuder, Deryck and Butler, Jeffrey. *op. cit.*, 43.
[440] Meredith, Martin. *op. cit.*, 321.
[441] National Archives, Harare, Zimbabwe, Earl Grey Papers GR 2/1/11.
[442] Parsons, Neil. *King Khama, Emperor Joe and the Great White Queen: Victorian Britain through African Eyes*, 208.

and Robinson were 'in it up to the neck', as Rhodes put it privately.[443]

W.P. Schreiner testified in mid-March and Charles Leonard in mid-May. Having prepared meticulously, Charles made a powerful case on behalf of the Uitlanders. Unfortunately, the members of the Select Committee were not particularly interested in what he had to say. Alfred Hillier rather disparagingly wrote: 'They confessed Charles Leonard rather bored them; but the missing cables – Miss Flora Shaw – here is matter indeed, my masters!'[444]

Charles was understandably disappointed with his reception. His evidence was given 'under great pressure' because the committee seemed tired of its work 'and I had literally to force the evidence on to the record. … Schreiner got six days; I got a little more than two hours. Schreiner has never been in the Transvaal for a fortnight; I have lived there for nine years but such is fate.'[445]

Since much of Charles's testimony has already been presented in relation to the events with which it deals, it is not included here. He did, however, reveal a few details about his personal circumstances, which are illuminating:

> 7972. …Have you property still at Johannesburg? – Yes, I have property under attachment there today.
> 7973. What does that mean? – It is interdicted. An injunction has been granted by the court restraining me from using or parting with that property; it is tied up so far as I am concerned.
> 7974. Why is that? – On the ground that I am charged with high treason.
> …
> 7976. I put the question because I want to understand your position here. Are you contemplating returning to the Transvaal? – I do not see why I should go back now.
> 7977. Then for you personally, do these economical and political grievances exist? – To me, individually, today, do you mean?
> 7978. Yes. – They are not affecting me today.
> 7979. And if you do not return to the Transvaal they are not likely to? – They are not likely to; but they are likely to affect the country generally, which is my native country, and which I love.

---

[443] Harlow, Vincent. *op. cit.*, 301.
[444] Hillier, Alfred P. *op. cit.*, 31.
[445] Leonard to Robins, 11 June 1897 (*Leonard Collection* M2999 pp. 261-262).

...

8086. If you had gone back there and been tried and paid the fine, you would have been able to continue your business? – Yes.

8087. I suppose you regret that you are not able to do that? – No, I have a deep-seated sense of wrong. I say that the oligarchy in Pretoria with our Hollander friends drove me into revolt. Fate put me outside of their hands, and as I am here and have been asked to stop here and fight the thing out, I do not see why I should voluntarily go back there; and I say further that I do not consider, as an Englishman, or a man with English sentiments, I could live in that country today.[446]

The Select Committee found Rhodes and Jameson to have been responsible for the Raid but recommended no further sanctions. A minority report rightly convicted Rhodes of 'double-dealing', but the rest of the members could not bring themselves to make this finding. Instead, the colonial officials Sir Graham Bower and Frank Newton were made the scapegoats and dismissed. As for Chamberlain, who had most to lose from the inquiry, this was the Select Committee's finding: 'Neither the Secretary of State for the Colonies nor any of the officials at the Colonial Office received any information which made them or should have made them or any of them, aware of the plot during its development.'[447]

No wonder that Bower later wrote: 'Everyone knows that ministers lie to parliament and the country. Chamberlain himself has, I believe, told some startling lies in connection with the negotiations that preceded the war.'[448] Arnold Morley, a former Liberal Party cabinet minister, put it more bluntly, famously describing the hearings as 'the Lying in State at Westminster'.[449]

However, it is Kruger's reaction which is most telling. Reporting on his conversation with 'Oom Paul' after the publication of the Select Committee Report, the Randlord J.B. Robinson wrote:

The old President then became irritable, and in a loud voice shouted at me, 'Do you mean to tell me, as an intelligent man, that you accept these statements, and that you believe in them? Do you think we are fools? Do you think for a moment that we do not know the true working of this

---

[446] Leonard, Charles. *op. cit.*, 403.
[447] House of Commons Report, Conclusions, cited by Leonard, Charles. *op. cit.*, 456-8.
[448] Schreuder, Deryck and Butler, Jeffrey. *op. cit.*, 65.
[449] Rotberg, Robert I. *The Founder: Cecil Rhodes and the Pursuit of Power*, 550.

Chapter 14

Raid? ... Do you think we are so innocent as not to know that Mr Rhodes, metaphorically speaking, held a pistol at the heads of certain men in England, and said to them, If you do not support me, I will denounce you and your complicity in the Raid?' The President at this stage became more excited, and shouted so loudly that the people in the street stopped to overhear the conversation.[450]

Chamberlain famously described Kruger as 'an ignorant, dirty, cunning and obstinate man'.[451] Perhaps so, but the old President proved to be particularly astute as well. Besides extracting more than £250,000 in cash in fines, President Kruger also secured damages in the amount in excess of £1,677,000 from the Chartered Company and the British Government for 'moral and intellectual damages'.[452]

Chamberlain had somehow emerged from the Jameson 'fiasco' with his career (if not his reputation) intact, but he was determined to put Kruger in his place. In May 1896, he acknowledged that 'war in South Africa would be one of the most serious wars that could possibly be waged. It would be in the nature of a Civil War. It would be a long war, a bitter war and a costly war...it would leave behind it the embers of a strife which I believe generations would hardly be long enough to extinguish...'[453] Yet, less than a year later, Chamberlain persuaded the Cabinet to increase the British garrisons in the South African colonies by three to four thousand men. Then, in August 1897, he appointed Alfred Milner as High Commissioner and Governor-General at the Cape in place of Sir Hercules Robinson, who, having been made Baron Rosmead, had returned to England a desperately sick man. He died on 28 October,[454] but his passing was unlikely to have been mourned by Charles Leonard, who must have watched with some alarm the growing tensions in South Africa. As one who had sought to unite the white factions, it must have disturbed him to see how the Jameson Raid had driven a wedge between them. The Boers (and Afrikaners in general) felt that they could no longer trust the British, and Kruger became even more recalcitrant towards the Uitlanders.

Milner had no time for the Boers or the Afrikaners and, within a year of taking office, had concluded that war with the Transvaal Republic was

---

[450] The *Daily News*, 16 January 1900.
[451] Meredith, Martin. *op. cit.*, 352.
[452] Hole, Hugh Marshall. *op. cit.*, 282.
[453] Pakenham, Thomas. *op. cit.*, 25.
[454] https://wikipedia.org>wiki>Hercules_Robinson Retrieved 24 January 2016.

inevitable. He helped Chamberlain swing British public opinion against Kruger so that by 1899, the majority of the population was supportive of a war.

When Woodford Leonard arrived in Australia in June 1899, a journalist interviewed him about the fraught situation in South Africa. Woodford said that if England declared war, every Boer would fight to the death. There would be civil war throughout South Africa directly the first shot was fired in the Transvaal. The Cape, he added, was full of secret agents of the Transvaal. In the event of war, he did not think the Boers would attack Johannesburg and the mines, except as a last resort. Neither would they destroy property on the Rand. He believed that the 'native states', particularly Basutoland and Zululand, would assist the British. In fact, all blacks would assist the Imperial Government against the Transvaal.[455]

Chamberlain, meanwhile, successfully appealed for further troops to be dispatched, so that by the beginning of October, nearly twenty thousand British troops were based in South Africa, with more *en route*. On 9 October, the Transvaal government issued an ultimatum that the troops be removed from her borders and that further troops bound for South Africa be recalled. When this ultimatum was ignored, the Transvaal and her ally, the Orange Free State, declared war on 11 October 1899.[456]

It is beyond the scope of this book to outline the course of the war, except to point out that before Britain and her colonies emerged victorious two years later, almost 25,000 Boer, 22,000 British and 12,000 African lives had been lost in the conflict. 'At a total cost of £200 million, it was not only the costliest war Britain had waged in almost a century, but also the bloodiest, longest and most humiliating.'[457] It was called the Anglo-Boer War, but in many respects, it was also a civil war between the British colonies of the Cape and Natal on the one hand and the Boer Republics of the Transvaal and Orange Free State on the other, just as Woodford Leonard had predicted. English- and Afrikaans-speaking whites found themselves on opposite sides (as did members of many families), and relations between them were so badly damaged that it has taken more than a century for mutual trust to be largely restored.

When the British realised the Boers could not be so easily defeated in

---

[455] *The Advertiser*, Adelaide, 30 June 1899.
[456] Packenham, Thomas. *op. cit.*, xv.
[457] Cruywagen, Dennis: *Brothers in War and Peace*, 7.

skirmishes, they turned to other methods, scorched earth and concentration camps. The camps were used to strike at the men psychologically: that they could not protect, feed, see or save their immediate families emasculated them... Of the 60,000 inmates, about 28,000 Boer women and children were estimated to have died in British concentration camps...

It is understandable that many who survived the concentration camps did not wish to talk about their experiences, but instead retreated into themselves, trapping their pain and memories, as they tried to hold themselves together. [458]

As the Afrikaners tried to rebuild their shattered lives, many nurtured a deep resentment towards the British, particularly as the victors sought to cover up their war crimes.[459] It was this fertile ground that organisations like the *Afrikaner Broederbond* (Union of Afrikaner Brothers), *Ossewabrandwag* (Ox-wagon Sentinel) and the *Gesuiwerde Nasionale Party* (Purified National Party) were later able to exploit in their plans to regain control of the country.

The war ended with the signing of the Treaty of Vereeniging on 31 May 1902. Cecil John Rhodes, who had played such a major role in events leading up to the war, did not live to see the end of hostilities. He died of heart failure at his seaside cottage in Muizenberg on 26 March 1902 at the age of 48. His funeral saw thousands of Capetonians lining the route of his cortege. He had decreed in his will that he was to be buried in the Matopo (now called Motobo) Hills, near Bulawayo, in the country that bore his name. On the long journey from Cape Town, the train stopped at every major town for the inhabitants to pay their respects. His burial was attended by Ndebele chiefs, who, for the first time, gave a white man the Matabele royal salute, *Bayete*.[460]

Rhodes bequeathed a large tract of land on the slopes of Devil's Peak to the South African nation. Part of this estate became the upper campus of the University of Cape Town, where his statue looked out across the Cape Flats to the north until the university authorities had it removed to a great cheer in 2015. Students opposed to colonialism and the perceived lack of transformation at the university had for some weeks demanded that 'Rhodes Must Fall'. One student had even drenched the statue in human excrement. Another part of Rhodes's bequest became the Kirstenbosch Botanical

---

[458] *Ibid.*, 10, 13-14.
[459] Packenham, Thomas. *op. cit.*, xvi.
[460] http://en.wikipedia.org>wiki>Cecil_Rhodes Retrieved 13 November 2015.

Gardens, and the rest of the estate was spared from development. The imposing Rhodes Memorial was erected on the mountain slope, facing north as he had done when envisaging an empire extending from the Cape to Cairo. He left his mansion Groote Schuur to the Cape Colony to be used as the official residence of the Prime Minister. After Union in 1910 and the country becoming a Republic in 1961, it became the official Cape Town residence of the country's Prime Ministers and Presidents. In his will, Rhodes also provided for the establishment of the Rhodes Scholarship which funded (and continues, as the Mandela-Rhodes Scholarship, to fund) the studies of selected young South Africans at the University of Oxford, where Rhodes himself had studied.[461]

Sir Graham Bower, who harboured justifiable bitterness towards his superiors after being unfairly dismissed from office for his insignificant role in the Jameson Raid, had nothing but praise for Rhodes, writing, 'I believe that the honestest [*sic*] politician I have met was Rhodes, and he shipwrecked his career from a sense of loyalty to his country and a determination not to play the part of Judas. He was so candid that he was constantly misrepresented and misunderstood, for people considered it impossible that any man in politics could be free from selfish or sordid or personal or corrupt motives.'[462]

Many of his contemporaries were not as charitable. Sir William Harcourt, addressing the House of Commons on 20 February 1900 (on a motion to have a new enquiry into the Jameson Raid), said, 'He [Rhodes] authorised the sending of that letter to *The Times*,[463] one of the most scandalous things I ever heard of. Nobody knew better than he did that the people of Johannesburg had countermanded the raid by sending men to order it not to take place, and yet Mr Rhodes authorised the letter to be sent with a false date to deceive the British people... All the world was deceived.'[464] Charles Leonard's friend, Sir David Graaff, later described Rhodes as one of the biggest thugs he had ever dealt with and prohibited his sons from ever applying for a Rhodes scholarship or accepting one.[465] President Kruger, speaking to his biographer in Holland as he neared the end of his life, said, 'In spite of the high praise passed upon him [Rhodes] by his friends and his countrymen, he was one of

---

[461] *Ibid.*
[462] Schreuder, Deryck and Butler, Jeffrey. *op. cit.*, 89.
[463] This was the notorious 'women and children' letter, published in *The Times* on 2 January 1896, to give the impression that Jameson was on a rescue mission.
[464] Schreuder, Deryck and Butler, Jeffrey. *op. cit.*, 128-9.
[465] Dommisse, Ebbe. *op. cit.*, 78.

the most unscrupulous characters that have ever existed.'[466]

In post-colonial Africa, of course, Rhodes is regarded in a far worse light, as a murderous, pillaging, racist jingo of the worst kind. While it is certain that Charles Leonard would not have sided with Rhodes's modern detractors, it does seem likely that he would have stopped short of calling Rhodes 'the honestest [*sic*] politician I have met'.

One hesitates to think what Charles would have called Chamberlain and his minion, Milner. Bower said of Chamberlain that he 'would embrace his enemies any day, if he was quite sure it would pay him to do so and would no more hesitate to do this than he would hesitate to desert his friends under the same circumstances.'[467] Dr Jameson put it more bluntly, saying, 'Chamberlain is a damned scoundrel.'[468]

At least Milner was forthright, even if he spoke with chilling equanimity: in June 1900, in conversation with Lord Roberts, he admitted, 'I precipitated the crisis, which was inevitable, before it was too late. It is not a very agreeable, and in many eyes, not very creditable piece of business to have been largely instrumental in bringing about a big war.'[469]

From his letters to Catherine, we know that Charles would have agreed with Bower's jaundiced verdict on politics: 'The rules of the game grant success to the man who takes all the credit to himself whilst he puts all the blame that is going on his adversaries or subordinates… This is to be accomplished by brazen lying on public platforms, or by equal effrontery in the House…'[470] Such Machiavellian expediency was not for someone with the integrity of Charles Leonard. No wonder he turned his back on politics!

---

[466] Crisp, Robert. *op. cit.*, 179.
[467] Schreuder, Deryck and Butler, Jeffrey. *op. cit.*, 140.
[468] *Ibid.*, 117.
[469] Pakenham, Thomas. *op. cit.*, 115.
[470] Schreuder, Deryck and Butler, Jeffrey. *op. cit.*, xvii.

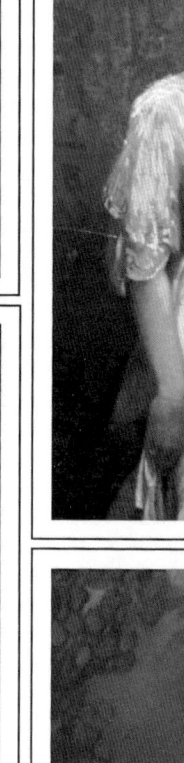

Portraits of the Leonard family, courtesy of the 12th Viscount Cobham of Hagley Hall: Charles (top left) and Daisy (bottom right), both painted by V.L. de Scerola. Violet (bottom left) is by Marshall and Catherine (top right) is by Fred Hall. All were painted c. 1908.

Chapter 14

The photograph of Daisy with an insulting caption on the back

Lady Cobham and Violet, photographed shortly before Violet's wedding in 1908

Gloria Farm, Villiersdorp, Cape

The view from Gloria Farmstead

Hagley Hall, Worcestershire

Biddlestone Hall, Northumberland

Hunting and fishing expedition, Northumberland, August 1908. Standing (l. to r.) Jim Leonard, Charles Leonard, Daisy Leonard, unknown, unknown. Seated (l. to r.) Jack Lyttelton, Violet Lyttelton (née Leonard) and Blanche Leonard (Jim's second wife). This is the last photograph taken of Jim before his death.

CHAPTER 15 : GAINING A SON AND LOSING A BROTHER
(1897-1909)

My hart verlang na die Boland

– Traditional Afrikaans folksong
('My heart longs for the Boland'[471])

Charles Leonard told the Select Committee that he saw no reason to return to South Africa and for the next six years he was true to his word. He took no further part in public affairs and lived in comparative obscurity with his family in Kent while his daughters completed their schooling and became refined young Englishwomen. His legal work kept him busy and was particularly lucrative.

Charles's brother Jim soon decided to join them. Following his release from gaol, he spent a few months wrapping up his affairs in the Transvaal and then, in September 1897, took the train from Pretoria to Delagoa Bay, where he boarded the mail ship bound for England via Cape Town.[472] His wife did not accompany him; in fact, Catharina (or Kate, as she was now known) sued him for divorce the following year.[473] It is interesting to note that Jim's

---

[471] Literally 'Uplands', the rural area beyond the Hottentots Holland Mountains, to the north-east of Cape Town.
[472] *Cape Times*, 12 September 1896.
[473] National Archives Repository of the former Transvaal Province and its predecessors (hereafter ZTPD) 5/846, 4067/1898. Illiquid Case, Divorce, Catherine Elizabeth Leonard versus James Weston Leonard, 1898.

stepdaughter Agnes named her child Doris Millicent Leonard Sandilands,[474] thus including the surname of her stepfather in the child's name. One wonders how her jilted mother felt about this.

Once Jim arrived in England, he prepared himself for joining the English bar by becoming a member of the Middle Temple, and soon acquired the rights of an English barrister under the privileges accorded to colonial advocates. In 1897, and again from 1899 to 1902, he practised at the English bar, but without the privileges of silk in the English courts.[475] He was not in England in 1898 as he returned to South Africa, where, on 15 December, he married Blanche Beresford Whyte in Cape Town.[476] She was 21 years his junior. The newlyweds then travelled to England, where they stayed with Charles and his family in Kent.[477]

However, once the Second South African War had ended in 1902, Jim took Blanche (as she preferred to be known) back to his beloved Johannesburg, to him the most congenial spot in the country. He at once recovered his position at the bar and enjoyed a most lucrative practice. 'During one year – we believe about 1906 – his fees came to more than £13,000. He avoided taking a very active part in politics, refusing to stand as a candidate for Parliament, yet, true to his old instincts, his eloquence was at the service of the Progressive [Association] – certainly the most distinctively British party.'[478] In January and February 1905, Jim made a number of speeches in the Wanderers' Hall, criticising General Louis Botha's constitutional proposals and describing his party, Het Volk (The People), as 'a pyramid of democracy standing on its head'.[479] Botha hit back at Jim in his speeches. Perhaps there was more than a little private antipathy in these speeches because Louis Botha and his family had become personal friends

---

[474] Marriage Register of St George's Anglican Church, Parktown, Johannesburg, 15 March, 1913.
[475] Anon. 'The Hon JW Leonard KC' (1905) 22 *SALJ* 132142.
[476] *The Era*, London, 17 December 1898, care of www.genesreunited.com.au/searchbna/results?...none...whyte... Retrieved 25 September 2015.
[477] "England and Wales Census, 1901," database *Family Search* (https://familysearch.org/ark:/61903/1:1:X9FS-KN2:29 August 2015), Charles Leonard, Chislehurst-, Kent, England; from "1901 England, Scotland and Wales census, "database and images, *findmypast* (http://www.findmypast.co.:n.d.; citing Chislehurst subdistrict, PRO RG 13, The National Archives, Kew, Surrey. Retrieved on 6 March 2017.
[478] Anon. 'The Hon JW Leonard KC' (1905) 22 *SALJ* 132142.
[479] DiSalvo, Charles R. *M.K. Gandhi, Attorney at Law: The Man before the Mahatma*, Endnotes, 179, 204, 209.

with Kate Leonard, Jim's jilted ex-wife.[480] As has already been noted, Jim also represented members of the Indian population in a number of high-profile cases at this time and was one of the signatories of the Manifesto of the Labour Importation Association.

Woodford Leonard also practised as an advocate in Johannesburg during the early years of the 20th Century. In 1903, he published a translation of a work by the young advocate J.B.M. Hertzog, who would later become Prime Minister of the Union of South Africa. Seeking to fill the gap between the last of the *Reports of the High Court of the South African Republic* in 1892 and the *Official Reports*, which commenced in 1894, Hertzog produced a volume of reports for the year 1893 in Dutch. Woodford Leonard's translation is entitled *Cases Decided in the High Court of the South African Republic during the year 1893*.[481] It was also in 1903 that Woodford and his wife, Alice, divorced.[482]

Woodford's elder brother Charles also had a book published that year, entitled *Papers on the Political Situation in South Africa, 1885-1895*. In the Preface, Charles writes: 'The papers which go to make up this book … may … possibly be of some use to the historians who, weighing testimony from all sides, shall seek to arrive at the truth.' An indication of how much it meant to him to leave these papers to posterity may be gathered from the final sentence of the Preface: 'To make these papers accessible, I am causing them to be reprinted, at my own expense, so that they may be placed on the shelves of every library in South Africa and of some libraries in Great Britain.'[483]

Early in 1903, Charles took his family back to South Africa, where they remained until April of the following year. There had been some interesting political developments at the Cape while the Leonards had been in England. In 1900, Dr Jameson had been elected to the Cape Parliament and in 1904, he became Prime Minister. This represented a truly remarkable comeback from the political wilderness. His career reached its pinnacle in 1911 when he was created a baronet.[484] One wonders what Charles thought of all this.

While he was in Cape Town, Charles looked up his old friend, David de Villiers Graaff, who had a lot to tell him. Graaff had resigned his seat in the Cape Parliament in 1897 in order to focus on growing his business. In 1899,

---

[480] *South Africa* magazine, Vol. CXL, 16 November 1923, 307.
[481] Published in London by Stevens and Haynes in 1903.
[482] National Archives Repository (Public Records of former Transvaal Province and its predecessors as well as of magistrates and local authorities) (hereafter, TAB) WLD 241/1903.
[483] Leonard, Charles. *op. cit.*, Preface.
[484] https://en.wikipedia.org/wiki/Leander_Starr_Jameson Retrieved 9 October 2014.

he and his brother had founded the Imperial Cold Storage and Supply Company, which eventually grew into one of the largest meat processing and distribution companies in the world, earning the Graaff brothers a fortune. Together with Sir Ernest Oppenheimer, Graaff had also succeeded in bringing all German mining interests together to form the Consolidated Diamond Mines of South West Africa, under the general control of the Anglo American Corporation. (C.D.M. is now the largest producer of gem diamonds in the world.) During the Second South African War, he had obtained lucrative contracts to supply the British Army in the field, but he had also made substantial donations towards alleviating the suffering of Boer prisoners of war and providing medical supplies to Boer women and children held under appalling conditions in British Army concentration camps. When the meat market slumped after the war, Graaff had invested in property in and around Cape Town. He had recently bought the farm De Grendel in Plattekloof, outside Cape Town, where he built up a Friesland cattle stud as well as breeding his beloved Arabian horses.[485]

It was almost certainly on Graaff's advice that Charles decided to buy some land just outside Villiersdorp (the rural village where the Graaff brothers had been born). After buying the farm Kale Ruggens, consisting of about 15 morgen, for £120 in July 1903, Charles extended his property by buying three adjoining farms, called Amandel River, Rust River and Amandel River Kom, which were transferred to him in May of the following year. (He was to acquire two more adjoining farms, called Palmiet Valley and Klipfontein, in July 1908.)[486] Charles called his farm Gloria Estate and one can understand why, commanding as it does a panoramic view across a tranquil lake to the majestic mountain range beyond. With its gracious farmhouse, it really is a glorious place to call home. When Jan Smuts visited Villiersdorp for the first time, in 1927, he was so impressed by the natural beauty of the place that he exclaimed, 'Can people sin here?'[487]

On 7 December 1903, Charles's mother Eliza passed away at the age of 77. The Leonards caught the train to the Eastern Cape in order to attend her funeral. She lies buried next to her husband in the Somerset East cemetery.[488]

---

[485] http://en.wikipedia.org/wiki/Sir_David_Graaff,_1st_Baronet. Retrieved 9 October 2014.
[486] KAB, MOOC 6/9/1894, 186. Leonard, Charles Henry Brandt, Estate Papers, 1921.
[487] Dommisse, Ebbe. *op. cit.*, 273.
[488] Gravestone of James and Eliza Leonard, Somerset East main cemetery.
eGGSA.library > Gravestones in South Africa > Eastern Cape: Ooskaap > Eastern

Chapter 15

Although it was a sombre occasion, Charles must have made the most of the opportunity to catch up with his siblings and their families. His sister Gertie had married Frederick Liesching, who had been captured and arrested with Dr Jameson at Doornkop. Now that the Second South African War was over, Fred was keen to take up farming, but lacked the means to do so. Charles proposed lending him the necessary capital. 'This assistance may have been in the nature of compensation for the part he played in the Jameson Raid, but, whatever the reason, the loan was a generous one.' Fred Liesching used this loan to put down a deposit on Milton Farm, situated about forty miles from Kokstad, and obtained a bond to cover the balance.[489]

Charles and his family sailed back to England aboard the *Kildonan Castle* in April 1904.[490] While there, Charles acquired a magnificent London mansion, 18 Kensington Palace Gardens, which he owned until 1911.[491] Today, it is the most prestigious home on 'Billionaires' Row' and is regarded as the fifth most expensive private home in the world. He also owned or rented a spacious Georgian home just a stone's throw from the sea in West Sussex, 18 South Terrace, Littlehampton.[492]

During the following summer, the Leonards visited other parts of the British Isles. Charles rented Maesllwch Castle, a mock 'medieval' castle at Glasbury-on-Wye in Wales, which was owned by the de Winton family. It is a grand and imposing house, with many towers, commanding a spectacular view of the Wye Valley. Set in a wooded park of about 300 acres, it also boasts extensive pleasure grounds. In August 1905, the famous writer Rudyard Kipling and his family joined the Leonards there.[493] Kipling had met Charles during a visit to Cape Town two years earlier and had written to him twice since.[494] The Kiplings' nine-year-old daughter Elsie became firm friends with Daisy, despite their fifteen-year age gap, while their fathers also enjoyed each

---

Cape, SOMERSET EAST/SOMERSET-OOS, Urban area > Eastern Cape, SOMERSET-EAST, Main cemetery > L-Vanne::Surnames L > LEONARD James 1823-1873 & Eliza HOWARD, 1826-1903. www.eggsa.org/library/main.php?g2-itemld=414443. Gravestone photograph contributed by Leslie de Klerk & Rosalean Flanegan, 12 May 2012.

[489] McMagh, Kathleen. *op. cit.*, 76.
[490] www.ancestorsonboard.com
[491] https://www.rbkc.gov.uk>planningedm Retrieved 14 November 2015.
[492] KAB, MOOC 13/1/4558, 264. Leonard, Charles Henry Brandt, Liquidation and Distribution Account, 1922.
[493] The Carrie Kipling Diary extracts, Kipling Society, www.kiplingsociety.co.uk/members/car_05.pdf
[494] Pinney, Thomas (ed.): *The Letters of Rudyard Kipling*, Vol. 3, Index. http://books.google.co.uk/books?isbn:0877456577 Retrieved 13 November 2015.

other's company while hunting and fishing. One suspects that at some stage Charles may have corrected his guest's erroneous impression of Dr Jameson, who is the subject of Kipling's most famous poem *If*.

Charles also spent some time in Scotland (in his papers, there is a letter addressed to him at Castle Road, Strathpeffer, Rosshire, dated 1905).[495] He was almost certainly there to attend the funeral of his eldest sister Margaret, who died that year.

Towards the end of the year, the Leonards packed up their home in Littlehampton (placing a Steinway piano in storage) and thence travelled to Southampton, where they boarded the mail ship and set sail for South Africa and their new home at Gloria Farm, Villiersdorp.

Having turned his back on the law and politics, Charles had to rely on his childhood experiences of helping his father on their farm and of his own brief experience of farming in the Great Karoo as he applied himself to his new occupation. Within a very short space of time, he had established himself as a leading livestock farmer. He imported the Wanganella strain of sheep from Australia with great success but resented the intemperate way in which some of the more established local farmers tried to emulate him.[496] Like his friend David Graaff, he also bred horses and is credited in Volume 1 of the *South African Stud Book* of 1906 with breeding the first Vlaamperde (Flemish horses) in South Africa.[497]

The same 1906 volume also identifies Charles Leonard as one of the first breeders of Friesland cattle at the Cape, recording that he owned three bulls and eight cows of this breed.[498] He also bred Berkshire boars, a classified advertisement in the *Agricultural Journal of the Cape of Good Hope* offering for sale 'pure-bred Berkshire boars, aged two to fifteen months, bred by Charles

---

[495] KAB, MOOC 13/1/4558, 264. Leonard, Charles Henry Brandt, Liquidation and Distribution Account, 1922.
[496] *The Kipling Journal*, October 1949, in which J.P. Collins writes about a *Cape Times* clip sent to him by Mrs Gertrude Chamberlain, recording how Charles Leonard had complained to Kipling of 'the coarse and greedy way this example of patience and far-sightedness had been thrown away on some of the rival farmers'.
[497] *Landbouweekblad* (Farmers' Weekly), Friday 8 September 2006, 51; and Friday 13 October 2006, 34.
http://m24lbarg01.naspers.com>2006/09/08 Retrieved 14 November 2015.
http://m24lbarg01.naspers.com>2006/10/13 Retrieved 14 November 2015.
[498] Nel, G.D. (1937). *Die Ontstaan en Ontwikkeling van Beesboerdery in Suid-Afrika en in Besonderheid van Friesveefokkery*, a thesis submitted in pursuance of the degree of Doctor of Agriculture, 99.

Chapter 15

Leonard Esq. on his well-known "Gloria" Estate'.⁴⁹⁹ He also grew oats and lucerne, his manager achieving excellent results with special mixtures of fertilizers, as recorded in an extensive study of soils of the Cape Colony:

> Three samples [of soil], Nos. 35, 36, and 37, were taken from a valley...on Mr Charles Leonard's stud farm, Kale Ruggens, now known as Gloria, which is situated about five miles south-west of Villiersdorp, on the River Zonder End. The estate is almost encircled by sandstone hills, and Mr Lange, the manager, declares that his best efforts have followed the use of guano from the Government islands, with a top-dressing of nitrate in the case of oats, and lime and sheep manure in the case of lucerne, which, under such conditions, thrives very well indeed. The surface soil at the locality where these samples were taken is a sandy loam, with a clay subsoil; the slopes adjacent to the valley consist of the usual alluvial soil, locally known as *klippers grond*.⁵⁰⁰

On 9 March 1906, Charles and Catherine celebrated their Silver Wedding Anniversary. After all the hardships and anxieties that they had endured in Johannesburg, followed by a decade of life in a foreign clime, they must have relished the prospect of a more settled and contented future now that they were at last back at the beautiful Cape.

In May 1907, Kipling and his family visited the Leonards at Gloria Farm. While there, he wrote a poem, which he autographed and gave to Charles, who had it framed and mounted on the dining-room wall. It reads:

> Work with the hope that lures us on
> Headlong to the game;
> This shall last when we are gone,
> This shall bear our name.
> When the tombstone tilts awry,
> When the date is blurred,
> This shall bear abundantly
> Mower, flock, and herd.⁵⁰¹

---

⁴⁹⁹ *Angora And* by M. Rams, journals.co.za>AJA0000018_1121. Retrieved 31 May 2017.
⁵⁰⁰ Juritz, C.F. (1909). 'The Agricultural Soils of Cape Colony', *Agricultural Journal of the Cape of Good Hope*, January 1909, 6. reference.sabinet.co.za/webx/access/journal_archive/0000018/1121.pdf. Retrieved 1 June 2017.
⁵⁰¹ *The Kipling Journal*, October 1949, in which J.P. Collins writes about a *Cape Times* clip sent to him by Mrs Gertrude Chamberlain, recording how Mr C.H. Ferrandi had taken a copy of the poem.

Kipling also gave Daisy a signed copy of his book *The Seven Seas*, writing a dedication on the title page: 'Daisy Leonard, from her obliged & obedient servant, The Author. May, 1907.'[502] This may have been a gift in appreciation of the kindness she had shown his daughter, but, given his unhappy marriage, he may have been motivated by other considerations: Daisy was twenty-five and a very attractive woman. Charles kept in touch with Kipling after this visit, sending him gifts of dried fruit.[503] Later that year, Kipling became the first English-language writer and, at 41, to date the youngest recipient of the Nobel Prize in Literature 'in consideration of the power of observation, originality of imagination, virility of ideas and remarkable talent for narration which characterize the creations of this world-famous author'.

Charles took his family to Johannesburg for the Christmas holidays so that they could spend some time with family and friends there. On Christmas Eve, Blanche Leonard gave birth to a daughter, who was named Angela.[504] Charles and his family had missed the birth of Jim and Blanche's first child because they had been in England when the boy was born on 26 January 1905. He had been named James Charles Beresford Whyte Leonard.[505]

That holiday in Johannesburg was to change young Violet Leonard's life. On Boxing Day, a young nobleman from England, John Cavendish Lyttelton, was introduced to the Leonards at the Johannesburg Races. Son of the eighth Viscount Cobham, Jack (as he preferred to be known) had served with the Rifle Brigade in South Africa during the Second South African War and had returned to the country in 1905 as Aide-de-Camp and Assistant Private Secretary to the High Commissioner to South Africa.[506] For Jack and Violet, it was love at first sight. It seems likely that Jack caught the train back to Cape Town with the Leonards and that at some stage the young lovers made a huge commitment to each other.

On his way back to England aboard the R.M.S. *Saxon*, Jack wrote passionate love letters to Violet. In the first, dated 29 January 1908, Jack

---

[502] Presentation Copy, Item 1758, advertised for sale by Maggs Brothers, Antiquarian Booksellers, 34 & 35, Conduit Street, London, in 1817.
https://books.google.co.uk>books Retrieved 14 November 2015.
[503] KAB, MOOC 13/1/4558, 264, 265. Leonard, Charles Henry Brandt, Liquidation and Distribution Account, 1922.
[504] Her full names were Marie Blanche Catherine Angela Leonard.
www.1820settlers.com/genealogy/getperson.php?personID=1152037&tree=master
[505] www.npg.org.uk>Collections. NPGx156497. Retrieved 24 January 2016.
[506] https://wikipedia.org>wiki>John_Lyttelton Retrieved 24 January 2016.

declares: 'For sure the pain of parting from you has already merged into the vision of the glorious golden future and I am radiantly happy in my love for my Violet.' The subsequent letters continue to convey his passion for Violet, although there is some evidence some days later that doubt begins to cross Jack's mind as to whether she feels the same way and to whether she is even thinking of him at all. He was writing these letters aboard ship, knowing that she would not receive them for some weeks and without hope of receiving a reply for some time. He assures her of his love: 'And I knew my Violet, I knew all the time that you were just the one and only girl in the whole wide world.'

On 5 February, Jack wrote of his intention to write to his 'future father and mother-in-law', indicating that he had already proposed to Violet and been accepted. In this letter, he describes how he 'drift[s] away into speculation of the glorious future which is before us — wonderful dreams like a tireless kaleidoscope.'[507] The happy couple arranged to be married during the English summer, just six months after they had met. This may seem a short courtship to us, but it was not unusual at the time. Jack and Violet certainly appear to have loved each other for the rest of their lives.

The following Christmas, Charles and his family once again visited friends and family in Johannesburg. One of those to spend time with them was Charles's niece, Kathleen Liesching, the daughter of his sister Gertie. She was studying to be a teacher at Normal College in Pretoria.

> My uncle, Charles Leonard, brought his family for a visit…that year and when I went to Johannesburg for the Michaelmas holidays I found them there, complete with French maids. These were gay times when we went to the races, when there were parties and when we went to the theatre.
>
> One day I sat in a sheltered corner of the balcony drying my hair when one of my cousins [probably Daisy] came out and sat chatting to me. She was kind enough to remark that I had beautiful hair and when I mourned the fact that the hard water was inclined to make it sticky, she said that I should boil lemons in the water as this helped to soften it and that the hair came out soft and glossy. Little did she know that I usually had to wash mine in cold water!
>
> It must have been difficult for my relatives to understand why I seemed to be such a country mouse and I expect that they put my

---

[507] These letters are kept at The Hive, Worcestershire Archive Service. They became open to the public in 2010 as part of the Acceptance in Lieu Scheme.

stiffness down to stupidity. Mother was very fond of saying that if a girl were her own sweet natural self she could hold her own in any society, but I had long since arrived at the conclusion that the trappings of wealth were far more necessary and without them I could not possibly feel at ease amongst those who possessed them.[508]

Kathleen had good reason to feel out of place. A few months earlier, during the Easter holidays, she had gone to stay with her aunt Susan and her family in Johannesburg. Susannah (Susie) Leonard was another of Charles's sisters. She had married the wealthy Charles Marx, who became Chairman of the *Argus* Company, was a stockbroker and was involved with Barnato's.[509]

I spent the Easter vacation with my relatives in Johannesburg and revelled once more in the luxury of rich living and remember especially the afternoon my aunt took Ilma [her daughter] and me to tea at the Carlton Hotel. It was beautiful in the Palm Court. Here an orchestra played soft music and discreet lighting flattered the guests so beautifully dressed, so impeccably groomed. This was the era of the ostrich-feather boa, of the large flowered hat and the flowing skirt.

Aunt Susan bowed to her friends and Ilma smiled at hers. How delightful it all was. The girls looked so charming with their hair curling softly about their fresh faces and, as I looked at them, I could not help contrasting the lives they led with those of us who were striving to become wage-earners. We had our being little more than thirty miles away but we might have been living in a different country, housed as we were in temporary structures of wood-and-iron with never a bit of heat to cheer us in winter, in bedrooms that grew cold, cold as ice in the small hours before the dawn. How pleasant it must be to be rich, I thought, and not have to wash one's woollen stockings in the wash-basin at night and dry them on the back of a bentwood chair before the window, not to have to 'iron' one's handkerchiefs on the mirror, not to have to wrap one's feet in one's underwear in the battle to keep warm in bed.

...

I had learned that if a woman was to hold her own as a leader in the

---

[508] McMagh, Kathleen. *op. cit.*, 135.
[509] Potter, Simon James. *News and the British World: The Emergence of an Imperial Press System, 1876-1922*, 102. https://books.google.co.za/books?isbn=0199265127 Retrieved 9 April 2017.

gilded society of the pretentious metropolis that was nouveau-riche Johannesburg, she had to be accomplished like my aunt, who had perfected her school-girl French and German by private study, who had kept up her music and who took the trouble to read the latest books and to be au-fait with world affairs and the arts.

…

I used to wonder why it was that Aunt Susan, the sister whom Mother adored, wrote so warmly of my visits. Did she really write so warmly or did my mother read in her letters a cordiality that was non-existent? Try as I would to believe otherwise, it seemed to me that my aunt did not regard me with the eyes of affection…'[510]

Charles and his family travelled to England ahead of the wedding and visited Lord and Lady Cobham at Hagley Hall in Worcestershire. It has been the Lyttelton family home since the Sixteenth Century. Out of interest, Jack's uncle, Alfred Lyttelton, who had been born there, had been sent to South Africa by Chamberlain as chairman of the committee planning reconstruction after the war. He had then succeeded Chamberlain as Secretary of State for the Colonies, despite his relative lack of political experience. When the British government's *Official History* of the war was in draft form, Lyttelton deleted all its political chapters, ensuring that there was no official record of the nation's war crimes in the concentration camps. He claimed in a confidential minute to have done so for fear of 'impeding the process of reconciliation'.[511] This was disingenuous since the Afrikaners remembered all too well the atrocities that had been committed there. Fortunately, a courageous Englishwoman named Emily Hobhouse had published her own report on what she had observed in the camps and campaigned for humanitarian relief. When she returned to England, she was vilified as a traitor by the British government and many of the media. However, she was made an honorary citizen of South Africa for her humanitarian work there and a town is named in her honour.[512]

After visiting Hagley Hall, the Leonards moved back into Pelham, Manor Park, Chislehurst, Kent. While staying there in May 1908, Charles signed his autograph in a book on hunting by Sir William Cornwallis Harris, which is today housed in the Yale University Library.[513] While in London, the family

---

[510] *Ibid.*, 132-6.
[511] Packenham, Thomas. *op. cit.*, xvi.
[512] https://wikipedia.org>wiki>Emily_Hobhouse Retrieved 24 January 2016.
[513] Harris, William Cornwallis, Sir: *The Wild Sports of Southern Africa*, British Art Center, Yale University Library.

lived in their mansion at 18, Kensington Palace Gardens. Shortly before the wedding, Jack's mother, Lady Cobham, wrote to Catherine Leonard requesting a meeting at her London home before 'the great day'. It must have been to finalise the guest list and to ensure that all the arrangements were to their mutual satisfaction.[514]

There is a rather poor-quality photograph taken at about this time of the Leonards with Jack. It is the only known photograph in which all four members of Charles's family appear together.[515] There is also a photograph of Violet with Lady Cobham taken shortly before or after the wedding.[516] Although she was slim and petite, with a fine head of hair, Violet did not have the soft features of her elder sister. She had straight, dark eyebrows, which gave her a slightly stern aspect, and her lips were thin and curved, making her appear to be sneering. Of course, it may just have been an unflattering photograph. She certainly looks more attractive in a painted portrait by Marshall which hangs in the Boudoir Room at Hagley Hall to this day.[517] There are also portraits painted by V. L. de Scerola of Charles, Catherine and Margaret (Daisy) on display at Hagley Hall.

Jack and Violet were married at St Peter's Church, Eton Square, Belgravia, on 30 June 1908. The church was decorated with masses of white blooms and broad palms. The service, which was fully choral, included the hymns *Holy, Holy, Holy, Lord God Almighty* and *Our Blest Redeemer ere He breathed*. One of the bridegroom's uncles, the Reverend Edward Lyttelton, headmaster of Eton, officiated. He was assisted by one of the bridegroom's cousins, the Reverend Edward Talbot. The bride was given away by her father, and George Lyttelton attended his brother as best man. The bridal gown was of white royale satin charmeuse, trimmed with old rose point and Brussels lace. Over a wreath of natural orange blossoms, she wore a veil of Brussels lace, the gift of her mother, and she carried a bouquet of white orchids, lilies of the valley and white heather. She wore a diamond and pearl pendant given her by her father. Eight bridesmaids attended her: her sister, Margaret (Daisy); her cousin, Winifred Taylor; Jack's sister, Rachel; his cousins Lady Helen Grosvenor and Bettine Cavendish; Ernestine Anne Leonard; Joan Preston-Whyte; and Winifred Hillier. Their dresses, made in the style of the First

---

http://orbexpress.library.yale.edu/vwebv/printResults.do?bibID=2256746&formjat=bri. Retrieved 03/07/2015.
[514] Hagley Hall Archives. No catalogue number.
[515] Hagley Hall Archives. No catalogue number.
[516] Hagley Hall Archives. No catalogue number.
[517] www.hagleyhall.com>the-state-rooms Retrieved 14 November 2015.

Empire, were of pink voile ninon over a foundation of pervenche blue, and had tucked net yokes and drapings of lace. Their hats were of pink straw to match, trimmed with pink and mauve tulle and shaded ostrich plumes of the same hue. Each carried a shower bouquet of mauve and pink sweet peas and wore a moonstone and green enamel pendant, the gifts of the bridegroom.

The guest list reads like a *Who's Who* of contemporary British High Society: it included the Prime Minister, H. H. Asquith and his wife; the former Prime Minister, Arthur Balfour; the British Ambassador to Germany, Sir Frank Lascelles; and so many members of the Peerage that the list would take up more than a page. Also present were the former British High Commissioner and Governor of Cape Colony, Lord Alfred Milner, the former Prime Ministers of Cape Colony, William Schreiner and Dr Leander Starr Jameson, the former Agent-General of Cape Colony in London, Sir Thomas and Lady Fuller, as well as his successor, Sir Somerset and Lady French. Then there were the legal luminaries, including the Chief Justice of Cape Colony, Sir Henry and Lady de Villiers, Sir James and Lady Rose-Innes, Sir Richard and Lady Solomon, and Sir Pieter and Lady Faure. Rudyard Kipling and his wife also attended.

A reception was hosted by the bride's mother at 18, Kensington Palace Gardens, at which there was a large gathering. Later in the afternoon, the newlyweds left for Hagley Hall, where they were to spend their honeymoon. In her earlier letter to Catherine, Lady Cobham had written, 'Everyone is so anxious the place should look its best & we are so delighted that Jack and Violet should start their new life together here…'[518] The bride travelled in a dress of sapphire blue voile embroidered with paler shades of blue, a shantung silk coat of sapphire blue, and a straw hat trimmed with ostrich plumes to match.

Besides the presents already mentioned, Violet was given a diamond tiara by her father, a star-sapphire and diamond and ruby pendant by her parents-in-law, a magnificent diamond and pearl ring by her husband, a set of sables by her mother, a sapphire and ruby brooch by her brothers- and sisters-in-law, and a silver toilet set by her sisters-in-law. Jack was given pearl and gold studs, cufflinks and waistcoat buttons by his wife, and a cigarette case by his sisters. The couple also received a dessert service, a Worcester china breakfast service, a Worcester china fruit bowl, a silver gravy boat, old gilt candelabra mirrors, a clock, two Brussels lace and tortoiseshell fans, an armchair, silver wine coolers, three silver salvers, an aneroid barometer, a silver dish, a china

---

[518] Hagley Hall Archives. No catalogue number.

powder pot, a leather writing set, a crystal and gold scent bottle, a crystal goblet, a vase, cut-glass decanters, a silver tea and coffee service, a picnic basket, an old print, and a number of books, including some inscribed by Kipling. The tenants and agent of Hagley estate gave them a silver salver, the villagers of Hagley gave them a mahogany office desk, the servants at Hagley Hall gave them a silver teapot, and the servants at Kensington Palace Gardens gave them Queen Anne candlesticks and an inkpot.[519]

After the wedding, Charles rented Biddlestone Hall, an ancestral pile not far from Chillingham in Northumberland. It has since been demolished after falling into disrepair. The Leonards invited a number of guests to stay while they were there. Mrs Carrie Kipling records in her diary that her family stayed there for a week or so in August 1908.[520] Kipling himself wrote to Charles on 12 August and again on 14 October.[521] Jim and Blanche also visited, as did the newlyweds Jack and Violet Lyttelton. From a photograph taken after a hunting and fishing expedition, it seems that Lord Cobham and another of his sons might also have enjoyed their company. It is interesting to note that Jack is the only male to be seated on a chair in this photograph, while his wife is seated on the ground at his feet, despite being pregnant![522]

Violet must have been grateful to have had her parents and sister in England during the first months of her married life because during September she suffered a miscarriage at nine weeks. Lady Cobham wrote to Catherine in London on 20 September, asking if she could spare Daisy for a few days to come and comfort her sister.[523] Once Violet was feeling better, her parents and sister returned to Cape Town, setting sail on 21 December.[524]

It must have been an emotional parting, particularly for Daisy, who had no other siblings. We do not know how close she and Violet were as sisters, but it would have been odd had they not formed a bond, particularly since much of their childhood had been spent cooped up in their home in Gus Street, Johannesburg. There is one telling clue, however, that there may have been some sibling rivalry, even in adulthood. It is a caption on the back of a photograph of Daisy, almost certainly written by Jack. It reads: 'Pretty of

---

[519] Hagley Hall Archives, scrapbook, including cuttings from *The Morning Post* and the *Worcestershire Echo* of 1 July, 1908.
[520] The Carrie Kipling Diary extracts, Kipling Society, www.kiplingsociety.co.uk/members_diaries.htm
[521] Pinney, Thomas. *op. cit.*, Index.
[522] Hagley Hall Archives. No catalogue number.
[523] Hagley Hall Archives 202/5.
[524] www.ancestorsonboard.com

Dardie, not plain of Gaga'. Violet, presumably, corrected the spelling by writing 'Dadi' underneath.[525] 'Dadi' was presumably the name given to Daisy by her nieces and nephew, while 'Gaga' must have been the children's name for their grandmother. In effect, Jack was suggesting that a pretty picture of Daisy might be mistaken for an unflattering one of Catherine. Why should he have written this insulting caption? It was surely not written for the amusement of their children! Did he write it because his wife was envious of her sister's beauty? Was she, perhaps, even jealous? Did Jack write it to reassure Violet that he did not find her sister attractive? If so, did she have cause to suspect him of having 'a wandering eye'? It is indeed a telling caption!

Perhaps Daisy was envious of Violet too. It must have been somewhat disconcerting that her younger sister had married before she had. After all, Daisy was already 27 by the time she and her parents set sail for home and most women – particularly attractive women from well-to-do families – were already married by that age. However, a second caption on the back of the same photograph provides us with the likely explanation: it reads, 'Was engaged, but her fiancé fell down a hatch while inspecting a ship and died'.[526] It would seem that Daisy was heartbroken and that this may explain why she remained a spinster for the rest of her days. Once again, one cannot but be struck by the insensitive or even heartless nature of the caption.

Sadly, before the Leonards returned to South Africa, they learned that Jim had been diagnosed with a malignant tumour in the brain. 'With his knowledge of medical subjects, which was considerable, he is said to have suspected its existence some time before he sought medical help. He underwent an operation while in England. Hoping to be able to carry on a consulting practice, he returned to Johannesburg. For a few weeks he was again to be seen in his old haunts, a pathetic figure. In the full vigour of his mental powers, the once facile speaker and charming conversationalist could now with difficulty articulate the simplest words.'[527]

On 5 March 1909, Jack wrote to Catherine, calling her 'Mamie', informing her of his political activities and that Violet (whom he calls Vi) was on a new diet 'which suits her amazing well. She has at this moment bright crimson cheeks, partly the result of good health and partly from the effects of a keen North wind'. He continues: 'Reports, which I am certain are much exaggerated, have come round to us concerning Jimmy's health. We both

---

[525] Hagley Hall Archives. No catalogue number.
[526] Hagley Hall Archives. No catalogue number.
[527] Anon. 'The Hon JW Leonard KC' (1905) 22 *SALJ* 132142.

however are perfectly content to think that he has overcome this further trouble as he overcame the last, and we shall continue to hope so until we hear definite news to the contrary. I do hope that by this time you are relieved of all anxiety concerning him.' [528] The almost flippant tone of these remarks suggests that it may have been Jack who wrote the captions on the back of Daisy's photograph.

On 17 July, Jim and Blanche arrived at Southampton, *en route* to Brussels, where he was to seek specialist treatment.[529]

There was also good news for the family, though: Violet gave birth to her first child, Charles John, on 8 August 1909. Lady Cobham wrote to Catherine on 12 August, thanking her for her letter 'about this most joyful event…in which *everyone* is rejoicing.'[530] The letter to which she refers must have been a telegram in order to have reached England so soon after the birth. She also sent a letter to Charles the following day, writing, 'It was very good of you to write to me in this trying time, but you know how much we are wanting to hear and how *deeply* we feel and sympathize in this great anxiety.' She then goes on to tell Charles about Jack's political aspirations and that some prominent politicians would be visiting their home to advise him in this regard. She adds, 'Violet will be a help, as she is so nice to all the neighbours & wins all hearts.'[531]

Sadly, despite these well-wishes, Jim did not recover.

It was perhaps well for one of his temperament that the end was not to be long delayed. A further operation at Johannesburg, though to a certain extent successful, failed to check the growth of the dread malady. He was persuaded to seek the services of an expert in Brussels as a forlorn hope. There, on 3rd September 1909, his illness terminated in death.[532]

The lives of Jim and Charles had been so intertwined, and they had been through so much together that Charles must have deeply mourned his elder brother's passing. He sailed to England alone and arranged for Jim's remains to be repatriated and buried in London's Brompton Cemetery, the funeral

---

[528] Hagley Hall Archives. No catalogue number.
[529] www.ancestry.com,rootsweb.Archiver>SOUTH-AFRICA-EASTERN-CAPE>2004-10>1096842737 Posted by Becky Horne. Retrieved 10 April 2017.
[530] Hagley Hall Archives 202/8.
[531] Hagley Hall Archives. No catalogue number.
[532] Anon. 'The Hon JW Leonard KC' (1905) 22 *SALJ* 132142.

Chapter 15

taking place on 8 September.[533] Blanche sent for her children, who arrived in England aboard the RMS *Armadale* Castle on 27 November and remained there with their mother.[534] Charles returned to South Africa aboard the same ship, setting sail on 12 February 1910.[535]

Jim was only in his mid-fifties when he died and left a grieving widow and two young children who would know their father only by reputation. But what a reputation! The *South African Law Journal* carried a fitting obituary:

> We do not think that the memory of Mr Leonard was altogether well served by the indiscriminate eulogy which some newspapers bestowed upon him at his death, and we wish to present a juster estimate of one who was undoubtedly a remarkable man. He was described as a great politician. Such a description is misleading. His eloquence, and the popularity resulting from his amiability, made him a force in politics. But he was not made of the stuff, perhaps often a somewhat coarse, if strong, material, of which the political leader is made. He was certainly not a *strong* man in politics, as was shown in the troubled times of 1896. And although he felt strongly on a great cause, and could sound a trumpet-call on its behalf, we doubt whether less stirring, but really more important political subjects, such as matters of social reform, excited in him more than a languid interest. His disposition strikes one as resembling the artistic disposition, and artists, using the word in its broadest sense, are not supposed to make good politicians.
>
> Mr Leonard's powers as a speaker cannot be praised too highly. He was a master of the art of expression. As the practised rider on his horse, the expert swimmer in the water, he was in his element in the use of language. He was controlled by his fine taste, his sense of proportion. While words came to him apparently at his command, he did not, as some speakers do, produce an unpleasing impression of volubility, of an excess of fluency. We have heard him in his later days at a noisy public meeting at Johannesburg, when his feelings were probably not very deeply engaged in the matter in hand. His address seemed to raise one

---

[533] www.deceasedonline.com Retrieved 19 July 2015.
[534] *South Africa* magazine, Shipping Lists, 4 December 1909. www.ancestry.com,rootsweb.Archiver>SOUTH-AFRICA-EASTERN-CAPE>2004-10>1096842737 Posted by Becky Horne. Retrieved 10 April 2017.
[535] *South Africa* magazine, Shipping Lists, 5 February 1910. www.ancestry.com,rootsweb.Archiver>SOUTH-AFRICA-EASTERN-CAPE>2004-10>1096842737 Posted by Becky Horne. Retrieved 10 April 2017.

for the moment to a higher level of taste; the epithet 'silver-tongued' would naturally come to one's lips, though it might also be reflected that the sledgehammer of the demagogue would prevail more with the crowd. The effect of his well-chosen language was heightened by a mellow and distinct voice, a sympathetic manner, pleasing features and a manly figure.

One should not forget how he excelled in a minor branch of speaking, namely, conversation. When we describe a person as a great conversationalist or talker, we are apt to think of one who monopolises the talk at a dinner-table or other gathering and looks for an audience that he considers worthy of him. But this was not the sense in which Mr Leonard was a conversationalist. Spontaneity and sympathetic responsiveness were his characteristics. He did not choose his occasions, nor his audience; he did not treat dullness with disdain. It is agreeable to think how many and diverse the persons must have been to whom he gave pleasure by his conversation. He had a wonderful memory for poetical quotations, and may be said to have brought poetry home to the unpoetical. But he was also an appreciative listener as well as a talker. Personally, as we look back to conversations with him under varying circumstances, in a railway carriage, at odd moments in court, it is the inspiring interchange of ideas, not his words, that we remember.

The utterances from the Bench at the time of Mr Leonard's death, which we print at the end of this sketch, are an authoritative record of his reputation in his profession, and we have little to add to them. The profession of a barrister has two aspects – that of the jurist or lawyer and that of the advocate. Mr Leonard was eminent in both aspects. He had a sound and deep knowledge of law, and the respect of a scientific lawyer for its principles. He entertained the objection of the true lawyer to arguing bad law. We have seen him refuse to appear in a case to uphold a contention which was repugnant to his legal instincts, although there was authority in its favour....

In advocacy he cannot be ranked too high. Mr Justice Mason in his allusions from the Bench pays tribute to his persuasiveness. One may also refer to his good taste and sense of proportion, which saved him from the extreme partisanship, the iteration, and long-windedness of so many members of the profession. It was a pleasure to collaborate with him in a case; and unless what he considered errors of taste jarred on his nerves, he was a sympathetic and courteous adversary. In his advocacy also it is pleasing to refer to the amiable elements in his character; the bullying of witnesses, for which the English common law bar has acquired an unsavoury reputation, was utterly alien to his nature.

There then follows a number of tributes from the Bench: The Judge-President, Mr J.G. Kotzé, mourned the passing of 'the greatest legal mind that South Africa has yet produced' and the Chief Justice of the Transvaal, Sir James Rose-Innes, as well as Mr. Justice Mason paid him similarly lofty tributes. Mr Esselen, K.C., at Pretoria and Mr Ward, K.C., at Johannesburg replied on behalf of the bar to the references from the Bench. They alluded to the forensic ability of the deceased and his amiable characteristics and expressed their sense of the loss sustained by the bar in his death.[536]

Charles may well have mourned, but he must also have been extremely proud of Jim's accomplishments. A bronze bust of James Weston Leonard stands in the foyer of the Law Court in Johannesburg[537] and his legacy was honoured by the University of the Witwatersrand, where the J.W. Leonard Memorial Law Library was housed until 24 December 1931, when the entire collection of over 2,000 volumes was destroyed in a fire.[538] Jim left a living legal legacy, however: his son James also studied law and went on to become a British judge. A portrait of him in his wig is housed in the National Portrait Gallery.

---

[536] Anon. 'The Hon JW Leonard KC' (1905) 22 *SALJ* 132142.
[537] McMagh, Kathleen. *op. cit.*, 73.
[538] 'The Wits Faculty of Law 1922-1989: A Story with a Personal Touch', published in *Consultus*, October 1989 (Vol. 002, No. 2, 106).

Catherine Leonard holding her third grandchild, Viola Maud Lyttelton, in 1912. Portrait painted by V.L. de Scerola

CHAPTER 16 : LOSING HIS WIFE AND LOSING HIS LIFE
(1910-1921)

*When you are away the place seems deserted,
and the sun does not shine as brightly.*

– Charles Leonard, writing to his future wife, Catherine, in 1880

Charles was back in England during the spring and summer of 1910. He no doubt visited Brompton Cemetery to pay his respects at his brother's grave. He would also have visited Jack, Violet and baby Charles. In the General Election held earlier that year, Jack had at last achieved his ambition by being elected to the House of Commons for Droitwich, a seat that he held until 1916.[539] The main reason for Charles's trip to England, however, was to attend a meeting of the London Committee of the Imperial Cold Storage Company (ICS).

After years of sustained growth, the company founded by the Graaff brothers had gone into decline and now faced bankruptcy. On 31 May, the day on which the Union of South Africa was born, the London Committee met to discuss ways of reviving ICS. Charles, who was a major shareholder in the company, wanted to disband the board and appoint a new one. When his plan met with opposition, he told a follow-up meeting on 21 June that there was only one other way out: winding down the company. Every member of the committee, except Sir James Sivewright, opposed this course of action.

---

[539] https://en.wikipedia.org>wiki>John_Lyttelton Retrieved 1/2/2016.

Undeterred, Charles returned to South Africa and lodged an application in the Transvaal Supreme Court for the disbandment of ICS. In this, he was supported by Sivewright. David Graaff, himself a major shareholder, vehemently objected, but Charles refused to back down and, on 21 December, an interim order for the liquidation of the company was granted.

At the subsequent board meeting in Johannesburg on New Year's Day, 1911, two directors in particular strongly opposed the demise of the company. Determined to rescue ICS, they proposed that the London directors resign with immediate effect and that a new board be constituted in South Africa. These two directors were the only ones initially appointed to the new board. They appointed a new managing director, under whom the fortunes of ICS began to improve, prompting him to request that the return date of the interim liquidation order against the company be postponed to 15 March.[540] Later, as ICS continued to rally, a settlement was reached with Charles and he withdrew his application in the Transvaal Supreme Court.[541] Charles and Graaff appear to have reconciled as a result.

Sometime that year, Graaff was rewarded with a baronetcy for his role in negotiating the Union of South Africa. Two years later, having married, Sir David bought Charles's former home in Sea Point, which he renamed Ostende. Like the Leonards, the Graaffs did not live there long, selling the place after they had left Cape Town in 1914. It is worth noting two further facts about this interesting house: between 1897 and 1908, when it was called Dent House, it was owned by Frank Fillis, the circus master whose Amphitheatre in Johannesburg had hosted the first meetings of the National Union; and, in 1913, while living there, Lady Graaff gave birth to a son, who as Sir de Villiers Graaff became Leader of the United Party and, as such, Leader of the Opposition in the South African Parliament.[542]

On 1 May 1911, Charles and Catherine became grandparents to their first granddaughter when Violet gave birth to Meriel Catherine. Rudyard Kipling, who had kept in touch with Charles, writing to him once again on 7 September 1910,[543] kindly agreed to be the child's godfather.

Charles, Catherine and Daisy again visited England in time for Meriel's birth because a letter that Charles's niece, Kathleen Liesching, had written to

---

[540] Archive Repository of the former Transvaal and South African Republic, Pretoria. TPD 8/36, 608/1911. Opposed application. Charles Leonard vs. Imperial Cold Storage Co. Ltd., 1911.
[541] Dommisse, Ebbe. *op. cit.*, 164-5.
[542] Murray, Marischal. *op. cit.*, 140.
[543] Pinney, Thomas. *op. cit.*, Index.

him was delivered to him there in July. Kathleen informed him that she had become engaged to Joseph Patrick McMagh. Joe (as he was known) had had a tough life, having arrived in South Africa from Ireland via Scotland when he was 6 years old. Both of his parents died when he was 19, leaving him with no money and three younger siblings to support. He gave up his ill-paid job on the mines at Barberton and accepted a job on the railways at Komati Poort, the last station in the Transvaal on the border of Mozambique. This was a post he was glad to accept because, situated as it was on the edge of a swamp in the hottest and most unhealthy part of the Lowveld, it carried an additional climatic allowance of 7/6 a day and he needed every penny to support his siblings, who were being cared for by his poor aunt in Durban. Joe spent ten years in that dreadful place, almost dying of malaria, but he faithfully fulfilled his duty and saw his siblings through school. He then accepted a transfer to cool, leafy Waterval Boven, where he fell in love with the young schoolteacher and she with him. They became engaged a few months later.[544]

Charles did not respond to Kathleen directly, but wrote instead to her mother, his sister Gertie. When next Kathleen visited her parents, she was somewhat chilled by her mother's reception:

> She was unusually silent and when we reached the house she handed me a letter, saying shortly, 'Read that...'
>
> 'That' was a letter from my mother's brother Charles, who was then living in England. It read: 'I have before me a letter from your second daughter Kathleen in which she tells me that she has become engaged to a common fellow who is obviously not her social equal. I thought that a child of yours would have been more sensible than to ally herself with a person like that and you may tell her from me that if she persists in concluding this disgraceful marriage I shall call up the bond on your farm immediately. Perhaps this may make her alter her foolish decision...'
>
> I looked at Mother for a long moment then, drawing a ribbon from around my neck, I showed her my wedding ring, thankful to be able to say, 'Joe and I were married in Johannesburg the day before yesterday so you may write and tell Uncle Charles that you no longer control me and, if you wish to add that you have washed your hands of me and are no longer responsible for my actions, you may do so.'[545]

---

[544] McMagh, Kathleen. *op. cit.*, 170-84.
[545] *Ibid.*, 187-88.

Kathleen had become painfully aware during her visits to Johannesburg that her relatives there moved in a different social circle, but this awful letter from her Uncle Charles, in which he harshly disparages her and her fiancé and spitefully threatens to penalise her parents for her decision, caused her so much hurt that she chose to end her memoirs with the incident. One can quite understand why Kathleen entitled her memoirs *A Dinner of Herbs*, quoting Proverbs 15:17:

> Better is a dinner of herbs where love is,
> Than a stalled ox and hatred therewith.

Although he no doubt meant well, Charles reveals himself for the first time in this letter not only as a snob, but as a bully too. When one considers that he had begun life as a poor *plaasjapie*, it is especially shocking that he should have adopted such a haughty tone and lofty position with poorer members of his family. Perhaps it was his great wealth or Violet's marriage into the aristocracy that had caused him to assume airs and graces. A few years before, in 1897, he had written to Catherine: 'I have met no end of Lords & Ladies, Members of Parliament, too, and am thoroughly sick of it.' Sadly, it apparently did not take long for Charles to feel at home amongst the aristocracy and for familiarity to breed contempt for the 'hoi polloi'.

The Lyttelton's third child and second daughter, Viola Maud, was born on 10 June 1912. Charles, Catherine and Daisy once again sailed to England to be there for the baby's birth and Meriel's first birthday. Kipling wrote to his son John on 1 May 1912: 'The Leonards came over yesterday with Bargee [Charles] and my small god-daughter Meriel.'[546] The Hagley Hall Archives contain photographs of young Charles and of Catherine Leonard looking into the pram containing her second granddaughter. They were beautiful children, judging by a studio portrait taken about a year later.[547]

Tragically, Catherine did not live to see her grandchildren grow up. After years of suffering, she succumbed to Bright's disease (a form of nephritis) and died in 1913 at the age of 53. She was buried alongside Jim in Brompton Cemetery.

Immediately after the funeral, Charles and Daisy returned to South Africa with heavy hearts, sensing Catherine's presence all about Gloria, yet aching with the void that her passing had left in their lives. As was the lot of

---

[546] Pinney, Thomas. *op. cit.*, Vol. 4.
[547] Hagley Hall Archives. No catalogue numbers.

Chapter 16

most women in Victorian and Edwardian times, Catherine had spent her adult life supporting her husband, raising her children and running a household. Yet she had brought to these three roles her own special qualities, particularly her stoicism during the tough times. She had also been a friend and confidante to Charles, who must have been enormously grateful to have had her wisdom and common sense to temper his sometimes impulsive instincts. To say that she had been a loving wife and mother would be to pay her a simple yet worthy tribute. Charles was heartbroken to lose her.

On 5 December 1913, Kipling wrote to Lieutenant W.H. Lewis, a career army officer whom he had met through Charles in South Africa:

> You will of course have heard the sad news about Mrs Leonard. It seems that she was suffering from Bright's disease for years. We went to her funeral in a London cemetery. Ghastly! Thank God the girls didn't come but stayed at home. Leonard came and was, as you can well believe, nearly heartbroken. They have all gone off now to the Cape as I expect Daisy will have written you by now. I am sorrier for Daisy than for anyone else. Vi has her husband and Leonard has his memories but poor Daisy has nothing – so it seems – but sorrow. She is a good girl.[548]

Charles and Daisy must also have missed Violet and her family. To help ease their pain, Jack, Violet and the children came to spend the summer with Charles and Daisy at the Cape.[549] The children must have enjoyed the hot summer weather and the chance to cool off in the lake. Jack returned to England on 3 March 1914, leaving his young family behind.[550] Violet and her children sailed home two months later, departing on 5 May.[551] Gloria must have seemed very quiet and empty without them.

The Great War broke out three months later and Jack enlisted. He fought at Gallipoli and in Egypt, the Sinai and Palestine, achieving the rank of Lieutenant Colonel.[552] It must have been a difficult time for Violet, wondering whether she would ever see her husband again. He came home on leave, of course, and Violet soon discovered that she was expecting another child. Perhaps it was this that caused Daisy to return to England to stay with Violet

---

[548] Pinney, Thomas. *op. cit.*, Vol. 4, 214. University of Sussex Library GB 181SxMs65. Courtesy of the National Trust, who own the copyright.
[549] www.ancestorsonboard.com
[550] *Ibid.*
[551] *Ibid.*
[552] https://wikipedia.org>wiki>John_Lyttelton Retrieved 24 January 2016.

and her children. They were now living in a mansion called Oakley House in Bromley Common, Kent, only a few miles from the Leonards' former home in Chislehurst.⁵⁵³ Violet gave birth to her third daughter, Audrey Lavinia, on 3 August 1918. After the war, Daisy continued living at Oakley House, no doubt helping her sister. Jack clearly had no objections. Violet gave birth to a fourth daughter, Lavinia Mary Yolande, on 21 August 1921. Charles provided each of his daughters with a very generous monthly allowance: £166, 13/- and 4d. for Daisy and half that amount, £83, 6/- and 8d., for Violet.⁵⁵⁴

During the Great War, Charles began growing wheat on his farm, which proved to be more profitable than keeping livestock. He applied modern methods to his agricultural activities and met with deserved success. In 1917, while staying at the stately Mount Nelson Hotel in Cape Town, he wrote a letter to the Minister of Agriculture, asking for his assistance. He explained that he owned four motorised ploughs, each capable of ploughing about a thousand acres in a season. Unfortunately, nobody in South Africa produced suitable shares for these ploughs and the agents who usually imported them from Britain could not do so because of the war. Without them, Charles said that he would be prevented from planting and growing any wheat. He argued that the production of food was a priority, both for the British and colonial governments, and asked the Minister for his help in persuading his British counterpart to authorise the production and export of these four ploughshares, claiming that this would have only a miniscule impact on the manufacture of armaments. After having to comply with the usual red tape, Charles was granted a Priority Certificate and the shares were duly delivered.⁵⁵⁵

Then, early the following year, he wanted to increase his wheat fields to 3,000 acres but could not obtain the required amount of fertiliser in South Africa, so once again he was advised by the Minister of Agriculture to complete a form applying for priority assistance from the British Government in procuring 100 tons of besic slag of a grade of 17% of phosphoric oxide. Charles motivated his request by explaining that he needed it urgently as he

---

⁵⁵³ KAB, MOOC 6/9/1894, 186. Leonard, Charles Henry Brandt, Estate Papers, 1921.
⁵⁵⁴ KAB, MOOC 13/1/4558, 264. Leonard, Charles Henry Brandt, Liquidation and Distribution Account, 1922.
⁵⁵⁵ KAB, MDC 34, 216, 217. Leonard, Charles, Mount Nelson Hotel, Cape Town. Apply for Priority Certificate, 1917.

Chapter 16

had to plough and plant the seeds during April and May.[556] He must have been relieved when the request was granted, and the fertiliser arrived just in time.

Besides farming, Charles also invested in property. Some years earlier, he had owned Grey Hill in Wynberg, which he had sold in August 1899, but he had had to sue the purchaser for £500, being the balance owed on the mortgage. The case was heard in the Supreme Court on 28 January 1908, with judgment in favour of the plaintiff. However, the defendant was unable to pay the debt and was declared insolvent in a final order of sequestration later that year.[557] One would have thought that it might have been a case of once bitten, twice shy, but in 1916, Charles bought Greeff's Buildings in Albert Road, Salt River, for £5,600. At first, this may have seemed a good investment as he received a tidy monthly rental income from the six tenants. However, with all the maintenance and municipal expenses associated with letting a residential property, the income was hardly worth the trouble.[558] In August 1920, a building inspector declared the second-floor balcony balustrade to be dangerous and the city sent a letter to the agents asking that it be repaired. The agents informed Charles, but he did nothing about it. A second inspection a month later found the condition of the building to be unchanged and a final notice was sent to the agents. Again, they informed Charles and again he did nothing. It was inspected again about a month later and a court order was obtained against Charles, compelling him to effect the repairs.[559]

In 1918, Charles became a founder member of the Van Riebeeck Society, which aimed to make primary sources available in a readable and enjoyable form to anyone interested in Southern African history. He was listed as a member in 1919 as well, although his address was now given as Cape Town, whereas it had been given as Villiersdorp the previous year. We know that he planned to write an account of the events before, during and after the

---

[556] KAB, MDC 48, 564/17. Application for Priority Certificate, Leonard, C. of Gloria, Villiersdorp, Caledon, Cape Province, 1917.
[557] KAB, CSC 2/2/1/297, 37 and CSC 2/2/1/298, 75. Record of Proceedings of Provisional Case, Charles Henry Brandt Leonard versus Jurgen Heinrich Friedrich Horstmann, 1908.
[558] KAB, MOOC 6/9/1894, 186. Leonard, Charles Henry Brandt, Estate Papers, 1921.
[559] KAB, 3/CT, 4/1/4/265, E370/4. C. Leonard, Dangerous balcony balustrade, 2nd floor, Greeff's Buildings, 468 Albert Road, Salt River.

Jameson Raid, and that he had already drafted an outline of the chapters.[560]

Perhaps Charles already knew or suspected that he did not have long to live because he revised his will in January 1918.[561] He visited England for the last time in 1919, leaving Cape Town on 5 September and returning nine months later, on 25 June 1920.[562] Sadly, it was the last time that his family would see their father and grandfather. During the latter half of the year, he underwent heart surgery in Cape Town, and stayed at the Mount Nelson Hotel while recuperating. However, he suffered a relapse in December so his personal physician, Dr Christian Lawrence Herman, had him admitted to the Tamboerskloof Nursing Home. Within a few days, he appeared to have regained his health, so he was discharged and returned to his hotel, where he was bright and cheerful, taking a keen interest in the affairs of the day, particularly the political developments relating to the forthcoming general election.

Just after noon on Thursday 13 January 1921, Charles left the Mount Nelson and set off down Government Avenue, either to have lunch in town or just for a stroll. Without any warning, he fell to the ground. People ran over to help him to his feet, but he was unresponsive. Doctor AD Ketchen, who happened to be making his way up the avenue, tried to revive him, but found life to be extinct. Charles had died of a massive heart attack.[563] He was only 64.

The City Late edition of *The Cape Argus*, published that very afternoon, contains a surprisingly detailed announcement of his passing, including an account of his collapse and a potted biography. News of his sudden death must have come as a dreadful shock to his friends and family, and particularly to his daughters far away in England.

The funeral was held two days later, at 3.30 p.m. on Saturday 15 January, in the Lutheran Church, Strand Street, Cape Town. The church was filled to capacity. The following report, though badly written, captures the essence of the eulogy:

---

[560] National Registers of Manuscripts and Photographs (NAREM and NAREF), National Archives' cartographic and library material, microfilms and copies TAB, Mikrofilm, M725. Charles Leonard-versameling, 1892-1921.
[561] KAB, MOOC 6/9/1894, 186. Leonard, Charles Henry Brandt, Estate Papers, 1921.
[562] www.ancestorsonboard.com
[563] https://familysearch.org/ark:/61903/3:1:33S7-95FH-YNB.jpg?ctx=CrxCtxPublicAccess&header:Content-Disposition&headerValue=attachments%3B%20filename%3Drecord-image_33S7-95FH-YNB.jpg Retrieved 26 February 2017.

Chapter 16

The Rev. F.J. Retief, in an able address, referred to the notable qualities of the late Mr Leonard's kindness of heart, and said he had never known him to refuse help in cases of genuine distress. Proceeding, the Predikant [Pastor] remarked that Mr Leonard's literary ability and attainments were of the highest. Whatever he set himself to do he did thoroughly. He possessed a legally and morally well-trained intellect, covering a wide range of knowledge; he was widely read and possessed a well-balanced judgment in matters of public interest. His one desire for South Africa was the satisfactory fusion of the two white races, the English and the Dutch. Hence he did whatever was in his power to strengthen the hands of General Botha, and supported with equal earnestness General Smuts in his zeal and earnest devotion for the peace and welfare of a united South Africa. Above all, the quality of character for which the deceased gentleman was most admired by his large circle of friends was his simple life and deep loyalty to the ties that bound him to those he loved. His heart was large and wide, and as unsullied as that of a little child. They loved him for what he was and now that he has gone they would cherish his memory to their dying day.[564]

Significantly, neither in the press report nor in the eulogy was there any mention of Charles's association with the notorious Jameson Raid, though *The Cape Argus* did allude to his chairmanship of the Transvaal National Union, which had campaigned against the injustices suffered by the Uitlanders, and to his having written and signed the famous Manifesto.

At the conclusion of the service, Handel's *Dead March* was played on the organ. There were 18 pallbearers, including Sir John Kotzé, Sir John Buchanan, Sir David Graaff, Sir Jacobus Graaff and Sir Carruthers Beattie. The mourners then proceeded to the Maitland Road Cemetery (as it was then known), where the mortal remains of Charles Leonard were laid to rest, the interment being conducted by the Reverend Alfred Daintree of Mowbray.[565] Three wreaths were placed on his grave: one from Daisy; one from Violet and Jack; and one from his grandchildren.[566] The grave is nondescript, listed as Number 676 in Block E of the Woltemade 1 Cemetery. The plain granite headstone bears the dates and locations of Charles's birth and death as well as

---

[564] *The Cape Argus*, 17 January 1921, 6.
[565] *The Cape Argus*, 17 January 1921, 6.
[566] KAB, MOOC 13/1/4558, 264. Leonard, Charles Henry Brandt, Liquidation and Distribution Account, 1922.

the following passage from the Scriptures: *And now abideth faith, hope and charity, these three, but the greatest of these is charity.*

In his will, Charles left £100 to each of his grandchildren and to sundry others. He bequeathed £250 to the Reverend Daintree as a fund to generate money in aid of missionary work in India (he had been contributing £12 per annum to this cause). He added: 'I do not make provision for charities as I have given freely during my life; my estate is reduced in value in consequence.'

To his son-in-law, the Hon. John Cavendish Lyttelton, he bequeathed his gold watch and chain, his guns, rifles, fishing rods, field glasses, and generally all his personal effects, or such of them as Jack might have desired to keep. Charles also left him all his books but asked that if there were any law books which he might not have wanted to keep, these were to be presented to the Incorporated Law Society of the Cape Province. He also left Jack the two largest Sevres vases in his collection, to be kept as an heirloom in his family, as well as the bronze equestrian statue of Napoleon the First, which Jack had always admired.

To his grandson, Charles John Lyttelton, he bequeathed the three-quarter length portrait (in oils) of his wife Catherine and hoped that he would keep it in remembrance of the grandmother who had loved him so devotedly. He added that he would like that portrait to find a permanent home at Hagley Hall (which it has). To his grandchildren Meriel and Viola, he bequeathed one each of the remaining portraits of his wife, which had been painted by Fred Hall. He declared, however, that his daughter Margaret (Daisy) was to have the life use of the three-quarter length portrait, and his other daughter, Violet, the life use of the other two portraits.

He left to his son-in-law, the Hon. John Cavendish Lyttelton, and after him to his eldest son, and after him to the eldest son for the time being who would inherit the title of Viscount Cobham, the sum of £500 in trust for the purpose of keeping beautified with flowers (with the income derived from the investment) the plot of ground in Brompton Cemetery in which his wife was buried. He added that he knew that his son-in-law and his son would never fail in that duty, and he begged their unknown successors to render him that kind office. This is an extremely touching testimony to the love that Charles had had for Catherine throughout their lives together and since her passing. Again, a few simple words convey so much.

He then turned his attention to his daughters, stating that he wished to treat them on an absolutely equal footing. In terms of a marriage settlement, Charles had promised to pay the sum of £30,000 to the Trustees for the benefit of his daughter Violet Lyttelton and others in terms of the Deed of

Chapter 16

Settlement. He now declared it his will that a corresponding sum be deducted from his estate for his daughter Margaret Leonard. He added that Violet should have no right to claim anything from his estate until her sister had received or had had secured for her this sum of £30,000, and he constituted Margaret to be the heiress of this sum. This is a strange condition, to say the least, suggesting that there might have been some suspicion on his part that Violet might try to take advantage of her sister's vulnerability.

He then appointed his daughters to be heiresses in equal measure of the residue of his estate, property and effects, both moveable and immoveable.

Charles and his brothers Jim and Woodie had also invested their separate inheritances from their late mother in a combined trust to help support their sister Emily, who had married a photographer, Thomas Hassall Howard. Besides caring for their mother until her death, Emily had also raised three sons in their home in Paulet Street, Somerset East. The family clearly struggled to make ends meet. Charles willed that this trust should continue to support Emily for the rest of her life. Thereafter, the trust was to help support the three daughters of his late sister Margaret.

With regard to his estate Gloria, he declared that it was to some extent in an experimental stage. He therefore gave his Executors a wide discretion in deciding whether to keep it or sell it. As Executors, he appointed Daisy, Violet, Jack and Dr Herman.[567]

An appraiser valued Gloria Estate at just over £6,000, while the property containing Greeff's Buildings in Salt River was valued at £5,600. This meant that the immovable property was valued at just over £11,600. The movable property, including shares, farm goods and Charles's Sunbeam motor car, was valued at £63,692. He had also left £9,317 in cash. After some claims had been deducted, the total worth of the estate was £85,771.

No immediate decision was made regarding Gloria Estate, but Greeff's Buildings were sold for £6,000 (after the balcony balustrade had eventually been repaired with funds from the Estate) and the Sunbeam motor car for £450. Once various costs and claims had been deducted, as well as the amounts bequeathed in the will, the residual value of the Estate was £13,190, which was shared equally between Daisy and Violet. They chose to have the entire value of their separate inheritances converted to Stock Market shares.

Gloria farm continued to be managed by Frank Bybee, assisted by three permanent labourers: Petrus, Andrews and Frikkie. The manager earned a

---

[567] KAB, MOOC 6/9/1894, 186. Leonard, Charles Henry Brandt, Estate Papers, 1921.

salary of £20 a month and the labourers received wages of between 2 and 3 shillings a day, which equates to about £5 each a month. In addition, every Friday, each labourer received his weekly 'dop' (the notorious yet ubiquitous helping of wine), although Charles had outlawed the practice while he was in charge. The farm also employed seasonal workers (mainly women) at planting time. Mr J.D.H. de Villiers was permitted to rent the farmhouse until 31 March 1922, pending a decision on its future.[568]

The farm was sold soon afterwards and has since been sub-divided so that a housing estate, known as Gloria Estates, could be developed. The original farmstead still exists and is now known as Gloria Guesthouse.

---

[568] KAB, MOOC 13/1/4558, 264. Leonard, Charles Henry Brandt, Liquidation and Distribution Account, 1922.

Chapter 16

Rudyard Kipling, family friend

Oakley House, the home of Jack and Violet Lyttelton and their family in Kent. Daisy stayed with them here.

The Mount Nelson Hotel, where Charles Leonard was residing when he died.

The last photograph taken of Catherine Leonard, admiring her third grandchild, Viola, in 1912, shortly before her death.

Charles Leonard's funeral was held in the Lutheran Church, Strand Street, Cape Town.

Charles Leonard's striking grandchildren, Meriel, Viola and Charles Lyttelton

CHAPTER 17 : KITH, KIN AND CO-CONSPIRATORS (1922-1987)

What we leave behind is a part of ourselves.

– Anatole France

Both of Charles Leonard's elder sisters, Margaret and Annie, predeceased him. His younger sister, Emily Howard, died at the age of 70 in 1928.[569] His younger brother Woodford, who had caused him so much anxiety, emigrated to New Zealand and died in Auckland at the age of 63 on 6 January 1930.[570] Another sister, Gertie Liesching, died in Somerset West, near Cape Town, at the age of 90 on 29 March 1955.[571]

Jack Lyttelton's father, the 8th Viscount Cobham, died seventeen months after Charles Leonard, in June 1922.[572] As the eldest son, Jack inherited his father's titles and entered the House of Lords. Violet was now known as Lady Cobham. Like his father and uncle before him, Jack was a successful cricketer. He represented Worcestershire County Cricket Club in three first-class matches in 1924-25 and was President of the Marylebone Cricket Club in 1935, again emulating his father and uncle.[573]

The Cobhams' son, Charles (nicknamed 'Bargie'), was also a keen sportsman. Like his father and grandfather before him, he played first-class

---

[569] KAB, MOOC 6/9/3448, 20971 Mary Emily Green Howard, Estate Papers, 1928.
[570] Auckland Council Libraries. Cemetery Records, 1930.
[571] www.wikitree.com/wiki/Leonard-3717 Retrieved 24 January 2016.
[572] https://wikipedia.org>wiki>Charles_Lyttelton Retrieved 24 January 2016.
[573] https://wikipedia.org>wiki>John_Lyttelton Retrieved 24 January 2016.

cricket, making his debut for Worcestershire in 1932 while in his final year at Trinity College, Cambridge, where he read for a degree in law. However, he then joined the Territorial Army and resumed his cricketing career only in 1934. He went on to play 104 First Class matches, his highest score being 162 and his best bowling figures 4/83. He captained the club between 1936 and 1939, when the outbreak of the Second World War effectively ended his cricketing career.[574]

While he was at university in 1930, tragedy struck the family when his eldest sister Meriel, who had already suffered two serious illnesses that year, succumbed to tubercular meningitis at the age of 19. It must have been a dreadful shock to her parents, aunt and siblings. She had been a lively young woman, taking part in sports, particularly hunting. She had also been a member of the prestigious (and later controversial) Mitford Society.[575]

Violet and her two eldest daughters had posed for celebrity photographic portraits shortly before Meriel's illness. Violet's features had softened, and she had filled out since her youth, but her daughters were both statuesque beauties.[576]

In 1939, Jack was appointed Under-Secretary of State for War in the government of Neville Chamberlain, a position he retained until May 1940.[577] His son Charles saw active service with the Expeditionary Force in France from 1940 and became commander of the 5th Regiment from 1943. He married Elizabeth Makeig-Jones on 30 April 1942 in Chelsea. They had four sons and four daughters.[578]

His sister Viola also served in the armed forces, gaining the rank of Flying Officer in the Women's Auxiliary Air Force, where she was mentioned in despatches. She married Robert George Grosvenor, fifth Duke of Westminster on 3 December 1946. They had one son and two daughters. From 1979 until her death in 1987, Viola, Duchess of Westminster, was Lord Lieutenant of Fermanagh. She died in a car accident near Dungannon, County Tyrone, on 3 May 1987, aged 74.[579]

John Cavendish Lyttelton, Lord Cobham, died on 31 July 1949, at the

---

[574] https://wikipedia.org>wiki>Charles_Lyttelton Retrieved 24 January 2016.
[575] https://themitfordsociety.wordpress.com>Meriel_Lyttelton Retrieved 24 January 2016.
[576] National Portrait Gallery. NPGx124642; Viscountess Cobham with her daughters, by Bassano Ltd, 26 June 1929.
[577] https://wikipedia.org>wiki>John_Lyttelton Retrieved 24 January 2016.
[578] https://wikipedia.org>wiki>Charles_Lyttelton Retrieved 24 January 2016.
[579] https://wikipedia.org>wiki>Viola_Grosvenor Retrieved 24 January 2016.

Chapter 17

age of 67.[580] Violet must have been heart-broken. Jack had apparently retained his sense of romance throughout the years of their married life, as one of his later letters to her attests: 'You and only you are just all the world to me.'[581] [There may have been some significance to his inclusion of the words 'and only you', but we shall let that pass.]

Their son Charles had intended following in his father's footsteps and entering the House of Commons, but his father's death precluded that. As the only son, he inherited his father's titles and entered the House of Lords. He became the ninth Governor-General of New Zealand on 5 September 1957, serving until 13 September 1962. In this position, he avoided commenting on contentious topics and established sound working relationships with the three Prime Ministers who served under him. Although an aristocrat, he proved popular. He was seen as an outdoors man with sporting prowess in cricket and golf, and an informed knowledge of rugby. He was also good with a gun and enjoyed fly fishing, all attributes that resonated well with New Zealanders. Like his maternal grandfather, he was a skilled orator, too, and a book of his speeches sold 50,000 copies. He donated the proceeds to the Outward Bound organisation, which he had established in New Zealand to encourage young people to experience the great outdoors. He was made Honorary Colonel of the Queen's Own Warwickshire and Worcestershire Yeomanry on 1 April 1969. He died in Marylebone, London, on 20 March 1977, aged 67.[582]

His mother, Violet Lyttelton, Lady Cobham, the younger daughter of Charles and Catherine Leonard, died on 28 February 1966, aged 80.[583]

And what of her elder sister, Daisy? After her father's death, she continued living in London, but for how long she lived with her sister's family is not known. In 1937, when she was 56, Daisy visited South Africa for the last time, setting sail for Cape Town on 19 November, apparently in order to wrap up her affairs there.[584] She signed her will in the Mother City on 24 March 1938[585] and then returned to her home at 13, Cheyne Walk, Chelsea.

This picturesque street with its tall and elegant Victorian houses overlooking the Thames Embankment has attracted famous people from all walks of life and continues to do so. Past and present residents include:

---

[580] https://wikipedia.org>wiki>John_Lyttelton Retrieved 24 January 2016.
[581] The Hive, Worcestershire Archive Service.
[582] https://en.wikipedia.org>wiki>Charles_Lyttelton Retrieved 24 January 2016.
[583] https://wikipedia.org>wiki>Violet_Yolande_Lyttelton Retrieved 24 January 2016.
[584] www.ancestorsonboard.com
[585] KAB, MOOC 6/9/23109, 5294/54.Margaret Elizabeth Catherine Leonard, Estate Papers, 1954.

writers George Eliot, T.S. Eliot, Henry James, Bram Stoker, W. Somerset Maugham, Hilaire Belloc and Ian Fleming; artists J.M.W. Turner, Dante Gabriel Rossetti and James Abbott McNeill Whistler; philosopher and pacifist Bertrand Russell; actors Laurence Olivier and Jill Esmond; pop stars Mick Jagger, Marianne Faithfull, Keith Richards , Ronnie Wood and Adele; professional footballers George Best and Sol Campbell; caricaturist Gerald Scarfe; and multi-millionaires John Paul Getty II and Roman Abramovich. Daisy's home had previously belonged to the composer Ralph Vaughan Williams from 1905-28.[586]

Sir de Villiers Graaff, the son of Charles Leonard's friend Sir David, was a frequent visitor to Number 13 as Daisy kept open house for South African students and those from other parts of the Commonwealth. 'She and I were great friends and I visited her on my way through England after the war when the houses next to her had both been bombed. She, however, was unshaken, and said she had slept on a sofa in the front hall throughout the war and had never been much affected by the bombing. "Of course," she said, "I am solid."'[587]

Daisy may have survived the Blitz, but she succumbed to breast cancer on 9 September 1954, shortly before her 73rd birthday. Her niece, Viola Grosvenor, was at her bedside at 10, Cheyne Walk, where Daisy was being nursed. Her funeral took place at Christ Church, Chelsea, on 14 September.[588] Tragically, none of the financial bequests that Daisy had made in her will could be disbursed because her estate was declared insolvent, her liabilities in England exceeding her assets.

Given my earlier speculation about possible friction between Violet and Daisy, the circumstances of the latter's death do seem to confirm some sort of estrangement. Why, as she neared her end, was Daisy not cared for in Violet's home? Why was Violet not present at her sister's deathbed? Why had the comparatively wealthy Cobhams not assisted Daisy financially? It is certainly poignant that Daisy, who had remained a spinster and had lost both her parents, should have died without her only sibling by her side, especially since Daisy had not hesitated to comfort and support Violet in her times of need. Whatever the reason may have been, it is a sad note on which to end this record of Charles Leonard's family.

---

[586] https://en.wikipedia.org>wiki>CheyneWalk. Retrieved 24 May 2017, and *Evening Standard*, 22 July 2014. www.standard.co.uk>News>Diary. Retrieved 24 May 2017.
[587] Graaff, Sir de Villiers. *Div Looks Back: The Memoirs of Sir de Villiers Graaff*, 51.
[588] KAB, MOOC 6/9/23109, 5294/54.Margaret Elizabeth Catherine Leonard, Estate Papers, 1954.

Chapter 17

Let us now turn our attention to Charles's co-conspirators to record what became of them.

Immediately after his release from gaol, Colonel Francis Rhodes was escorted out of the Transvaal and went to help his brother Cecil, who was engaged in the Second Matabele War in the region which had been given his name, Rhodesia.[589] Shortly after learning of the assassination of the Ndebele spiritual leader, Mlimo, by the American scout Frederick Russell Burnham, Cecil Rhodes walked unarmed into the Ndebele stronghold in the Matobo Hills and persuaded the warriors to lay down their arms, thus ending the war.[590] Colonel Rhodes then set sail for North Africa to join Kitchener's Nile expedition as war correspondent for *The Times*. At the Battle of Omdurman on 2 September 1898, he was shot and severely wounded in the right arm. For his services during this campaign, he was restored to the British Army active list. During the Second South African War, he continued to work as a war correspondent. He was trapped for the duration of the Siege of Ladysmith and participated in the relief of Mafeking. After his brother's death in 1902, Francis took possession of Dalham Hall in England, and erected a village hall in Cecil's memory. After retiring from the British Army in 1903, he served as managing director of the African Trans-Continental Telegraph Company until his death in 1905 at his brother's former Cape Town estate, Groote Schuur.[591]

Lionel Phillips also left South Africa after his release from gaol and settled in England until the end of the Second South African War, when he was persuaded to return to Johannesburg. He was once again elected Chairman of the Chamber of Mines and in 1910 was elected to the first Union House of Assembly. In 1912, he was created a baronet. On 11 December 1913, he survived an assassination attempt when he was shot at five times by a trade unionist. The following year, he moved to London as Managing Director of the Central Mining Company and advised the British Government on the metal industry during the First World War. He returned to South Africa in 1924 and settled on the farm Vergelegen near Somerset West, where he died on 2 June 1936. He and his wife Florence left South Africa a major legacy through their art collections.[592]

John Hays Hammond, who had almost died while imprisoned at Pretoria, also left South Africa after his release, but never returned. Back in

---

[589] https://wikipedia.org>wiki>Cecil_Rhodes Retrieved 24 January 2016.
[590] *Ibid*.
[591] https://wikipedia.org>wiki>Frank_Rhodes Retrieved 1 February 2016.
[592] https://wikipedia.org>wiki>Lionel_Phillips Retrieved 1/2/2016.

the U.S.A., he became a close friend of President William Howard Taft and was appointed a special U.S. Ambassador. He became Professor of Mining Engineering at Yale University from 1902 to 1909, and from 1903 to 1907 was employed as general manager and consulting engineer for the Guggenheim Exploration Company, developing mines in California and Mexico. In 1923, he made a fortune while drilling for oil with the Burnham Exploration Company. He became personal friends with Presidents Grant, Hayes, Roosevelt and Coolidge and was featured on the cover of *Time* magazine in the issue of 10 May 1926. He died on 8 June 1936. His son, John Hays Hammond Jnr, patented over 400 inventions and is widely regarded as the Father of Radio Control.[593]

George Farrar, who had been interested in horses since his time as Chairman of the Johannesburg Turf Club, raised two regiments of South African Horse during the Second South African War, and was appointed Major in the Kaffrarian Rifles. He saw service in the Orange River Colony, took part in the defence of Wepener and saw action at Wittebergen, south of the Orange River. He was mentioned in despatches and was awarded the Queen's South Africa Medal, a D.S.O. for his military service during the Second South African War and was knighted in 1902. After the war, he became Chairman of the Chamber of Mines and became an ardent supporter of the controversial scheme to solve the labour problems of the mines by importing cheap Chinese workers on three-year contracts. Despite strong opposition, the plan was implemented in 1904 and over 60,000 Chinese were brought into the country over a period of three years. Farrar represented Boksburg East in the Legislative Assembly of the Transvaal in 1906 and was Leader of the Opposition. He represented Georgetown in the first Union Parliament in 1910-11 and was created a baronet in 1911. He withdrew from politics that year and devoted all of his time to his business enterprises on the East Rand. Farrar was visiting England when the First World War began. He enlisted and was ordered to German South West Africa as Assistant Quartermaster-General to Brigadier Duncan McKenzie's force with the rank of Colonel. Based in Lüderitz Bay, he was in charge of the restoration of the railway and of supplying the forces with water, critically important in that semi-desert region. On 19 May 1915, while returning from a tour of inspection, his motor trolley collided with a construction train at Kuibis, near Gibeon, and he succumbed to his injuries the following day. He was buried in

---

[593] https://wikipedia.org>wiki>John_Hays_Hammond Retrieved 1/2/2016.

his family's Bedford Farm Cemetery east of Johannesburg.[594]

James Percy Fitzpatrick wrote a history of events leading up to the Jameson Raid, entitled *The Transvaal from Within*, which was published in 1899 and greatly influenced public opinion in Britain in the years leading up to the Second South African War. It emphasised the grievances of the Uitlanders against the Boer Government and advocated British intervention on their behalf. At the outbreak of the Second South African War, Fitzpatrick helped establish the Imperial Light Horse Regiment. Prevented by ill health from active service, he became Official Adviser on South African Affairs to the British Government. In 1902, he was appointed Knight Commander of the Order of St Michael and St George. He served as an M.P. in the Transvaal Legislature and successfully defended his Pretoria seat in 1906 and 1910. His famous novel *Jock of the Bushveld* was published in 1907. He was one of eight Transvaal representatives at the National Convention of 1908-9, which resulted in the formation of the Union of South Africa in 1910. He and General J.B.M. Hertzog worked out the agreement that recognised English and Dutch as the official languages of the Union. He also helped establish citrus farming in South Africa. It was Fitzpatrick who suggested that a moment of silence be observed annually on 11 November in honour of the dead of the First World War. King George V approved and, on 7 November 1919, proclaimed 'that at the hour when the Armistice came into force, the 11th hour of the 11th day of the 11th month, there may be for the brief space of two minutes a complete suspension of all our normal activities…so that in perfect stillness, the thoughts of everyone may be concentrated on reverent remembrance of the glorious dead'. Fitzpatrick died in Uitenhage in 1931, aged 68. Some of the wild animals that he had brought back to Johannesburg after hunting trips formed the first stock of the Johannesburg Zoo.[595]

Whatever one may think of his politics or professional life, each of these men made a significant impact on the society in which he lived. Each was a leader in his own right and yet all five of them were happy to acknowledge Charles Leonard as their leader during the tumultuous events of 1894-5. What was it about this man that made him stand head and shoulders above the rest?

The final chapter will attempt an appraisal of Charles Leonard's significance, both to those fortunate enough to have known him during his lifetime and to those of us seeking to learn something from him a century later.

---

[594] https://wikipedia.org>wiki>George_Farrar Retrieved 1 February 2016.
[595] https://wikipedia.org>wiki>James_Percy_Fitzpatrick Retrieved 1 February 2016.

The author placing flowers on the grave of Charles Leonard in the Woltemade Cemetery, Maitland, outside Cape Town. It is a humble monument for such a great man, but he would not have wanted anything more elaborate. R.I.P.

CHAPTER 18 : A GREAT SON OF SOUTH AFRICA (1856-1921)

> *I pray you, in your letters,*
> *When you shall these unlucky deeds relate,*
> *Speak of me as I am; nothing extenuate,*
> *Nor set down aught in malice.*
>
> – *Othello*, V, ii, 340-344

Significantly, Charles Leonard chose to begin his will with the following words: 'I declare first of all that I have always regarded South Africa, where I was born, as my home and my domicile.'[596] He may have deemed this appropriate from a legal perspective, but this assertion is also significant in underlining his lifelong loyalty to the land of his birth.

Throughout the conflicts and crises which consumed his energies, strained his relationships and impaired his health, Charles Leonard always tried to do what was best for his country, whether it was attempting to unite what he called the white 'races', striving to avert a civil uprising by campaigning for equal rights, leading a revolutionary movement aimed at overthrowing a corrupt regime by force of arms, demanding justice for those unjustly charged with treason, or trying to avert a potentially bloody, costly and divisive war. The fact that his efforts were largely unsuccessful is a reflection not on his commitment to these causes, but on the power, guile and

---

[596] KAB, MOOC 6/9/1894, 186. Leonard, Charles Henry Brandt, Estate Papers, 1921.

duplicity of those ranged against him. Throughout it all, we have seen how Charles was guided by his principles and acted with the utmost integrity, which is more than can be said for most of the other leading players. That simple affirmation at the start of his will informs the world, in typically understated fashion, that Charles Leonard was first and foremost a patriot.

Let us for a moment indulge in some speculation as to what might have occurred had things gone according to plan and the Jameson Raid succeeded in ousting President Kruger and his regime. As the leader of the National Union, Charles Leonard would – so it was claimed – have acted as Interim President until a plebiscite could determine the way forward.[597] Given the political climate in the Transvaal at the time, it is likely that some form of qualified franchise would have been instituted (perhaps permitting every adult white male who had resided in the Transvaal for at least two years to vote). Given his popularity and the respect he commanded amongst the Uitlander community, Charles would almost certainly have been elected Leader of the National Unionist Party (or whatever the Uitlander party came to be called), which, based on its popular following and the role it had played in ousting the Kruger regime, would undoubtedly have swept to victory in the polls. Charles Leonard would then have become President of the Transvaal Republic. Of course, all of this would depend upon his having agreed to stand for election, which, given his professed reluctance to seek public office, is by no means a certainty.

As an 'Afrikander' who was sympathetic to the fears and insecurities of the Dutch inhabitants of the Transvaal, Charles would no doubt have gone out of his way to reassure them that their rights would be guaranteed in the new Constitution and he would have worked tirelessly to unite the English- and Dutch-speaking factions. Such was the nature of the man. This would have reassured the political leaders in the Orange Free State of his bona fides and would have earned him plaudits in the Cape Colony, where he had influential friends in the Afrikander Bond and in the Cape Parliament. IF – and it is a capital IF – he could have persuaded the governments of the Cape Colony and Orange Free State that they and their people would benefit by accepting the Transvaal's proposal to form a united South Africa, it is likely that Natal, 'the last outpost of the British Empire', would have felt obliged to

---

[597] Henry Labouchère published a copy of the proposed provisional government, drawn up by the Reform Committee, which identified Charles Leonard as President. The first Prime Minister of the Union of South Africa, General Louis Botha, also made this claim on a public platform in 1910. (*Cape Times Weekly Edition*, 7 September 1910, 15)

follow suit. Who knows? Charles Leonard might well have become the first Prime Minister of the Union of South Africa – at least a decade before union was actually accomplished. In fact, given his republican views, he might well have become the first President of the Republic of South Africa, seventy-odd years before the country actually became a republic.

If this scenario had come to pass – and I honestly believe it to be entirely plausible – the tensions which led to the outbreak of the Second South African War (the Anglo-Boer War) would almost certainly have been diffused and almost 70 000 lives could have been spared as a result. Furthermore, the consequent rift between Afrikaans- and English-speaking South Africans could have been averted, with the result that the rabidly racist National Party would not have been able to muster sufficient support to come to power.

How President Leonard and his government would have dealt with the thorny issue of race relations is a matter of conjecture, but it is tempting to believe that our country would have taken a less confrontational path. In his Manifesto of 1895, Charles devotes a section to Native Affairs, which sheds some light on his views:

> The administration of native affairs is a gross scandal, and a source of intense loss and danger to the community. Native Commissioners have been permitted to practise extortion, injustice, and cruelty upon the natives under their jurisdiction. The Government have allowed petty tribes to be goaded into rebellion. We have had to pay the cost of the 'wars', while the wretched victims of their policy have had their tribes broken up, sources of native labour have been destroyed, and large numbers of prisoners have been kept in gaol for something like eighteen months without trial. ... We have had revelations of repulsive cruelty on the part of the field-cornets. ... The Government is enforcing the *plakkerswet*,[598] which forbids the locating of more than five families on one farm. The field-cornets in various districts have recently broken up homes of large numbers of natives settled on 'Uitlanders" lands, just at the time when they had sown their crops to provide the next winter's food. The application of this law is most uneven, as large numbers of natives are left on the farms of the Boers. ... The sources of the native labour supply have been seriously interfered with at the borders by Government measures, and difficulties have been placed in the way of transport of natives by railway to the mines. These things are all a drain

---

[598] Literally, squatters' law.

upon us as a State, and many of them are a burning disgrace to us as a people.⁵⁹⁹

While he certainly condemns some of the atrocities perpetrated against black people, Charles also regards blacks as a cheap labour force and criticises government policies that hamper their 'supply'. He may well have outlawed some of the cruel treatment meted out to blacks, but he is unlikely to have protected them from labour exploitation.

Of course, back in 1895, there was no organised black liberation movement (the African National Congress was founded only in 1912), but the drafting of a national Constitution would have presented its architects with the opportunity to consider the rights of the black population, and particularly the vexed question of extending the franchise, or at least granting the 'natives' democratic representation in the all-white parliament. More than anything else, it was Kruger's reluctance to extend the franchise to the Uitlanders that had driven Charles into politics. It was only because this right was persistently denied that, in desperation, he became a revolutionary. As someone who knew what it was like to be denied the vote, he – more than most – might have understood the risks of denying the black majority this right. He might even have foreseen that continued intransigence might drive others to become revolutionaries. He was, in his own words, a man who 'stood up for justice and liberty at the risk of everything in the world'.⁶⁰⁰

However, such speculation pushes conjecture beyond the bounds of credibility. Although Charles did include an occasional critique of the Kruger government's 'native' policy in his speeches, it was his brother Jim who came to enjoy a much greater reputation as a 'negrophile', based on his opposition to the 1882 Cape Diamond Trade Act and his calls for Britain to 'fulfil its obligations to the native tribes of the Protectorate of Bechuanaland'.⁶⁰¹ At best, Charles Leonard showed only a passing interest in improving the lot of his black compatriots. As a man of his time, he would almost certainly have shared the prevalent view of white South Africans that any talk of extending the franchise to the black population would be foolhardy or, at best, premature.

So much for conjecture. Let us now return to our appraisal of what

---

⁵⁹⁹ Leonard, Charles. *op. cit.*, 31-32.
⁶⁰⁰ Hagley Hall Archives 203/31/1, letter of 4 March 1896.
⁶⁰¹ Mmegi Blogs. The establishment of the protectorate (part 13) - "The syndicate" http://www.mmegi.bw/index,php?aid=53546&dir=2015/august/24 Retrieved 3 April 2017.

Chapter 18

Charles Leonard did manage to accomplish during his lifetime.

After being admitted to the Cape bar as a young man, he soon came to be regarded as one of Cape Town's leading attorneys and was offered a partnership in a prominent law firm. His proposals on divorce law reform in cases of malicious desertion were taken up by others in the legal profession and led to the scrapping of the preliminary court order for restitution of conjugal rights, at first in Cape Colony, but eventually throughout South Africa. He also played a leading role in the establishment of the Incorporated Law Society in the Cape, which was the forerunner of the Law Society of South Africa. After moving to Johannesburg, Charles became one of the foremost lawyers there and established a very lucrative practice, which he was later able to continue in England.

He had already shown an interest in social reform while living in Cape Town when he wrote an article urging the English- and Dutch-speaking sections of the population to unite rather than become polarised, and to share a commitment to a common destiny. Whether his article had the desired effect we shall never know, but the Afrikander Bond in the Cape did become less strident in its demands for independence from the British Empire after its publication. It was in Johannesburg, however, that his public-spirited inclinations really came to the fore and led him to speak out against political injustices and corruption. He proved to be a powerful orator and gained the respect and admiration of the English-speaking populace to such an extent that he was elected Chairman of the Transvaal National Union, the organisation campaigning for the democratic rights of the Uitlander population. He drafted the Union's Manifesto and fearlessly challenged the notoriously prickly and irascible President Kruger. He even won the admiration of some of the progressive Dutch citizens, such as the editor of *Land en Volk*, Eugène Marais, who wrote to Charles in August 1893, urging him not to do anything to alienate Boer sympathies and praising the magnetism of his personality, which, he said, would give Charles practically limitless influence among the Boers.[602]

It was only in desperation at Kruger's intransigence that Charles gave his support to Rhodes's conspiracy to overthrow the Boer government by armed insurrection. It was not a role that came naturally to him as he was a mediator by nature, but he felt that he and his organisation had exhausted all legal channels of seeking justice and redress of their grievances. As the leader of the planned insurrection in Johannesburg, Charles must be held partly

---

[602] *Leonard Collection* M3002 (Marais to Leonard, 23 August 1893)

accountable for the coup's failure, even though the majority of the blame must be attributed to Cecil John Rhodes and Dr Jameson, who precipitated the crisis. Charles proved too gullible in trusting Rhodes (who had ulterior motives), and in trusting John Hays Hammond and Colonel Francis Rhodes with the military preparations (which they grossly neglected), and in trusting the impetuous Dr Jameson with leading the force that was to come to their aid (when he proved to be impulsive, cocksure, headstrong, and entirely unsuited to leading such a campaign) and in trusting Jameson (and Rhodes) with the 'women and children' letter (which they duplicitously misused for their own ends). To be fair to Charles, though, he was not to know that all four of these co-conspirators would let him and his comrades down so calamitously. To his credit, he refrained from publicly criticising any of them after the Raid and seems not to have borne any grudges. He even invited Dr Jameson to his daughter's wedding!

His nervous breakdown after the Raid will be considered a weakness only by the most insensitive of commentators. One has only to consider the following: the strain of planning an armed insurrection and of having to keep the preparations secret; the strain of knowing that the requisite arms and ammunition had failed to reach Johannesburg, even at the eleventh hour; the strain of having his co-conspirators threaten to pull out when rumours surfaced that Jameson intended coming in under the Union Jack; the strain of having to endure a long train trip in order to seek reassurances while the whole enterprise was about to implode; the relief of having the rebellion deferred, only to suffer the shock of discovering that Jameson had disobeyed orders and had set off on his march; the strain of having to remain in Cape Town against his better judgment in order to try to reduce the political fallout; the strain of worrying about his family's safety both in Johannesburg and on the train to Cape Town; and the strain of having to leave his family in Cape Town in order to return to Johannesburg to stand by his comrades, despite the enormous risks involved, only to have to turn back *en route*. No wonder he suffered 'congestion of the brain and nervous prostration'! It was this mental aberration that caused the editor of the *Cape Times*, Edmund Garrett, to claim that Charles lacked the strength of character to lead a revolution. While I respect his right to hold this opinion, I beg to differ.

It was during his time in England shortly after the Raid that Charles revealed that he did indeed possess admirable strength of character. He refused to disclose the truth of Jameson's role in the Raid in order to avoid prejudicing his trial, even though Jameson did nothing to counter the accusations of cowardice levelled at Charles and the people of Johannesburg, which 'the good Doctor' could quite easily have squashed, without any prejudice to himself or his confederates. Charles even resisted the temptation to have his wife and children join him in England, fearing that this might play into the hands of the Transvaal authorities and prejudice those still in prison there because it would signal that he had no intention of returning to stand trial with them. He devoted most of his time, a great deal of his energy and much of his money to campaigning on behalf of those in prison and helping to counter the propaganda being disseminated by Kruger's emissaries in Europe. Sceptics may argue that Charles was trying to salve his conscience for having deserted his followers, but there is sufficient evidence to assert that his intentions were entirely honourable.

He appeared before the House Select Committee and testified honestly, which is more than can be said for others involved in the planning and execution of the Raid. Some of his testimony bears repeating: '…let me state emphatically that I personally not only had no selfish or monetary object, but that on the contrary I risked everything, that I have lost a practice worth ten thousand a year, while a considerable amount of my property in the Transvaal in under interdict, and that I had not directly or indirectly any motive except the establishment of right.'[603]

Once he had returned to South Africa and turned his hand to farming, Charles met with almost immediate success. His introduction of the Wanganella strain of sheep from Australia was such a masterstroke that other farmers immediately followed his example. His first attempt at breeding horses led to an entirely new breed (Vlaamperde) being registered in the South African Stud Book and this continues to be a popular breed of horse to this day. He also had the foresight to convert much of his land to the cultivation of wheat during the First World War, when food became scarce. Because he used modern farming methods, his yield was considered sufficiently significant that he was granted two Priority Certificates to receive agricultural assistance from the British government.

Charles fathered two daughters, the elder of whom was by all accounts a most delightful person and the younger of whom married a nobleman and produced highly successful children. Charles continued to love and support his daughters financially even in adulthood. As a husband, Charles was unapologetically romantic and sentimental, and his marriage to Catherine was one of enduring mutual love and devotion. As a brother, he helped support his less fortunate siblings and he enjoyed a particularly close relationship with

---

[603] Leonard, Charles, *op. cit.*, 71.

his elder brother Jim. He also supported numerous charities and worthy causes.

The crucial question, of course, is 'So what?' Charles Leonard may well have lived an extraordinary and largely exemplary life and have participated in some momentous events, but of what relevance is all of that today? Are there any lessons that we in the 21st Century can learn from his life or those times? I contend that we can learn a great deal from both the man and the times in which he lived.

Dame Rebecca West once said, 'It is sometimes very hard to tell the difference between history and the smell of skunk.'[604] Anyone who reads the story of the politics of imperialism in South Africa from the discovery of gold to the end of the Second South African War will see an example of democracy gone wrong.

> Since Plato, as Janet Smith has reminded us, there have been available to those of power and influence the notions of deception, of concealment, of secret decisions and of misleading statements, which were to be justified on the theory that such actions were ultimately in the name of the general good of society. Implicit in this notion is the attendant supposition of an elite that they, and only they, in making decisions, can make them with safety or surety.[605]

Democracies, however, rely on transparent government in order for the electorate to hold their representatives to account. When governments try to hide what they are up to from the prying eyes of the media and the public at large, they are undermining democratic principles and processes. And when leaks do occur, as is their wont, the subsequent attempts by the guilty to cover their tracks result in what we today euphemistically call 'spin' but is in reality a pack of lies. As Abraham Lincoln so pithily noted, 'You can fool all the people some of the time, and some of the people all the time, but you cannot fool all the people all the time.' The events which form the background of this book 'offer a lesson for states claiming to be democracies, whether in South Africa or more globally. Open processes in democratic politics [ought to] remain at the very heart of modern government in the 21st Century as well'.[606]

---

[604] https://www.brainyquote.com/quotes/authors/r/rebecca_west.html Retrieved 24 January 2016.
[605] Schreuder, Deryck and Butler, Jeffrey. *op. cit.*, lvi.
[606] *Ibid.*, xii.

Chapter 18

And what of Charles Leonard himself? He provides us with a fine example of how ordinary citizens need to respond when they see democratic principles and processes under threat or direct attack. Charles spoke out against Kruger's abuses of power and, when legal channels of protest were exhausted, took the courageous decision to resort to armed struggle. In this sense, he was a forerunner of those who took up arms against the apartheid regime. Their motivations were remarkably similar. They were not prepared to roll over and back down when confronted by the abuse of power and the denial of their legitimate rights, and neither should we.

Charles entered politics for the right reasons, too: he was motivated by the desire to serve those whom he represented. He did not seek personal aggrandisement, or wealth, or power, as so many of today's politicians do. He sought to right the wrongs that were afflicting the oppressed. Oh, for politicians who would emulate his example in South Africa and the world today!

He also provides us with an example of courage and tenacity in the face of defeat and of scurrilous attacks on his integrity. He may have seethed inside, but he maintained a dignified silence and steely composure in public, withstanding the temptation to defend himself or offer excuses or pin the blame on others. People in prominent public positions, and even the man in the street, could benefit by emulating his example of stoicism.

The most pressing lesson, however, is the need for South Africans and others in areas of conflict to unite for the sake of peace. Charles Leonard spent his entire adult life trying to unite English- and Dutch-speaking South Africans. He foresaw the dreadful consequences of a rift between them and spoke out against extremists on either side of the divide who sought to polarise people for political ends. It has taken more than a century for that particular rift to heal, but there is another, potentially far more destructive wedge that now threatens to drive South Africans apart.

The world marvelled at South Africa's relatively peaceful transition to democracy in 1994 and Nelson Mandela won universal acclaim for his focus on nation-building and social cohesion. For a while, South Africans and the world at large joined Archbishop Tutu in celebrating our having become 'a rainbow nation'. However, this optimism failed to take into account the deep divisions which still exist in our society, the legacy of more than three hundred years of oppression, exploitation, violence and deprivation during the colonial and apartheid eras. Today, there is a new breed of extremist, no longer characterised by home language, but by race. Passionately angry and bitter people, both black and white, are once again seemingly intent on driving

South Africans apart. Racist invective and vitriol have become far more prevalent over the past few years, spewed out by extremists on both sides of the divide. Now more than ever, we need mediators like Charles Leonard, who have one foot in each camp, to step forward and appeal to reason rather than emotion in re-envisioning a united nation and striving to make it a reality. Our country cannot afford another bloody and divisive civil war!

In conclusion, I hope that I have succeeded in presenting Charles Leonard as a truly remarkable son of South Africa – one who merits far greater public acknowledgement than he has received. It is, I believe, a travesty that his reputation has been tarnished by historians who judged him prematurely, that his bones lie in an obscure and neglected grave, and that his compatriots have never heard of him. It is my fervent wish that, having read this book, the reader will agree that Charles Leonard deserves, belatedly, to be accorded his rightful place amongst the leading figures in this nation's history and that his memory ought to be honoured.

ACKNOWLEDGMENTS

As I pieced together Charles Leonard's biography after its subject's near-century of undisturbed repose, I was pleasantly surprised to find that my research yielded a much more comprehensive corpus of relevant sources than initially anticipated. Though I worked on my own, I have incurred debts to a number of people who assisted me, and it is only fitting that I should acknowledge them here.

I am particularly indebted to Charles Leonard himself, who, as a founder member of the Van Riebeeck Society, sought to make primary sources available to those interested in South African history and ensured that copies of his correspondence, articles, speeches and other papers were preserved for posterity. Without them, his authentic 'voice' would have been lost. Wherever possible, I have allowed him to tell his story through his own words.

I also owe a huge debt of gratitude to Joyce Purnell, volunteer archivist at Hagley Hall, the ancestral home of the Lyttelton family in Stourbridge, Worcestershire, and by extension to the 12th Viscount Cobham, for allowing me to make copious use of the family records, many of which have only recently been catalogued. Joyce not only responded to my numerous requests for assistance, but did so promptly and professionally, often providing me with more than I had requested, scanning and e-mailing copies of private letters, family photographs and portraits. I frankly acknowledge that, were it not for her help, this book could not have been written.

I also thank Erika le Roux, Head of Client Services at the Cape Archives Repository, for her helpful advice and friendly assistance in accessing relevant archival material, as well as her colleague, Jaco van der Merwe, who pointed me in the right direction to begin with. The National Automated Archival Information Retrieval System (NAAIRS) website also proved indispensable and I extend my thanks to all those who compiled this extensive online facility. For anyone wanting to research family history in South Africa, this is the place to start.

The staff of the National Library in Cape Town were also most helpful, even providing me with a magnifying glass to read virtually illegible newspaper text on microfilm!

It would be remiss of me not to pay tribute to those writers whose works I have found to be particularly helpful: May Bell for her seminal work on the 1820 Settlers; Guy Butler for his record of growing up in the Karoo; Thelma Gutsche for her fascinating history of the Wanderers Club and early Johannesburg; Martin Meredith for his coverage of South African history from the discovery of gold to the Second South African War; and Owen Rogers for his dense history of the Johannesburg lawyers in a time of turmoil.

I also acknowledge the work done by Shirley Paladin in transcribing early Johannesburg street directories and by Becky Horne and Sue Mackay in administering a variety of Eastern Cape and 1820 Settler message boards, both of whom do so on behalf of RootsWeb, an Ancestry.com community. I found these websites very helpful.

Credits for the photographs and illustrations are included in the list of illustrations. Every effort has been made to obtain the necessary permissions with reference to copyright material, both illustrative and quoted. I apologize for any omissions in this respect and will be pleased to make the appropriate acknowledgements in any future edition.

Some of the illustrative material is understandably of inferior quality as it was sourced from old postcards, photographs and newspapers.

Constructive criticism, as usual, came from my younger daughter, Janice, currently completing her doctorate in politics at the University of Oxford. Her firm yet tactful suggestions were heeded in every instance. Thankfully, she gave me plenty of encouragement as well!

I also thank my wife, Lee, for her love, patience and understanding as I repeatedly withdrew into a bygone era.

Lastly, I thank my publisher, David Hilton-Barber, for putting his faith in this book, and the graphic designer Anthony Cuerden for the cover design and page layout.

SELECT BIBLIOGRAPHY

Ackroyd, Peter (2000). *London: The Biography*. London: Vintage.

Anonymous (1896). *Jameson's Heroic Charge, A True Story: A Complete Vindication of the Reform Movement*. Publisher not identified.

Argus Editorial Team (1896). *From Manifesto to Trial. A Full History of the Jameson Raid and the Trial of the Members of the Reform Committee and of Dr Jameson and His Staff*. Cape Town: Argus Printing and Publishing Company.

Austin, Alfred (11 January 1896). *Jameson's Raid*. London: *The Times*.

Ayliff, John (1963). *The Journal of Harry Hastings – Albany Settler*. Grahamstown: Grocott & Sherry.

Beinart, William (2003). *The Rise of Conservation in South Africa: Settlers, Livestock, and the Environment 1770-1950*. Oxford: Oxford University Press.

Bell, May. (1963). *They Came from a Far Land*. Cape Town: Maskew Miller.

Bell, W. H. Somerset (1933). *Bygone Days*, London: H. F. & G. Witherby.

Bickford-Smith, Vivian (1987). *Cape Town at the Advent of the Mineral Revolution (c. 1875): Economic Activity and Social Structure*. Johannesburg: Wits History Workshop Papers. URI: http://hdl.handle.net/10539/7698.

Butler, Guy (1981). *Karoo Morning: An Autobiography 1918-35*. Cape Town: David Philip.

Cape of Good Hope (South Africa) Parliament, House Select Committee on the Jameson Raid (1896). *Majority Report of the Select Committee on the Jameson Raid into the Territory of South African Republic*. Cape Town: W.A. Richards.

Creswicke, Louis (1900). *South Africa and the Transvaal War*, Vol. 1, 143. Edinburgh: T.C. & E.C. Jack.

Crisp, Robert (1964). *The Outlanders: The Men Who Made Johannesburg*, London: Peter Davies.

Cruywagen, Dennis (2014). *Brothers in War and Peace: Constand and Abraham Viljoen and the Birth of the New South Africa*. Cape Town: Zebra Press.

Davis, Richard Harding (1897). *Dr Jameson's raiders vs the Johannesburg reformers*. New York: Robert Howard Russell.

DiSalvo, Charles R. (2013). *M.K. Gandhi, Attorney at Law: The Man before the Mahatma*. California: University of California Press.

Dommisse, Ebbe (2011), *Sir David Pieter de Villiers Graaff: First baronet of De Grendel*, Cape Town: Tafelberg.

Fitzpatrick, J. Percy (1900). *The Transvaal from Within: A Private Record of Public Affairs*. London: William Heinemann.

Gandhi, Mohandas K. (trans. Desai, Mahadev) (1948). *Gandhi's Autobiography: The Story of My Experiments with Truth*. Washington D.C.: Public Affairs Press.

Gandhi, M.K. (1962). (Compiled and edited by Kher, S.B.). *The Law and the Lawyers*. Ahmedabad: Navajivan.

Gandhi, M.K. (1999). *The Collected Works of Mahatma Gandhi (Electronic Book)*. 98 volumes. New Delhi: Publications Division Government of India.

Garrett, Fydell Edmund. (ed. Shaw, Gerald) (1984). *The Garrett Papers*. Cape Town: Van Riebeeck Society.

Garrett, Fydell Edmund, and Edwards, E.J. (1897). *The Story of an African Crisis: Being the Truth about the Jameson Raid and Johannesburg Revolt of 1896, Told with the Assistance of the Leading Actors in the Drama*. Westminster: Archibald Constable.

Graaff, Sir de Villiers (1993). *Div Looks Back: The Memoirs of Sir de Villiers Graaff*. Cape Town & Johannesburg: Human & Rousseau.

Great Britain Colonial Office (1899). South African Republic: correspondence relating to the claim of the South African Republic for damages on account of Dr Jameson's raid. London: Printed for H.M. Stationery Office by Darling. (page images at HathiTrust)

Select Bibliography

Great Britain, Parliament, House of Commons, Select Committee on British South Africa (1897). *Second Report with the proceedings of the Committee.* London: H.M. Stationery Office.

Gutsche, Thelma (1966). *Old Gold: The History of The Wanderers Club.* Cape Town: Howard Timmins.

Hammond, John Hays and Ireland, Alleyne (1918). *The Truth about the Jameson Raid.* Boston: Marshall Jones.

Hammond, Mrs Natalie Harris (1897). *A Woman's Part in a Revolution.* New York: Longmans, Green.

Harlow, Vincent (April 1957). 'Sir Frederic Hamilton's Narrative of the Events relating to the Jameson Raid' *The English Historical Review* Vol LXXII No 283 (April 1957) 279-305.

Hillier, Alfred P. (1898). *Raid and Reform: By a Pretoria Prisoner.* London, New York: MacMillan.

Hole, Hugh Marshall (1930). *The Jameson Raid.* London: Philip Allan.

Jameson, Sir Leander Starr, et al. (1896) *Regina v Leander Starr Jameson, Sir John Christopher Willoughby, bart., Henry Frederick White, Raleigh Grey, Robert White, and Charles John Coventry.* London: Eyre and Spottiswoode.

Kipling, Rudyard; Pinney, Thomas (ed.) (1990-2004). *The Letters of Rudyard Kipling, Volumes I-VI.* London: Palgrave Macmillan.

Krout, Mary Hannah (1899). *A Looker on in London.* New York: Dodd, Mead and Company.

Leonard, Charles (1903). *Papers on the Political Situation in South Africa, 1885-1895.* London: Arthur L. Humphreys.

Longford, Elizabeth (1982). *Jameson's Raid: The Prelude to the Boer War.* London: Weidenfeld & Nicolson.

MacSymon, Robert Massey and Linnegar, John (1990). *Fairbridge, Arderne and Lawton: A History of a Cape Law Firm.* Kenwyn (Cape Town): Juta.

McMagh, Kathleen (1968). *A Dinner of Herbs: Being the Memoirs of Kathleen McMagh.* Cape Town & Johannesburg: Purnell.

Meredith, Martin (2008). *Diamonds, Gold and War: The Making of South Africa.* London: Pocket Books (an imprint of Simon & Schuster).

Mouton, F.A. (2009). '"The good, the bad and the ugly': Professional historians and political biography of South African parliamentary politics, 1910-1990" Inaugural address at Unisa, 27 October 2009.

Murray, Marischal (1964). *Under Lion's Head*. Cape Town: Balkema.

Nash, M.D. (1982). *Bailie's Party of 1820 Settlers: A collective experience in emigration*. Cape Town: Balkema.

Nash, M.D. (1987). *The Settler Handbook: A New List of the 1820 Settlers*. Diep River (Cape Town): Chameleon Press.

Nathan, Manfred (1932). 'The Republican Bench and Bar' *The South African Law Times* 1932 (1) 88.

Pakenham, Thomas (1979). *The Boer War*. London: Abacus.

Parsons, Neil (1998). *King Khama, Emperor Joe and the Great White Queen: Victorian Britain through African Eyes*. Chicago & London: University of Chicago Press.

Patterson, Sheila (1957). *The Last Trek: A Study of the Boer People and the Afrikaner Nation*. Abingdon: Routledge.

Phillips, Dorothea Sarah Florence Alexandra (Ortlepp), lady. (1899). *Some South African Recollections*. London: Longmans, Green.

Potter, Simon James (2003). *News and the British World: The Emergence of an Imperial Press System, 1876-1922*. Oxford: Clarendon Press.

Pringle, John and Hudson-Reed, Sydney (1997). *1820 Settler Sails and Tales*. South African Baptist Historical Society.

Regina v Leander Starr Jameson, Sir John Christopher Willoughby, bart., Henry Frederick White, Raleigh Grey, Robert White, and Charles John Coventry (1896). London: Eyre and Spottiswoode.

Rhoodie, Denys (1967). *Conspirators in Conflict: A Study of the Johannesburg Reform Committee and its role in the conspiracy against the South African Republic*. Cape Town: Tafelberg Publishers.

Roberts, Edmund (1837). *Embassy to the Eastern Courts of Cochin-China, Siam, and Muscat*. New York: Harper & Brothers.

Rogers, Owen (2020). *Lawyers in Turmoil: The Johannesburg Conspiracy of 1895*. Cape Town: Stormberg Publishers.

Rotberg, Robert I. (1988). *The Founder: Cecil Rhodes and the Pursuit of Power.* Oxford: Oxford University Press.

Schreiner, Olive (2004) (ed. Emslie, T.S.). *Karoo Moon.* St. James (Cape Town): Stonewall Books.

Schreuder, Deryck and Butler, Jeffrey (eds) (2002). *Sir Graham Bower's Secret History of The Jameson Raid and the South African Crisis, 1895-1902.* Cape Town: Van Riebeeck Society.

Select Committee of the British House of Commons (1897). *Report of the Select Committee of the House of Commons inquiry into the origin and circumstances of the incursion into the South African Republic of an armed force.*

South African Law Society (1887). *Cape Law Journal, Volume 1.*

South African Law Society (1910). *South African Law Journal, Volume 1.*

Stead, W. T. (1902). *The Americanization of the World.* New York & London: Horace Markley.

The Editors (1906). *Men of the Times: Old Colonists of the Cape Colony and Orange River Colony.* Johannesburg: The Transvaal Publishing Company.

Van Onselen (2017). *The Cowboy Capitalist: John Hays Hammond, the American West & the Jameson Raid.* Johannesburg: Jonathan Ball Publishers.

Webb, C. (1952). 'The Uitlander Movement in the South African Republic Before the Jameson Raid', being a thesis presented in pursuance of the B.A. (Hons.) course at the University of the Witwatersrand. wiredspace.wits.ac.za>webb,c,1952

LIST OF ILLUSTRATIONS AND SOURCES

Cover image

Portrait of Charles Leonard by VL de Scerola, courtesy of Lord Cobham, Hagley Hall
Background image: Trial of the Reform Committee, Second Raadsaal, Pretoria
Antique print from *The Graphic*, 1905. Copyright expired.

Facing Chapters

Contents		Charles Leonard
		The story of an African crisis: being the truth about the Jameson Raid and Johannesburg revolt of 1896 by Fydell Edmund Garrett and EJ Edwards. Copyright expired
Preface	xiv	18-19 Kensington Palace Gardens, London
		Courtesy of www.trendingtopmost.com
Ch. 1	6	*Gin Lane*, an etching by William Hogarth
		https://en.wikipedia.org/wiki/File:William_Hogarth_-_Gin_Lane.jpg
		Public domain
Ch. 2	24	Fertile farmlands of Somerset East
		Courtesy of www.goingsomewhereslowly.com
Ch. 3	40	Longmarket Street, late 19th Century
		Courtesy of Hilton Teper, HiltonT at Flickr
Ch. 4	56	Fresnaye and Sea Point c. 1887
		Courtesy of Hilton Teper, HiltonT at Flickr
Ch. 5	68	Private residences, Jeppes Township, 1888
		Gold: The History of the Wanderers Club 1888 to 1968 by Thelma Gutsche. Copyright expired
Ch. 6	80	Founding of the Transvaal National Union
		The Illustrated History of South Africa by D Marquard and PW Wheeler, the Johannesburg *Star*, 1972
Ch. 7	98	'Slow and Sure', a political cartoon by JM Staniforth
		Evening Express (Wales), 5 April 1899. Public domain
Ch. 8	112	Statue of President Paul Kruger, Church Square, Pretoria
		Pretoria East Rekord, 7 April 2015. Photographer unidentified
Ch. 9	128	Committee of the British South Africa Company
		British Imperialism in Rhodesia, a blog by Ryan Thompson (www.rythompsonmicds18.weebly.com)
Ch. 10	144	Arrest of Leander Starr Jameson
		Petit Parisien 1896. Public domain

Ch. 11	158	The Reform Committee, Johannesburg, 1896
		Antique print from *The Illustrated London News*, 23 May 1896, from the original photograph by Barnett and Co., Johannesburg
Ch. 12	170	Postcard of the *Guelph*
		Simplon – The Passenger Ship Website (www.simplonpc.co.uk)
Ch. 13	186	The Grand Hotel, Trafalgar Square, London
		The Graphic, 5 June 1880
Ch. 14	200	Satirical cartoon of the House Select Committee Inquiry into the Jameson Raid
		The Westminster Gazette, 15 July 1897
Ch. 15	218	Hunting party, Northumberland, 1908
		Courtesy of Hagley Hall Archives
Ch. 16	238	Portrait of Catherine Leonard and her granddaughter, Viola Lyttelton
		Courtesy of Lord Cobham, Hagley Hall
Ch. 17	252	The Hon. Charles, Meriel and Viola Lyttelton
		Courtesy of Hagley Hall Archives
Ch. 18	260	The author placing flowers on the grave of Charles Leonard
		Copyright the author

Inserts

23	James and Eliza Leonard (Charles Leonard's parents)
	Courtesy of Hagley Hall Archives
23	Annie, Eliza and Charles Leonard
	Courtesy of Hagley Hall Archives
23	Postcard of Reverend Templeton's Public School, Bedford
	Courtesy of Ivor Markman (www.ivormarkman.wix.com)
39	Charles Leonard
	Courtesy of Hagley Hall Archives
39	Caricature of Jim Leonard
	From the JW Schroder Scrapbook, 1880. Public domain.
	https://J_W_Leonard_QC_Cape_Colony_Parliament_MLA_for_Oudtshoorn.jpg
39	Cape Town, c. 1876
	Courtesy of the George Washington Wilson Collection, Hilton Teper, HiltonT on Flickr
54	Charles Leonard's boarding house and St Mary's Roman Catholic Cathedral
	Source unknown
54	Mrs JJ (Margaret) le Sueur
	Courtesy of Hagley Hall Archives. Original photograph by Akkersdyk Studios, Cape Town
54	Weston Cottage, Kloof Road, Cape Town
	Copyright the author

List of Illustrations and Sources

55	Catherine, Charles and Daisy Leonard c. 1884
	Courtesy of Hagley Hall Archives
79	President Paul Kruger addressing the crowd at the Wanderers Club, 1890
	Thelma Gutsche, *Gold: The History of the Wanderers Club 1888 to 1968*, Howard Timmins, 1966, Copyright expired
79	Fillis's Amphitheatre
	https://johannesburg1912.files.wordpress.com/2013/07/fillis-circus.jpg
97	President Paul Kruger
	Archiv Christensen, Hamburg. Public domain
97	Cecil John Rhodes
	www.archive.org (Unattributed). Public domain
97	John Hays Hammond
	From an antique print, 'The Johannesburg Reform Committee', by The Rembrandt Intaglio Printing Co., Ltd., now in the possession of the author. Elliott & Fry took the original photograph
97	Dr Leander Starr Jameson
	Public domain
97	Colonel Francis (Frank) Rhodes
	From an antique print, 'The Johannesburg Reform Committee', by The Rembrandt Intaglio Printing Co., Ltd., now in the possession of the author. Elliott & Fry took the original photograph
97	Lionel Phillips
	From an antique print, 'The Johannesburg Reform Committee', by The Rembrandt Intaglio Printing Co., Ltd., now in the possession of the author. Goch of Johannesburg took the original photograph
97	President Kruger granting an audience to a deputation
	Antique print, 'Never Again', *The Graphic*, 14 December 1901
111	George Farrar
	From an antique print, 'The Johannesburg Reform Committee', by The Rembrandt Intaglio Printing Co., Ltd., now in the possession of the author. Duffus Brothers of Johannesburg took the original photograph
111	Joseph Chamberlain
	Courtesy of Auckland Libraries, Sir George Grey Special Collections (AWNS-19020605-1-2)
111	Mohandas Gandhi
	https://commons.wikimedia.org/wiki/File:Gandhi_London_1906.jpg Public domain
111	Groote Schuur, the home of Cecil John Rhodes
	TD Ravenscroft (photographer) Public domain
127	Postcard of the library at Groote Schuur
	TD Ravenscroft (photographer) Public domain
143	Jameson's Last Stand, the Battle of Doornkop, 2 January 1896
	Antique print of the painting by R. Caton Woodville

156	Sir Hercules Robinson
	Powerhouse Museum Collection, Gift of Freemans Studios, 1969. No known copyright restrictions
156	Sir Graham Bower
	https://en.wikipedia.org/wiki/Graham_John_Bower#/media/File:Sir_Graham_Bower.png Public domain
156	David Pieter de Villiers Graaff
	https://af.wikipedia.org/wiki/David_Pieter_de_Villiers_Graaff#/media/File:David_Pieter_de_Villiers_Graaff_1909.jpg Public domain
156	Bordeaux, the Graaff home on the Sea Point beachfront
	Source unknown
157	Prisoners playing marbles inside the Pretoria Gaol
	Cartoon by Melton Prior
157	The crowd outside the Goldfields Building
	Source unknown
185	Preliminary investigation of the Reform Committee in the Market Hall
	Antique print from *The Illustrated London News*, 14 March 1896, Zeiler Bohlmann Wess IS4J342
185	Trial of the Reform Committee, Second Raadsaal, Pretoria
	Antique print from *The Graphic*, 1905
193	Prisoners playing cards inside the Pretoria Gaol
	Source unknown
199	Dr Jameson and his officers appear at the Bow Street Court
	Antique print from the Supplement to *The Illustrated London News*, 25 February 1896
199	Dr Jameson disembarking from the transport at Plymouth
	Antique print from *The Illustrated London Times*, 1896
199	Pelham, Manor Park, Chislehurst, Kent
	Courtesy of jdm Estate Agents, advertising on www.rightmove.co.uk. Photographer unknown
199	Henry Labouchère
	British Political Leaders by Justin McCarthy, p. 101, published as an e-book by Project Gutenberg. Original photograph by Elliott & Fry. No copyright
199	Percy Fitzpatrick
	From an antique print, 'The Johannesburg Reform Committee', by The Rembrandt Intaglio Printing Co., Ltd., now in the possession of the author. Elliott & Fry took the original photograph
199	James (Jim) Weston Leonard
	Men of the Times: Old Colonists of the Cape Colony and Orange River Colony, The Transvaal Publishing Company, Johannesburg, 1906, p. 599. Copyright expired. Courtesy of the South African Library, Cape Town. A.920.068 FOL/MEN

List of Illustrations and Sources

216 Portrait of Charles Leonard
Courtesy of Lord Cobham, Hagley Hall
216 Portrait of Catherine Leonard
Courtesy of Lord Cobham, Hagley Hall
216 Portrait of the Hon. Violet Lyttelton
Courtesy of Lord Cobham, Hagley Hall
216 Portrait of Daisy Leonard
Courtesy of Lord Cobham, Hagley Hall
217 Daisy Leonard, aged about 25
Courtesy of Hagley Hall Archives. Original photograph by Duffus Brothers, Cape Town
217 Lady Cobham and Violet Leonard
Courtesy of Hagley Hall Archives. Original photograph by Barony and Co., Ltd
217 Gloria farmstead, Villiersdorp
Copyright the author
217 The view from Gloria farmhouse
Copyright the author
217 Hagley Hall, Worcestershire
Courtesy of www.chrismillsconsulting.co.uk
217 Biddlestone Hall, Alwinton, Northumberland
Courtesy of www.lostheritage.org.uk
251 Rudyard Kipling
Rudyard Kipling, a biography by John Palmer. Original photograph by Elliott & Fry. Public domain
251 Oakley House, the Lyttelton family home
Courtesy of www.theosophy-nw.uk
251 Mount Nelson Hotel, Cape Town
Courtesy of the George Washington Wilson Collection, Hilton Teper, HiltonT on Flickr
251 Catherine Leonard admiring her granddaughter Viola in her pram, c. 1912
Courtesy of Hagley Hall Archives
251 Lutheran Church, Strand Street, Cape Town
Cropped image. Licensed to debbielouise on Wikimedia Commons

INDEX

1820 Settlers 9-20, 28-29, 31, 43, 272
A Dinner of Herbs 242
Adler, H 86
Afrikaans (formerly Afferkaans) 62-63, 212, 219, 263
Afrikander (later Afrikaner) 29, 63, 121, 138, 155, 262
Afrikander (later Afrikaner) Bond 62-63, 65, 86, 109, 138, 155, 168, 262, 265
Afrikaner Broederbond 213
Algoa Bay (Port Elizabeth) 14-16
Anglo American Corporation 222
Arderne Gardens (formerly Claremont Public Gardens) 45
Arderne, Henry Mathew 44
Armadale Castle 235
Asquith, HH (British Prime Minister) 231
Auret, JG 86
Austin, Alfred 160
Ayliff, John (aka Harry Hastings) 12
Bailie, John 9-11, 13, 16
Bain, Charles 74
Balfour, Arthur 202
Barberton 241
Barnato, Barney 76, 114, 228
Barry, Captain 176
Basutoland 212
Baviaans River 31
Beattie, Carruthers, Sir 247
Bechuanaland Protectorate 100, 132, 138, 141, 145, 147, 150, 208, 264
Beckam, William 61
Bedford 31-32, 35, 42
Beit, Alfred 113, 116, 190
Belgravia 72
Bell, William Henry Somerset 43, 47, 204
Bettelheim, Henri, Captain **158**, 166, 183
Biddlestone Hall, Alwinton, Northumberland **217**, 232
Biddulph, Louisa 12-13
Biesjes Fontein Farm, Somerset East 34-35

285

Bishop, F 168

Bloemfontein 152, 173

Boers 29-30, 64-69, 90-92, 94, 99-100, 109, 120, 136-137, **143**, **144**, 146, 151, 153, 160-161, 163-165, 168, 172-174, 179, 183, 211-213, 262

Boer War concentration camps 213

Boksburg 96

Bordeaux, Sea Point 1, **156**, 164, 167

Boschberg Mountains 19, **24**, 27

Botha, Louis, General 220, 247

Bouquet Street, Cape Town 62

Bower, Graham, Sir 139, 151, **156**, 207-208, 210, 214-215

Braamfontein Station 152

Brakfontein Farm, Somerset East 35

Bridge, John, Sir 202

Brilliant 14

British South Africa (BSA) Company (or Chartered Company) 3, 114-115, 119, **128**, 130, 145, 148, 167, 176, 208, 211

Brompton Cemetery 234, 242-243, 248

Brownlee, Charles 37, 42-43

Buchanan, John, Sir 247

Buissinnè, Cornelis Johannes 52

Buissinnè, William Templer 52

Bulawayo 213

Burgersdorp 20

Burlington Hotel, Cork Street, London 201

Burnham, Frederick Russell 257

Butler, Guy xii, 17, 25, 30

Bybee, Frank 249

Campbell (née Taylor), Mrs 27

Cape Argus 140, 128, 246-247

Cape Government Railways 152

Cape Law Journal, The 47

Cape Times 121, 150, 167, 196, 204-205, 266

Cape Town 1, 14, 19, 36-37, **39**, **40**, 41-44, 46-47, 51-52, 57-59, 61-63, 67, 69-70, 75, 86, 93, 108, 113-116, 120, 123, 131-135, 137, 140, 149, 152-153, 164, 165, 168, 171, 173-174, 180, 182-183, 189, 191, 202, 205, 212-213, 219-223, 226, 232, 240, 244-246, 253, 255, 257, 265-266

Cape Town Botanical Gardens 34

Carlton Hotel, Johannesburg 228

Index

Cases Decided in the High Court of the South African Republic during the year 1893 221
Castle Road, Strathpeffer, Rosshire, Scotland 224
Cavendish, Bettine 231
Central Hotel, Johannesburg 77
Chamber of Mines 71, 83, 116, 120, 257-258
Chamberlain, Joseph (Secretary of State for the Colonies) 3, **98**, **111**, 119, 129-130, 137-139, 147-148, 155, 161-162, 174, 176, 178-179, 202, 209-211, 214, 229
Chapman 12-15, 42
Charles Street, Somerset East 21, 35
Chase, John Centlivres 15
Cheyne Walk, Chelsea 255
Claremont 44
Clarke, George Somers 202
Cobham, Lady **217**, 229-230, 232, 234
Cobham, Lord (Eighth Viscount) 226, 229, 232, 253
Cochrane, Thomas 202
Coghlan, Charles 173
Combrinck, Jacobus Arnoldus 46
Commercial Advertiser, The 51
Consolidated Diamond Mines of South West Africa 222
Corner House 83
Corunna 201
Coventry, Captain 176
Cowper, William 16
Cradock 16-18, 29, 43, 99
Cradock, John, Sir 16
Cradock Place 16
Crane, Francis 74
Currey, John Blades 44
Cuylerville 16
Daggaboersnek 17
Daintree, Alfred, Revd 247-248
Dale, Langham, Sir 33
Danckwerts, William Otto 32
Darragh, John, Revd 72
Darwin, Charles 67
De Beers Consolidated Mining Company 114

De Grendel Farm, Durbanville 222
de Jager, Gert 109
de Jager, Lodewyk 109
de Villiers, JDH 250
de Villiers, Henry, Sir 231
de Wet, Jacobus 146
de Wet, Miss 59
Delagoa Bay 10, 114, 219
Dempers and van Ryneveld 62
Dempers, Herman J 62
Dent House, Sea Point 240
Department of Native Affairs 37, 42-43
Devonshire, Duke of 180
Diamonds 35, 76, 114, 222, 230-231, 264
Difaqane 10
Divorce Reform 47-51, 66
Doornfontein 76, 164
Doornkop **143**, **144**, 160, 207, 223
Dormer, Francis 121-122
Drew, DW, Revd 86
Drifts Crisis 114
Dumat, FC 86
Duning, EH 86
Eckard, Johannes Henricus 35
Eckstein, Hermann 78, 83
Edwards, EJ 150
Ellis, John 181-182
Empire League 63, 86
End Street, Doornfontein 76
England in South Africa 63-66
Esselen, Ewald 109-110, 165-166, 183-184, 237
Fairbairn, John 51
Fairbridge and Arderne **40**, 43
Fairbridge, Charles Aiken 44, 47, 51
Fairfield, Edward 208
Farrar, George 78, 82, **111**, 120, 129-130, 165, 179, 203, 258-259
Farrar, Mrs Helen Howard 179
Faure, Pieter, Sir 231

Feltham, Henry 206
Fiddes, George 202
Fillis, Frank 78, 240
Fillis's Amphitheatre 78, **79**, 84, 240
First South African War (First Anglo-Boer War) 63
Fitzpatrick, James Percy **80**, 150, 161, 175, **199**, 203, 259
Ford and Jeppe 69
Fordsburg 71
Fort Hare, Alice 43
Fort Willshire 20
Fraser, WP 86
Fraser's Building, Commissioner Street, Marshall's Township 70
French, Somerset, Sir 231
Fresnaye 58
Fresnaye Villa, Sea Point 58, 167
Frontier Wars (Wars of Dispossession) 10
Fuller, Thomas, Sir 231
Gandhi, Mohandas (Mahatma) **111**, 124-125
Garrett, Fydell Edmund 121, 150, 204-205, 266
Genootskap van Regte Afrikaners, Die 62-63
Germany 178, 231
Germiston 96
Gesuiwerde Nasionale Party 213
Gill College 33, 203
Gill, William 33
Glen Avon Farm 21
Glencoe rail disaster 152
Globe Theatre 74
Gloria Estate, Villiersdorp **217**, 222, 224-225, 242-243, 249-250
Gold xii, 69-70, 76, 82-83, 92, 114, 152, 231-232, 248, 268
Goldfields South Africa 114-115, 149-151, 153, **157**, 161
Government Avenue, Cape Town 246
Graaff, David Pieter de Villiers, Sir 46, 155, **156**, 159, 164, 167-169, 191, 193, 195, 205, 214, 221-222, 224, 239-240, 247, 256
Graaff, de Villiers, Sir 234, 250
Graaff, Jacobus Arnoldus 46-47, 247
Graaff, Lady 240
Graaff-Reinet 18, 36, 62

Grahamstown 19-20, 33, 43
Grand Hotel, Cape Town 188-189, 191
Grand Hotel, Trafalgar Square, London 176, **186**, 189
Great Trek 28-29, 90-91, 99-100, 110
Great War (First World War) 243-244, 257-259, 267
Greeff's Buildings, Albert Road, Salt River 245, 249
Gregorowski, Reinhold 203
Grey Hill, Wynberg 245
Grey, Earl 208
Griqualand East 43
Griqualand West 75
Groote Schuur **111**, 116, 118, **127**, 134, 139-141, 196, 214, 257
Grosvenor, Helen, Lady 231
Grosvenor, Robert George, Fifth Duke of Westminster 254
Guardian, The 202
Guelph **170**, 171, 176, 180
Gus Street, Johannesburg **68**, 71, 233
Hagley Hall, Worcestershire xi, **216**, **217**, 229-232, 242, 248
Hall, Fred 216, 248
Hamilton, Frederic (Fred) 120, 131-135, 137, 139-141, 150, 154-155, **158**, 165, 182, 184
Hammond, John Hays **97**, 114-116, 120, 132, 165, 175, 203, 257-258
Hammond, John Hays jnr 258
Hancock, E 86
Harcourt, William, Sir 214
Harlech Castle 176, 201
Harris, Frederick Rutherfoord, Dr **128**, 130, 132-134, 136
Harris, William Cornwallis, Sir 230
Hartebeest Leegte Farm, Somerset East 33, 35
Hawksley, Bouchier 176, 202
Hay, James 86, 95, 101
Hayes, Captain 74
Heany, Maurice, Captain 133-134, 136
Heavyside, John, Revd 19
Heidelberg 96
Henry VIII 8
Herman, Christian Lawrence, Dr 246, 249
Hertzog, JMB 221, 259

Index

Het Volk 220
Hillier, Alfred 182, 209
Hillier, Winifred 230
Hobhouse, Emily 229
Hockly, Daniel 16
Hofmeyr, Gysbert Reitz 28
Hofmeyr, Jan (Onze Jan) Hendrik 155, 159, 182
Holland, Thomas 34
Holloway Gaol 207
Holt, D 86
Hoole, James 10-11
Howard, John Hassell 20
Howard, Sarah Ann 20
Howard (née Brandt), Susannah 21
Howard, Susannah Brandt 20
Howard, Thomas Hassel 249
Huguenots 57
Imperial Cold Storage and Supply Company 222, 239-240
Incorporated Law Society 47, 51-52, 248, 265
Jameson, Leander Starr, Dr
    photographs and illustrations **97**, **128**, **143**, **144**
    discusses fraught situation in Johannesburg with Rhodes and Hammond 115
    visits Johannesburg 115, 119-123
    conspires with Rhodes 116
    decision to invade Transvaal from Pitsani Potluga in Bechuanaland 119
    persuades Charles Leonard to write 'women and children' letter 119-120, 123
    rumour of his plan to come in under Union Jack 130-131, 266
    plan to set off on 28 December 1895 131
    telegrams to and from 131-135, 151
    messengers sent to 132, 135, 146-147
    Rhodes agrees to delay invasion 134-135
    reads letter to troops 136
    sets off on Raid 137
    Joseph Chamberlain learns of his advance 137-138
    Rhodes learns of his advance 136
    Charles Leonard and Fred Hamilton learn of his advance 139, 266
    Rhodes's reluctance to stop him 141-142, 148-149
    responds to Boer protest 145-146

    High Commissioner tries to stop him 146-148
    Chamberlain tries to stop him 148
    Reform Committee learns of his advance and repudiates him 149, 153
    Boers move to intercept him 145, 153
    Chief Justice refuses to include him in peace negotiations 155
    defeated by Boers 160
    allegations that Reform Committee deserted him 161-162
    his life at risk, claims High Commissioner 163
    imprisoned at Pretoria 165
    Rhodes sails for England to negotiate on his behalf 167
    uses letter to defend himself 168
    taken to Port Natal and thence to England 174-175
    British public behind him 176, 201
    news leaks out that he disobeyed orders 192
    Charles Leonard refuses to prejudice him before his trial 195, 266
    terms of surrender guaranteed his life 196
    preliminary hearing 202
    remand hearing 203
    goes fishing in Norway 203
    Cape House of Assembly finds him responsible 206
    trial and sentence 206-207
    early release and return to South Africa 207
    Select Committee finds him and Rhodes jointly responsible 210
    calls Chamberlain a scoundrel 215
    Member of Cape Parliament 221
    Prime Minister of the Cape 221
    Kipling's veneration of him in 'If' 224
    guest at Violet's wedding 231
    Charles Leonard's error of judgment in trusting him 266-267
Jameson Raid 130-155, 160-162, 175-176, 203-204, 206-211, 214, 223, 247, 259,
            262, 266-267
Jameson Raid, Cape House of Assembly inquiry into the 206-207
Jameson Raid, House of Commons Select Committee inquiry into the 166-167, 174-
            175, 180-184, **200**, 204-205, 207-211
Jameson Raid, trial of prisoners 201-204, 206-207
Jameson, Samuel (Sam) 131-132, **158**
Jeppe, Carl 86, 109, 196
Jeppe, J jnr 86

Index

Jeppe's Town (later Jeppestown) 71-72

Joel, Solly B 166, 183

Johannesburg viii, 3, **68**, 69-81, **79**, 83-88, 90, 93, 95, 101-102, 104-109, 114-116, 118-121, 123, 129, 131-132, 134, 136-144, 145, 147-150, 153-155, 159-164, 166-167, 169, 172-174, 177, 181, 184, 189-190, 192-193, 196-197, 202, 205, 208, 212, 214, 220-221, 225-228, 233-234, 236-237, 240-242, 257-259, 265-266

Johannesburg Turf Club (Races) 78, 226, 258

Joubert, General 145, 160

JW Leonard Memorial Library, University of the Witwatersrand 237

Kaga Mountain, Bedford 31

Karoo xii, 17-18, 36-38, 69-70, 224

Kei Apple Grove, Sea Point 51

Kenilworth 59

Kensington Palace Gardens **xiv**, 1, 223, 230-232

Khoekhoe (also known as Khoikhoi) 63

Kildonan Castle 223

Kimberley 35-36, 70, 75-76, 114, 167

Kipling, Carrie 232

Kipling, Elsie 223, 226

Kipling, John 242

Kipling, Rudyard 159, 223-226, 231-232, 240, 242-243, **251**

Kirstenbosch Botanical Gardens 213-214

Klerksdorp 96

Kloof Road, Sea Point 51

Kloof Street, Cape Town 61

Kok, JHM 154

Kokstad 223

Komati Poort 241

Korsten, Frederick 16

Kotzé, John Gilbert, Sir 110, 237, 247

Kroonstad 152

Kruger, Stephanus Johannes Paulus (Paul), President
  birth and participation in the Great Trek 99
  photographs, cartoons and statue of **79**, **97**, **98**, **112**
  visits to Johannesburg 81-83
  negotiations with Transvaal National Union 100-107
  refusal to make concessions 110

    two political blunders (conscripting Uitlanders and Drifts Crisis) 111-113
    opposition to him 122
    gives Jim Leonard 'Windhond' nickname 123
    allusion to tortoise 145
    negotiations regarding peace terms after Jameson Raid 154
    dealings with Afrikander Bond 155-157
    negotiations with Robinson, High Commissioner 155-159, 162-164
    negotiations with Chamberlain, Colonial Secretary 162-163, 174, 178-179
    negotiations regarding Reform Committee prisoners 175, 178
    telegram from High Commissioner 177, 197
    Charles Leonard's opinion of him 179, 269
    Charles Leonard's suspicion of him 189
    terms of Jameson's surrender 196
    commutes death sentences and releases some Reform prisoners 203-204
    allegation of Charles Leonard's compact with him 204-205
    deteriorating relations with Britain 210-211
    response to Select Committee's findings 211-212
    plot to overthrow him 3, 95, 262, 265
    Charles Leonard's objections to his racial policies 263-264
Krugersdorp 96, 147, 160, 176
Labouchère, Henry 160, 174-175, 180-181, 183, **199**, **200**, 206, 262 (footnote)
Labour Importation Association 221
Langermann, H 86
Lascelles, Frank, Sir 231
Lawley, Arthur 149
le Sueur, Jacobus Johannes, jnr 57
le Sueur, Margaret **54**, 57
le Sueur, François, Revd 57
le Sueur, Ryk 58
Leader, James 9-10
Leibbrandt, Johann Sebastian (Bassie) 66-67
Leonard (formerly Eckard), Agnes Sophia 36, 220
Leonard (née Pearson), Alice Frances Mary 76, 196, 221
Leonard (later Nel), Ann (Annie) Charlotte 21, 27-28, 63, 67, 257
Leonard (née Whyte), Blanche Marie Augusta Diendonne (Emma) Beresford 151, **218**, 220, 226, 232, 234-235
Leonard (formerly Eckard, née Coetzee/Kotze), Catharina (Kate) Elizabeth 36, 41-42, 52, 108-109, 175, 219-220

Index

Leonard, Charles Henry Brandt
    ancestors and parents 5, 7-22, **23**, 26, 33-35
    birth 22
    appearance 21, **23**, 27, **39**, 42, **55**, **216**, **218**, **276**
    an Afrikander 29, 90
    attitude towards Dutch/Afrikaners/Boers 30, 62, 64-69, 90-91, 94, 122, 262-263, 265, 269
    attitude towards blacks 30-31, 73, 263-264
    schooling 31
    first attempt at farming 36
    moves to Cape Town 37, 41-42
    boards in Roeland Street, Cape Town 42
    civil servant 37, 42
    father dies 45
    articled clerk 43
    qualifies and begins practising as a lawyer 46-47
    writes article on divorce reform 47-51
    partner in law firm 51
    falls in love with Catherine le Sueur 58-61
    wedding 61-62
    buys Weston Cottage 61
    sues William Beckam 61
    birth of daughters Margaret (Daisy) and Violet 62
    buys Sea Point home 66
    sister Annie Nel dies 67
    moves to Johannesburg 69
    establishes own law firm 70
    buys house in Gus Street, Jeppe's Town 71
    social life in early Johannesburg 71-78
    helps arrange English cricket tour 77
    meetings with President Kruger 82, 100-103, 107
    committee member of Transvaal National Union 84
    political speeches 89-95, 105-107
    drafts Manifesto 95, 117-118, 153-154
    presents programme of action 107
    elected Chairman of Transvaal National Union 108
    first visit to England 108
    sues Andries van Niekerk 115

Charles Leonard

meetings with Cecil John Rhodes 116-118, 133-135, 139-140
outline of plot 118-119
writes 'women and children' letter 119-120
'unsuitable for leader of armed rebellion' 121
hears rumour of Union Jack 129-130
travels to Cape Town with Fred Hamilton 131-133
learns of Jameson Raid 139-140
sends reassuring telegrams to Reform Committee 133, 149, 154
meets newspaper editors in Cape Town 140, 150
receives telegram from Reform Committee 153
collaborates with David de Villiers Graaff 155, 159
heads back to Johannesburg 163
heads back to Cape Town 164
given refuge by Graaff 165
nervous breakdown 165
warrant for arrest and extradition 166, 174-175, 183, 197
exchanges telegrams and letters with Ewald Esselen 165-166, 183-184
escapes in disguise 168, 171
aboard the *Guelph en route* to England 171-176
at the Grand Hotel, London 176-210
letters to and from wife 176-180, 187-198
accusations of cowardice 177, 180-183, 197, 204-205
interventions on behalf of Reform prisoners 177-182, 192, 195-198, 202
allegations of wanting to denounce Rhodes 196, 205
joined in England by wife and daughters 202
buys Pelham, Manor Park, Chislehurst, Kent 202
testifies before House Select Committee 140-141, 163-164, 166-168, 174-175,
                              180-184, 204-205, 209-210
turns his back on politics 215
practises law in England 219
publishes papers 221
returns to South Africa 221
buys farms to comprise Gloria Estate 222
mother dies 222
returns to England 223
buys 18, Kensington Palace Gardens 223
buys 18, South Terrace, Littlehampton 223
rents Maesllwch Castle 223

Index

    hosts Rudyard Kipling and family 223-234, 225-226, 232
    sister Margaret Taylor dies 224
    returns to South Africa 224
    takes up farming 224, 244-245
    celebrates Silver Wedding Anniversary 225
    visits brother Jim and family in Johannesburg 226-228
    returns to England 229
    gives daughter Violet away at her wedding 230
    rents Biddlestone Hall, Alwinton, Northumberland 232
    returns to South Africa 232
    birth of first grandchild, Charles 234
    brother Jim dies 234
    returns to England for the funeral 235
    returns to South Africa 235
    returns to England 239
    dispute with ICS board 239-240
    returns to South Africa 240
    birth of second grandchild Meriel 240
    returns to England 240
    writes hurtful letter to niece Kathleen 241-242
    birth of third grandchild Viola 242
    wife dies 242-243
    returns to South Africa 242
    Lytteltons visit Gloria Estate 243
    birth of fourth grandchild Audrey 244
    birth of fifth grandchild Lavinia 244
    invests in property 245
    Co-founder of Van Riebeeck Society 245
    last visit to England 246
    illness and death 246
    funeral and burial 246-248, **260**
    will and bequests 247-248
    tributes 247, 259, 261-270
Leonard, Edward Chapman 14
Leonard (née Howard), Elizabeth (Eliza) 20-23, **23**, 26-27, 45, 232
Leonard (née Taylor), Elizabeth 8-11, 14-17, 19-21
Leonard (later Wade), Elizabeth 21
Leonard, Ellen Martha 18

Leonard, Ernestine Anne 230
Leonard, Frances Hannah 19
Leonard, Francis Phipps 19, 31
Leonard (later Liesching), Gertrude (<u>Gertie</u> Amy) Alice Sophia 26, 154, 185, 223, 227, 241-242, 253
Leonard, Harry 19
Leonard, Hassell Bruce 26
Leonard, James 21
Leonard, James Charles Beresford Whyte 226, 235, 237
Leonard, James (Jim) Weston
   birth 20
   schooling 31-32
   appearance **39**, 52-53, **199**, **218**
   diamond digger 35-36
   marries Catharina (Kate) Eckard and adopts her daughter Agnes 36
   journalist and editor of *Richmond Era* 36
   obtains Ll.B 36.
   moves to Cape Town 37, 41-42
   advocate 45
   first trip to England 52
   buys part of Rustenburg estate 52
   Member of Parliament 52
   Attorney-General 52
   Cabinet Minister 52
   personality 53
   helps found Empire League 63, 86
   moves to Johannesburg 76
   buys house in End Street, Doornfontein 76
   establishes law firm 76
   President of the Political Reform Association 82
   committee member of Transvaal National Union 84-85
   meets President Kruger 101-102, 123
   employs brothers Charles and Woodford 123
   'Windhond' nickname 123
   assists Gandhi 124-125
   becomes member of Reform Committee 149
   addresses angry mob 151
   insulted by colonial officials 151

Index

    falls in love with Emma Blanche Beresford Whyte 147
    arrested with other members of Reform Committee 164
    writes to Charles from gaol 165
    released from gaol 204
    writes to *Cape Times* 205
    visits England with Blanche 219
    first wife divorces him 219
    becomes an English barrister 220
    marries Blanche Whyte 220
    returns to England and stays with Charles in Kent 220
    returns to Johannesburg 220
    represents Indians 221
    birth of first child from second marriage, James 226
    birth of second child from second marriage, Angela 226
    Charles and family visit him in Johannesburg 226-227
    visits Charles in Northumberland 232
    diagnosed with brain tumour 233
    returns to Johannesburg 233
    seeks treatment in Europe 234
    death and burial 234-235
    tributes 235-237

Leonard, James Weston snr 18, 20-22, **23**, 25-27, 33-35, 45-46

Leonard, Jane 19

Leonard, John 18

Leonard, John William Weston 8-17, 19-21

Leonard, John Woodford (Woodie) Stoney 26, 53, 76, 123, 177, 188, 191-195, 212, 221, 249, 253

Leonard (née le Sueur), Katharina (Catherine) Aletta Renina
    birth 57
    falls in love with Charles Leonard 58-61
    appearance **55**, **216**, **238**, **251**
    wedding 61-62
    birth of daughters Margaret (Daisy) and Violet 62
    moves into Sea Point home 66
    reluctance to move to Johannesburg 70, 190
    moves into house in Gus Street, Jeppe's Town 71
    social life in early Johannesburg 71-78
    first trip to England 108

confidante 123, 129
flees Johannesburg with daughters 152
moves in with friends Dot and Eric in Sea Point 153
at Charles's sickbed 164
coping without Charles 172, 187-189
letters to Charles 172, 174, 187-189, 190-191
joins Charles in England 202
moves into Pelham, Manor Park, Chislehurst, Kent 202
returns to South Africa 221
moves into Gloria Estate, Villiersdorp 222
returns to England 223
moves into 18, Kensington Palace Gardens 223
holidays in Wales 223
entertains Kiplings 223, 225-226
returns to South Africa 224
celebrates Silver Wedding Anniversary 224
holidays in Johannesburg 226-227
returns to England 229
prepares for Violet's wedding 229-230
attends Violet's wedding and hosts reception 230-231
holidays in Northumberland 232
returns to South Africa 232
Receives letter from son-in-law 233-234
birth of first grandchild Charles 234
receives letter from Lady Cobham 234
birth of second grandchild Meriel 235
returns to England 235
birth of third grandchild Viola 242
death 242-243
funeral and burial 243, 248
tribute 242-243

Leonard, Margaret (Daisy) Elizabeth Catherine 55, 62, 72, 129, 187-190, 193-194, 202, **216**, **217**, **218**, 223, 226-227, 230-233, 240, 242-244, 246-247, 249, 251, 255-256

Leonard (later Taylor), Margaret Eliza 21, 26-27, 224, 249, 253

Leonard, Marie Blanche Catherine Angela 226, 235

Leonard (later Theys), Mary Anne 8

Leonard (later Howard), Mary Emily Green 26, 46, 249, 253

Leonard, Phipps Weston 8

Index

Leonard (later Marx), Susannah (Susie) Brandt 26, 188, 228-229
Leonard, Susannah Elizabeth 21
Leonard, Tryphena 19
Leonard (later Lyttelton), Violet Yolande 62, 72, 129, 187-189, 194, **216**, **217**, **218**, 226-227, 230-234, 239-240, 242-244, 246-249, 251, 253-256
Leonard, William 8
Leonard, William Weston 19
Lewis, WH, Lieutenant 243
Leyds, Willem 178
Liesching, Frederick 160, 223
Liesching (later McMagh), Kathleen 227-229, 240-242
Liesching, William 160
Lindsay (née Taylor), Mrs 27
Lippert, Edouard 178
Lisdale Flats, Sea Point 67
Loch, Henry, Sir 113-114, 116
Lockwood's Company 151
London 1, 7-9, 32, 44, 63, 130, 148, 176, 188-189, 192, 201-203, 205, 208, 223, 230-232, 235, 239-240, 243, 255, 257
Longford Farm, Albany 43
Lovedale College 32
Loveday Street, Johannesburg 71
Loveday, Richard 109
Lutheran Church, Strand Street, Cape Town 246, **251**
Lyttelton, Alfred 229
Lyttelton, Audrey Lavinia 244
Lyttelton, Charles John (10th Viscount Cobham) ('Bargie') 234, 239, 242, 248, **252**, 253-255
Lyttelton, Edward, Revd 230
Lyttelton (née Makeig-Jones), Elizabeth 254
Lyttelton, George 230
Lyttelton, John (Jack) Cavendish (9th Viscount Cobham) **218**, 226-227, 229-234, 239, 243, 247-249, 251, 253-255
Lyttelton, Meriel Catherine 240, 242, 248, **252**, 254
Lyttelton, Lavinia Mary Yolande 244
Lyttelton, Rachel 231
Lyttelton (later Grosvenor), Viola Maud **238**, 242, 248, **252**, 254, 256
Lyttelton-Leonard wedding 230-232

MacOwan, Peter 33-34
MacWilliam, Professor 188
Mafeking (now Mafikeng) 114, 131, 137, 146-147, 149, 257
Malaboch 113
Malan, Abraham 153
Malan, François 140
Malays 63
Malcomess, C 86
Malmani 145
Mandy, John 12
Manifesto of the Transvaal National Union 95, 116-117, 150, 153-154, 162, 247, 265
Manikus, Dr 164, 172
Marais, Eugène 109, 153, 265
Marico 145
Market Hall, Pretoria 203
Market Square, Johannesburg 152
Marx, Charles 228
Marx, Ilma 228
Mashonaland 115
Masllwch Castle, Glasbury-on-Wye, Wales 223
Mason, Justice 236-237
Matabele 13, 257
Matabeleland 115
McMagh, Joseph Patrick 241
McMagh, Kathleen (see Liesching)
Mein, Thomas, Captain 130, **158**
Mercantile Buildings, Simmonds Street, Johannesburg 76, 123
Meyer, Jan P 77, 85
Meyer, Lucas 109
Middelberg 160
Milbank, John 14
Milner, Alfred 211-212, 215, 231
Milton Farm, Kokstad 223
Mimosas, Sea Point 44
'Missing' telegrams 207
Mozambique 241
Molteno, John 42
Morley, Arnold 210

Mossel Bay 76
Mount Nelson Hotel, Cape Town 244, 246, **251**
Murray, Andrew, Dr 28
Natal 212, 262
Natal Indian Congress 125
Natal Spruit 71
Nautilus 12
Ndebele 213, 257
Nel, JJ 35
Nel, Leonard Weston 28
Nel, Lorna 28
Nel, Louis (or Lewies or Luis) 'Waterval' 28
Nel (later Hofmeyr), Ydie 28
Netherlands Railway Company 114, 153
New Review 180-181, 196, 202
New Zealand 253, 255
Newton, Frank 146-147, 209
Nigel 96
Nobbs, William 10
Norham Castle 109, 202
Oakley House, Bromley Common, Kent 244, **251**
O'Flinn, Daniel, Dr 14
Oliver Road, Sea Point 62
Ons Land 140
Oppenheimer, Ernest, Sir 222
Orange Free State (formerly Republic of the Free State) 63, 65, 93, 132, 152, 164, 203, 212, 262
Ossewabrandwag 213
Ostende, Sea Point 67, 240
Otto, CB 109
Oudtshoorn 52, 67
Outlook 202
Owen, George 8
Pall Mall Magazine 202
Papenkuils Fontein (later known as Cradock Place) 16
Papers on the Political Situation in South Africa, 1885-1895 221
Park Station, Johannesburg 131
Park Street, Johannesburg 72

Paulet Street, Somerset East 46, 249
Pelham, Manor Park, Chislehurst, Kent **199**, 202, 229
Phillips, Florence 71, 73, 179, 257
Phillips, Lionel 71, 77, **80**, 83, **97**, 116, 119-121, 133, 149, 161, 165, 203, 257
Phipps, Elizabeth 8
Phipps, Robert 8
Phipps, William 8
Pistorius, JFE 101
Pitsani Potlugo 119, 137
Political Reform Association 82-83
Port Natal (later Durban) 152, 174, 176, 241
Potchefstroom 96
Powell, Edmund 140
Press, The 179
Preston-Whyte, Joan 231
Pretoria 85, 87-88, 90, 94, 96, **97**, 100-101, 105, 113, 118-119, 124-126, 134-135, 137, 145-146, 153, 155, **157**, 160, 164-165, 172-173, 175-176, 180, 182-183, **185**, 187, 190, **199**, 202-203, 210, 219, 227, 237, 257, 259
Pringle, Thomas 14-15, 31
Progressive Association 220
Rand Club 76, 78, 120, 164-165
Reed, Henry Byron 173-174
Reed, Sarah 14
Reform Committee 149-154, **158**, 161-166, 175-176, 180-182, **185**, **199**, 203-204
Reform Committee trial **185**, 203
Regent Road, Sea Point 51
Reid, AH 86
Reid, HA 86
Retief, FJ, Revd 247
Retreat Farm, Bedford 42
Rhodes, Cecil John
  High Commissioner Loch broaches plan to invade Transvaal with him 113
  at the height of his power 114
  employs John Hays Hammond 115
  broaches plot with Charles Leonard and then also with Lionel Phillips 116-118
  his real intention 121-122, 130
  photographs and cartoons **97**, **126**, **200**
  William Schreiner visits him 138-139, 141-142

learns of Jameson's advance 139
asks Charles Leonard and Fred Hamilton to stay in Cape Town 140-141, 182
tries to prevent Robinson from issuing proclamation 149
sends telegram to Flora Shaw criticising Chamberlain 148-149
Fitzgerald accuses him of 'selling out' 161
resigns as Prime Minister 164
sails for England 167
negotiates with Chamberlain 176, 210
pays fines of Reform Committee prisoners 204
allegation that Charles Leonard planned to denounce him 205
Cape House of Assembly all but exonerates him 206
testifies before House Select Committee 207
Select Committee finds him jointly responsible, but imposes no sanction 210
death and burial 213
bequests 213-214
appraisals of his life 214-215
courage in ending Second Matabele War 257
Charles Leonard's relationship with him 265

Rhodes, Francis (Frank), Col. **97**, 116, 120, 130, 132-133, 162, 165, 203-204, 257, 266

Rhodes Memorial 214

Rhodes Scholarship (now Mandela-Rhodes Scholarship) 214

Rhodesia 100, 115, 173, 257

Richmond 36-37, 52

Richmond Era 36

Rietfontein Farm, Somerset East 28

Roberts, Lord 215

Robinson, Hercules, Sir (British Governor of the Cape and High Commissioner) 138-139, 146-149, 151, 153-155, **156**, 159-163, 168, 177, 196-197, 208-209, 210-211

Robinson, JB 210

Roeland Street 42, **54**, 57

Rogers, WH 86, 101, 107

Rondebosch 52

Rose Villa, Sea Point 168

Rose-Innes, James 32, 231, 237

Ross (later Darragh), Mary 72

Russell, Lord 206

Rustenburg 96, 137

Rustenburg, Rondebosch 52
Rutherfoord, Howson 51
Rynheath, Sea Point 62
Salisbury, Lord (British Prime Minister) 202
Salisbury 173, 191
San 31
Sandilands, Doris Millicent Leonard 220
Sandilands, Gordon 204
Sans Souci 71
Saturday Review 192
Saxon, RMS 227
Scanlen, Charles 43
Scanlen, Thomas Charles, Sir 43-44, 52, 191
Schreiner, Olive 29, 32
Schreiner, William (WP) 32, 138-139, 141-142, 206, 209, 231
Sea Point 1, 44, 51, **56**, 58, 62, 66-67, 72, 153, **156**, 164-165, 168, 171, 240
Sea Point Contact, The 67
Seafield, Banffshire, Scotland 27
Searelle, Luscombe 78
Second Chamber (Second Raadsaal) 91-93, 102-103, 176, **185**
Second South African War (Second Anglo-Boer War) 173, 211-212, 220, 222-223, 226, 229, 257-259, 263, 268
Seven Seas, The 226
Shaw College 33
Shaw, Flora 148, 208-209
Sivewright, James, Sir 239-240
Slaves 11, 28-29, **39**, 51
Smit, General 102-103, 105
Smith, Charles Aubrey 75
Smuts, JJ 67
Smuts, Jan Christiaan 137, 222, 247
Solomon, Edward 32
Solomon, EP 86
Solomon, H 86
Solomon, Richard 32
Solomon, William 32
Somerset East 19-21, **24**, 25, 27-28, 31, 33, 35, 37, 45-46, 99, 203, 222, 249
Somerset, Charles, Lord 19, 28, 51-52, 62

Index

South Africa Journal 202
South African Law Journal 235
South Terrace, Littlehampton, Sussex 223-224
Southey, Richard, Sir 35
Sprigg, Gordon, Sir 52
St Mary's School 72
St Peter's Church, Eton Square, Belgravia 230
St Stephen's Club 179, 190
Staatscourant 166
Standard and Diggers' News 94, 100
Star, The 72, 120, 122, 137, 149, 202
Stead, WT 122
Stellenberg 59
Stringfellow, Thomas 14
Stuart, John 163
Swellendam 51
Talbot, Edward, Revd 230
Tamboerskloof Nursing Home 246
Tancred, Augustus Bernard (AB) 76, 173
Tancred, Mrs 173
Taylor, Bertram Alexander Leonard 27
Taylor, Harry James Charles 27
Taylor, James B 77
Taylor, William Brown 26
Taylor, Winifred 231
Templeton (née Calderwood), Elizabeth 32
Templeton, Robert, Revd 31-32
Templeton School, Bedford **23**, 31-32
Theatre Royal 78
Thornhill's Party 20
Times, The 9, 137, 148, 180, 196, 202, 208, 214, 257
Transvaal (formerly and officially, Zuid-Afrikaansche Republiek) 32, 63-65, 69-70, 75-76, 82, 90, 92-96, 99-100, 109, 113-115, 118-119, 121, 125, 131, 133, 135-136, 139, 141, 146, 149, 153, 162-167, 173-174, 177-180, 183-184, 189-190, 192-193, 195, 203, 205-206, 208-209, 211-212, 219, 237, 240-241, 257-259, 262, 267
Transvaal International Political Association 83
Transvaal National Union 3, **79**, **80**, 84, 86, 94-95, 100-101, 106-109, 113, 115-116,

118-120, 123, 129, 131-132, 137-138, 140, 150-153, 159, 166, 173, 182, 240, 247, 262, 265

Treaty of Vereeniging 213
Trekboers 10
Trull, HC 77
Tudhope, John 84-89, 101-105, 108
Turner, Alice 35
Turner, William 35
Uitenhage 16, 26, 32, 259
Uitlanders **79**, 83, 86, 90, 92-93, **98**, 99-101, 108-110, 113, 115, 120, 122, 126, 155, 163, 166, 178, 183, 209, 211, 247, 259, 262-265
Union of South Africa 32, 135, 239-240, 255-259, 262-263
'Union Jack' controversy 65-66, **128**, 129-130, 132-134, 145, 266
United Party 240
University of Cape Town (formerly South African College) 34, 213
University of the Cape of Good Hope 46
Upington, Thomas, Sir 45, 47, 172, 174-175, 197
Vaal River 92, 114, 152
van Hulsteyn, Willem 124, 172, 191, 206
van Niekerk, Andries 115
Van Riebeeck Society 245
van Ryneveld, Anthony 62
van Ryneveld, Daniel Johannes 62
van Zyl, Buissinne and Leonard 51
van Zyl, Casper Henry 51
van Zyl, Gideon Brand 51
van Zyl, GP 51
Vereeniging 163, 213
Victoria H.M.T. 175, **193**, 201
Victoria West 163
Vierkleur (Flag Incident) 65-66, 82-83, 105, 122, 149
Villiersdorp 46, **217**, 222, 224-225, 245
Vine Park, Uitenhage 26
Visserhoek, Durbanville 115
Volksraad (Boer/Transvaal Government) 3, 82-84, 87-88, 91-95, 99, 101-103, 105-110, 114, 118, 120-122, 125, 136, 145, 153-155, 162-163, 166-167, 175, 178-179, 183-184, 205, 210, 212, 259, 263-265
von Brandis, Captain 82

Wade, Edward 21
Walford (née Taylor), Mrs Frederick 27
Wanderers Club xii, 74-75, 77, 79, 81, 83, 150, 220
Waterval Boven 241
Waverley 72
Weinkal, (newspaper editor) 179
Wernher, Beit and Company 180 (footnote), 188, 196
Weston Cottage **54**, 61-62
Weston, John 8
Weston, Sarah 8
White, Henry Frederick, Col. 203
Willoughby, John, Colonel 147, 203, 207
Winterslust Farm, Sea Point 58
Wisden Cricketers' Almanack 173
Wither, Peter, Revd 31
Witwatersrand (more commonly, the Rand) 69-71, 74, 81, 113, 122, 146-147, 177, 212, 237, 258
Woltemade Cemetery, Maitland 247, **260**
Women and Children letter 119-120, 123, 136, 148, 214, 266
Woodrooffe, Henry Reade, Revd 37
Wormwood Scrubs Gaol 207
Wynberg 52
Xhosa 10, 16, 42
Yarnton Manor, Oxford 8
Younghusband, Francis 137
Zeerust 137, 145
Zoroaster 20
Zululand 100, 212

ABOUT THE AUTHOR

Simon Winter was born in London but has spent most of his life in South Africa. He was educated at Bishops and the University of Cape Town, where he obtained the B.A. and B.Ed. degrees. He then taught English and history at Plumstead High School for many years. He served as headmaster from 2000 to 2009. During that time, the school won the National Most Improved School Award in the category of Racial Integration and Simon Winter received the National Teaching Award for Excellence in Secondary School Leadership in the Western Cape.

He was then promoted to Deputy Chief Education Specialist, co-ordinating the professional development and performance management of 5,000 teachers in 200 schools. In 2014, he received the Premier's Service Excellence Silver Award in the category Best Overall *Batho Pele* (Citizen-centric) Public Servant.

He retired in 2015 and now indulges in his pastimes of reading, writing, painting and watching sport. He has been married to Lee for 43 years and they have two daughters and two grandchildren.

He may be contacted via e-mail at simwinsol@gmail.com